DATE DUE			
Dec 9 '74			
Dec 3 7 8			
Feb 23 '81			
Mar 18			
AUG 1 3 1987			

Problems in Intellectual Freedom and Censorship

PROBLEMS IN INTELLECTUAL FREEDOM AND CENSORSHIP

· ·

by A. J. Anderson

R. R. Bowker Company
New York & London, 1974
A Xerox Education Company

XEROX

363.31
Aл2p
90220
oct 1974

Published by R. R. Bowker Co. (A Xerox Education Company)
1180 Avenue of the Americas, New York, N.Y. 10036

Printed and bound in the United States of America.

Library of Congress Cataloging in Publication Data

Anderson, Arthur James.
   Problems in intellectual freedom and censorship.

   (Problem-centered approaches to librarianship)
   Includes bibliographical references.
   1. Libraries—Censorship—Case studies.   I. Title.
Z711.4.A63   363.3'1   74-4107
ISBN 0-8352-0677-7

For Victoria

"Those who expect to reap the blessings of freedom must undergo like men the fatigue of supporting it."

—THOMAS PAINE

CONTENTS

· · · · · · · · · · ·

Contents

FOREWORD

· · · · · · · · · · ·

A. J. Anderson's *Problems in Intellectual Freedom and Censorship* is the eighth title to appear in Bowker's Problem-Centered Approaches to Librarianship series. It is also the fourth volume in this series written by a member of the faculty of the School of Library Science at Simmons College, which, for more than two decades, has been a leading center for experimentation with and development of problem-oriented teaching materials and methods in the pre-service and in-service education of library personnel. It was at Simmons College, as well, that a semester-length course devoted entirely to the concepts and problems of intellectual freedom and censorship was introduced into the curriculum—the first such course to be offered in any graduate library school. In preparing the present volume, Professor Anderson has been able to draw upon a rich background of experience as a teacher of this and other related courses, as a frequent leader of in-service and continuing education programs for practicing librarians, and as a library administrator.

Problems in Intellectual Freedom and Censorship constitutes an innovative and highly original contribution to an area of the literature of librarianship that, while great in volume, has often been disappointingly thin in substance, and better calculated to stir the emotions of readers than to stimulate their intellects. Far too many of those who have to date contributed to this literature have failed to recognize that while it is vital there be a strong personal commitment on the part of every librarian to the highest ideals of free access to information, the mere making of such a general commitment in the abstract does not, in and of itself, reduce either the complexity or the difficulty of the problems encountered in practice in dealing with controversial materials. Nor, as we have often noted with dismay, will high oaths of allegiance to the noblest principles of free inquiry, freely sworn in the safety of classroom or conference hall, be consistently honored by librarians in the dim arenas of daily decision-making. As one former student, whose promising career may have been permanently blighted by the traumatic consequences of an especially hysterical and unsavory censorship battle that led ultimately to his summary dismissal from the directorship of a small public library, ruefully remarked, "It sure is a lot more complicated in real life than I thought it would be when we discussed this in class."

And the simple fact is that it *is* more complicated in real life, where questions of freedom and censorship are concerned, than we have generally been willing to recognize. The great value of this collection derives in large part from Professor Anderson's sensitivity to the complexity of problems that do arise in practice, along with his skill in conveying to the reader the ambiguities that so often surround these issues, and the personal conflicts they so frequently engender. These case studies provide a vehicle through which the individual can test, in application, the limits of both personal and professional concepts of free access to information. They are intended, among other things, to compel both students and practicing librarians to recognize that libraries exist within the varied fabric of a pluralistic social order, where neither individual nor collective value systems can function in isolation. Thus, the cases are not limited to questions about controversial materials, but record, as well, problems arising out of conflicts among professional goals, institutional objectives and client needs.

Most challenging of all, perhaps, are the questions raised by Professor Anderson in several case studies concerning means and ends. Under what circumstances, if any, he asks, may the rights of individuals—librarians, trustees, teachers, students—properly be subordinated to the greater good, real or anticipated, of society at large? What are the actual or potential points of conflict between the concept of free access to information and opinion and other individual freedoms or societal goals? These are indeed apt questions to ask of those who practice a profession that can exist only in an institutional setting which is itself a product of the social order and can flourish only if, and to the extent that, society wills.

These case studies offer a clear recognition that in a heterogeneous society, creative interaction becomes obligatory among individuals whose attitudes reflect a wide range of tastes and values. They are designed to prepare librarians to work effectively with clients and citizens whose views will not always be in accord with their own. Through individual and group analysis of the issues posed in this collection, both students and practitioners should achieve a deeper understanding of the assumptions, attitudes, opinions, and prejudices that govern not only their own actions, but the actions of others with whom they must work. One would hope, for example, that the public librarian reading Case 1, "A Time to Speak Out," would not only ask himself or herself "How would *I* respond to the plea of the Corregia Family?," but would ask both trustees and staff colleagues "What response would *you* expect of me in a situation of this kind?" The results of such inquiry may prove invaluable, although the process is not without potential hazard, for with the case approach, there is little, if any, room for rationalization in accounting for action.

The Problem-Centered Approaches to Librarianship series is designed to make case studies and related materials available for both formal and informal teaching purposes in the several subfields of librarianship, as well as to demonstrate the value of the case method as a technique for presentation and analysis of contemporary problems of professional practice. Future volumes in this series will appear at regular intervals, and will be concerned with such areas as the simulation approach in teaching library management; selection and utilization of the newer media in libraries; public library service to children and youth; and the role of libraries and information centers in service to the disadvantaged. As series editor, I take genuine pride in presenting *Problems in Intellectual Freedom and Censorship* as the work of a talented, thoughtful, humane, and compassionate teacher which should prove both enlightening and provocative to all who are concerned with the library's role in preserving basic human freedoms.

THOMAS J. GALVIN
Series Editor

PREFACE

• • • • • • • • •

Most librarians are haunted by the feeling that they should be championing all points of view and all forms of expression—even if they themselves cannot endorse some of them. And often they find themselves between the rock of upholding a commitment to intellectual freedom's principles and the whirlpool of catering to the wishes of the people they work with and serve, which may be at variance with these principles. There is a small voice which whispers disturbing questions in their ears as they perform their jobs: Will I, by taking this stand, creating this policy, sponsoring this program, acquiring this book, film, periodical, or whatever, upset my governing authorities, my co-workers, and members of my community? And will these people make trouble? Am I letting my personal antipathies or prejudices interfere with my decisions? Is what I am thinking of doing legal? Is some form of censorship necessary under certain circumstances? How do I balance the interest of freedom of expression against the possible ill effects of that expression? Am I "copping out?"

These are not simple questions to answer. It is little wonder (though not always excusable) that many librarians habitually look for the easy way out—for reasons against purchasing controversial material and thereby not getting involved in issues, rather than for reasons for doing so. They tend to "play it safe," rarely becoming entangled in disputes or moving faster in defense of freedom than their communities will tolerate. Every now and then, however, some librarians do muster up sufficient courage to strike a blow for freedom, but invariably they suffer in their professional and personal lives for their actions.

In no other area do librarians seem so unprepared to handle themselves as in the knotty areas of intellectual freedom and censorship. Most librarians are at a total loss to know what to do before, when, or after the censor comes. It is for these reasons that this book was written. The thirty instructional cases presented attempt to expose librarians and library science students to as many manifestations as possible of the kinds of intellectual freedom and censorship problems that occur or could occur in all types of libraries—public, academic, school, and special. There are cases on the effects on people of reading and viewing pornographic and violence-oriented material; on whether librarians' personal philosophies and political or other beliefs are relevant to the successful discharge of their duties; on whether libraries should lend their weight to one side over another on controversial issues; on what community standards mean and what effects they can have on the selection of material; on whether librarians should turn over borrowing records to the police and other officials; on whether there should be "restricted shelves" and "adults only" sections; on how to inform school boards, trustees, or communities about the *Library Bill of Rights* and other documents on intellectual freedom; on how to convince a staff that a collection needs to become more contemporary; on whether libraries do indeed have an obligation, as many feel, to represent all points of view; and much more.

The purpose of this collection is to help librarians and students formulate personally satisfying and workable philosophies of freedom which will guide them in their professional careers and help them to make decisions with confidence, understanding, and forethought, rather than on the basis of fear, ignorance, or panic. They will be better prepared to approach the questions of selection or retention of controversial material, and involvement or noninvolvement in controversial issues, with a fuller realization of what it means to take a stand or *not* to take a stand. The book is intended for use by library educators in the classroom, by administrators for in-service coaching and developing of their staffs, by leaders of workshops, institutes, and the like—indeed, by anyone involved in the decision making and materials selection processes.

In solving the cases, analysts are compelled to become thoroughly familiar with and to understand the implications of the American Library Association's guidelines on the library's role in intellectual freedom—the *Library Bill of Rights*, the *Freedom to Read Statement*, etc.,—and the First Amendment to the Constitution and its various interpretations.

There is no other book in library literature that deals exclusively with these problems in this way. True, numerous books and articles have been written on the subjects of intellectual freedom and censorship, but they do not force their readers to solve problems as if they were their own. "A man has not seen a thing who has not felt it," Thoreau wrote. This is the beauty of the case method. It presents incidents which readers can relate to, and comes as close as possible to enabling them to become involved in—to have a "feel" for—a situation.

Several of the problem situations described are based on actual occurrences, suitably camouflaged to protect those involved; others are taken from questions raised in library literature. Any similarity between the names of the characters or the descriptions of the libraries or communities and actual people and places is purely coincidental. Two sample student solutions are included at the end of the book to show how variously the cases can be analyzed and solved. The prefix Ms. has been used throughout as a matter of editorial style, and not as a reflection of political or social preference.

The author expresses thanks and appreciation to the Macmillan Publishing Company for permission to quote from *A Sign for Cain* (copyright © 1966) by

Fredric Wertham, and to Holt, Rinehart & Winston, for permission to use material from *Seduction of the Innocent* (copyright © 1953, 1954), also by Dr. Wertham.

To Kenneth R. Shaffer, Director of the School of Library Science at Simmons College, who first introduced the case method into library education, I owe a great debt; he was the impetus behind this book. I am also deeply indebted to Thomas J. Galvin, editor of the Problem-Centered Approaches to Librarianship series, for his extremely valuable assistance and wise counsel. In addition, I am most grateful to Kenneth F. Kister, who created a course in Intellectual Freedom and Censorship at Simmons College; his influence upon my thinking has been profound.

I also owe a vote of thanks to several colleagues who listened to my ideas and offered valuable suggestions—Jane A. Hannigan of Columbia University, Leigh S. Estabrook and James M. Matarazzo of Simmons College, Whitney Smith of the Flag Research Center in Winchester, Massachusetts, and Harry Sagris of Memorial Hall Library in Andover, Massachusetts.

I am also most appreciative of the sensible advice and help which Patricia Glass Schuman and Madeline Miele of the publisher's staff gave me.

I want to thank two former students, Dorothy S. Hirshfield and James Hogan, for permitting me to include their analyses of two of the cases.

Finally, words cannot adequately convey my gratitude to my wife, Victoria, for all her help.

A. J. ANDERSON
School of Library Science
Simmons College

INTRODUCTION

· · · · · · · · · · · · · ·

Our age is experiencing a diversity of modes of expression unprecedented in the history of the world. Never before has there been so much controversy over what is and what is not acceptable. And librarians, whose job is to choose which expressions will be represented in his or her library, find themselves at the very center of this controversy. In spite of its many detractors—both within and without the profession—librarianship is a high calling; it carries with it tremendous responsibility. "Whoever determines what alternatives shall be known to man," Ralph Barton Perry has written, "controls what man shall choose *from*. He is deprived of freedom in proportion as he is denied access to *any* ideas, or is confined to any range of ideas short of the totality of relevant possibilities." A profound responsibility, the harried librarian acknowledges, but does it mean that we should be attempting to satisfy every vagary of human taste in our libraries? Does it mean that we must applaud equally every experiment in expression—however bold, however unrestrained, however pathological?

There are two points of view about freedom, not necessarily mutually exclusive, which have been widely debated in recent times. One says, in the eloquent words of William Ernest Hocking: "If society grants a freedom, it knowingly accepts a degree of risk, a statistical probability of mistaken action; it accepts this as a necessary price for an indispensable social good arising from the undictated explorings of its individual members." The other says, in the cautious words of Will and Ariel Durant: "The first condition of freedom is its limitation; make it absolute and it dies in chaos." The first statement connotes initiative, the second responsibility. The first says that if restrictions are placed upon man's imaginings, life becomes sterile and controlled; the second, that freedom cannot be complete because some men will abuse it beyond what is tolerable and life will become chaotic. None but the most obtuse or naive would deny that freedom can be abused by men and women of evil intent. There are no guarantees in a free society that some people will not act irresponsibly; but neither, as George Steiner wisely observes, are there guarantees that once censorship is made a tool of society it won't be used to suppress all unpopular ideas within that society. The dangers of the cure must always be balanced against the dangers of the disease. The greatest hope for resolving the tension between the two views of freedom is through Hegelian dialectic: thesis and antithesis are "sublated" to beget a higher condition—synthesis. A solution is to be found not by one side triumphing over the other, but rather by the two being lifted up together and merging into a new kind of productive relationship.

One of the problems of our age is to know where to set limits on freedom, if indeed we agree that limits should be imposed. And one of the chief problems for librarians is to know where to set limits on how much freedom shall be allowed in their collections and programs. It is not easy to be a conscientious and dedicated librarian—one who takes his or her work seriously. It *can* be easy to be a librarian; but those who find the work easy must ask themselves if they are doing what they should be doing. Librarians have been notoriously timid, and, like so many Hamlets, have stood irresolute before the act of making a decision. "How far do I go?" is not an easy question to answer; but librarians must resolve it to their own satisfaction—given his or her own particular situation and set of circumstances. Do librarians deny total freedom of expression in their libraries because there is no merit to the particular expression under consideration? Or do they do it because of their personal partialities and because they fear the censor? The answer is of utmost importance. When one listens to the excuses given for not including a sampling, at least, of all varieties of expression (lack of space, no demand, insufficient funds, poor reviews, not suitable to the needs of the community), one perceives a conscious or unconscious rationalization of an elemental impulse in life—an impulse, if one may call it that, of fear. Sometimes these excuses are legitimate, but sometimes they are cover-ups for the two real reasons—fear of the censor, and the librarian's personal feeling of indignation. Neither the censor's nor the librarian's sensibilities can be the final arbiter of what is suitable for a library's collection and practices; there is much more to be considered.

In spite of the idealistic tone of the *Library Bill of Rights* and other noble statements which advocate free expression, there is no way that librarians can be coerced into accepting their urgings unqualifiedly. To be oblivious to the potential implications of taking a stand for principle is to be hopelessly simple. Financial support may be withdrawn, jobs may be jeopardized or lost, and library service may be retarded. An intelligent and well-informed librarian must have a keen sense of logic—an awareness of the possible repercussions of his or her actions—and then make decisions accordingly. There may be times when the wisest course of action might be to do nothing; there may be other times when the wisest course might be to state, like Martin Luther, "Here I stand—I cannot do otherwise." But librarians who *always* lower their standards to match those of the censor, or who *never* put principle before prejudices, are unfit for the profession.

The case studies in this book are intended to help librarians arrive at solutions to the intricate questions intellectual freedom and censorship problems raise. They are designed to provoke a close examination of many practices and beliefs, and thus help clarify purposes and shape philosophies. In achieving these objectives, the question might be raised by those who have not had a great deal of experience teaching by the case method: Why not simply ask librarians and students what they think generally about certain issues rather than involve them in a particular situation? For example, why not ask what they think are the effects on young people of viewing pornographic material—the essential question in Case 18? Or why not ask them whether they think borrowing records should be turned over to the police—the question in Case 12? Or if librarians should move from a passive role to an active one and take sides on controversial issues—the question in Case 22? A well-constructed case contains, in addition to these basic questions, a number of related issues and variables which have to be considered. Thomas J. Galvin has dealt with this question in a paper entitled "A Case Method Approach in Library Education," which appears in *Library School Teaching Methods: Courses in the Selection of Adult Material*, edited by Larry Bone (Urbana, Ill.: Graduate School of Library Science, 1969). Galvin points out that if students are required to make a decision in terms of a particular library in a particular community, a generalized question is put in specific terms and students can then consider all the ramifications of their decision. The context in which a problem arises can have the same influence upon its solution in the classroom as it would in real life.

No case ever describes exactly the circumstances in which readers might find themselves; but when they face similar problems on their jobs they should be able to make the necessary connection between what they have learned from the experience of analyzing a case and their own dilemma—and they should be in a better position to avoid making some of the blunders the characters in the case have made. Because many neophyte librarians and students sometimes find it difficult to assume the role of an experienced administrator, several cases in this book have been written to provide problem-solving roles for people with little or no library experience; in one instance (Case 6), the main character has been on the job only two days. But in most instances, the issue is of pivotal importance and the characters of secondary importance. Because there may be times, however, when the *sex* or *race* of a character might have something to do with the situation, or have some effect upon the outcome, the case entitled "The Confrontation" has been written with the protagonist as male in one instance (Case 29) and female in another (Case 30); in the case entitled "The Other Side," the key character in one instance is black (Case 27) and white in another (Case 28). The facts are identical in both situations. Case analysts are thus given the opportunity to determine whether sex and race *are* important factors in some problem situations.

Some analysts claim they find it difficult to identify with case characters who, in their opinion, are stupid or who make what they think are silly errors of judgment. The case studies in this book attempt to mirror life as nearly as possible. In real life, as everyone knows, all librarians make occasional errors of judgment and some librarians make them frequently. It is axiomatic, however, that we often can discover what should be done by examining what should not have been done. Cases should not only describe ideal characters—people with no flaws (if there be such people)—but also very human ones with human frailties. In another effort to simulate real life in this book, all elderly librarians are not depicted as fools nor all young ones as wise—or vice versa—because that, too, is not the way life is. Also, the male characters are not all portrayed as competent and the female characters as incompetent, nor are all the men supervisors and the women subordinates—or vice versa. With one or two exceptions, stereotypes have been avoided; but stereotypes do exist in the real library world, and so have been described occasionally.

In some of the cases, it is relevant to the solution to know something about the community and the setting; in others, the location is of no consequence. Again, Galvin has dealt with this question in the introduction to his *Problems in Reference Service* (New York: R. R. Bowker, 1965): "One must provide enough details about the environment in which a problem occurs," he says, "and allow the individual characters in the case to reveal themselves through dialogue, so that the student can get a clear sense of *what the specific situation is*. Failure to sketch out the circumstances surrounding a problem in some detail results only in vague, generalized or meaningless student solutions."

In the Intellectual Freedom and Censorship course at Simmons College, the case method is used in conjunction with a body of literature which students read and then discuss in class. The literature, which consists of monographs, essays, novels, plays, and articles, is designed to accomplish three things: (1) to illustrate the continuous struggle over the years of liberty against repression, ignorance, and vested interests; (2) to identify the various rulings and interpretations which have been handed down by the courts on constitutional provisions affecting libraries and librarians; and (3) to alert students to the meaning of democratic ideals and intellectual freedom concepts.

In a given semester at Simmons, students are assigned approximately twelve cases. They are asked to prepare solutions on their own—the two appended student analyses are *samples*, not models, of how this is often done—which they are then requested to share with their instructor and fellow students when they get together in class. What a student may regard as the best course of action before the class meets frequently undergoes considerable alteration when it is discussed. Although there is no single, correct, or "official" solution to the cases, there are many times when, through the interplay of thoughts and the pooling of resources, a concensus is reached on how best to proceed.

Solutions to problems do not come, as a rule, like shafts of lightning out of nowhere; rather, they come after much debate, experimentation, and weighing of possibilities. How much better it is to test out possible solutions in the safe confines of the classroom or the training room than in the harsh crucible of the real world! This book affords the reader the opportunity to do just that.

Problems in Intellectual Freedom and Censorship

1.
A Time to Speak Out

· · · · · · · · · · · · · · ·

The May 7 edition of the Vallins *Sentinel* carried the following letter to the Editor:

To the Editor:

When we read that Walter Berle had recently confessed to committing the brutal rape–murders of the four young women in town, one of whom was our daughter, we felt impelled to break our silence and do our part to warn people of the evil effects of too much permissiveness.

It has been revealed in the media that Berle owned several books dealing with gruesome and ghastly themes and a large collection of photographs and descriptions of sado-masochistic behavior.

We feel that publishers, librarians, editors, theater owners, and television and movie producers must take a serious look at what they are offering the public. Is the freedom to have literature such as Berle collected worth human lives? Will society be hurt if it is not available? Is the suffering of parents who have lost loved ones of less importance than the suffering of society because some of its members who relish depictions of violence might not be able to get it? If hundreds of people were killed, would we then listen to the voice of reason? Obviously, no one is going to get upset and do anything because our daughter was killed—she is only one person. Everybody says it is too bad, but no one does anything about it.

Because we cannot accept our daughter's death, we have been attempting to understand the mind of a madman like Berle. We have recently looked into accounts of the lives and habits, including the reading habits, of others who have committed similar atrocious acts. "I read a lot of sexy stuff," the Boston Strangler said in Gerold Frank's book. Would Arthur Bremer have attempted to assassinate George Wallace if he had not read *RFK Must Die?* Did Charles Whitman read Ford Clark's *The Open Square,* as some think, before he undertook his mass murders? Did the reading of de Sade's *Justine,* Gorer's *Life and Ideas of the Marquis de Sade,* Hitler's *Mein Kampf,* and Robbins' *Carpet-baggers* cause Ian Brady and Myra Hindley to torture and beat to death the children (and tape-record the pitiful screams of the helpless little girl in her final moments before she expired) in the celebrated Moors murders, as Pamela Hansford Johnson and Emlyn Williams suggest? Would the brutal torch-burning of Evelyn Wagler in Boston have occurred if the movie *Fuzz* had not been shown on television a few days earlier? These are questions we must ask ourselves. And what about the reading habits of Lee Harvey Oswald, Charles Manson, Richard Speck, and James Essex? When will the madness end?

We lost a daughter at the hands of a maniac. We have another daughter age sixteen, and we are terrified that the same thing might happen to her. Unthinking libertarian intellectuals would probably say we are "overreacting" and that our fears are unfounded, and they would recommend that we see a psychiatrist whose job is to accommodate us to this sick society. How easy it is to dismiss our plight. Would the reader of this letter be willing to give up *his* or *her* life, so that some mentally deranged person can read and view some of the sadistic and violent material to be found in our libraries, bookstores, movie houses, theaters, magazines, and newspapers? Don't the people who work in these places have feelings? As long as it's not their daughters, they don't care. Can society afford to ignore the social and moral consequences of pathological minds? The standard response to our questions and comments is to say that this is a price we pay for democracy. Is this form of democracy worth it? Can't a democracy act responsibly? Does democracy mean irresponsibility? Will Durant has written that "Civilization begins with order, grows with liberty, declines with license, and dies with chaos." Are we declining with license? Or even reaching a chaotic state? It is time for someone to speak out. Why must someone who speaks out be a Cassandra, never to be believed? Another response is to say that we must change and reform society. What an easy way to avoid the problem. Are defenders of free expression to be found in the vanguard of movements to change and reform society? Do librarians, for instance, ever do anything besides defend the right of all sorts of material to be in their libraries? Or editors? Or bookstore dealers? Or publishers?

We say that responsible people must learn to censor responsibly. We are speaking out on behalf of others who might be concerned with the surfeit of violent, sadistic, and pornographic material that is finding its way into our communities.

Louis and Maria Corregia

On the same page was an editorial commenting upon Mr. and Ms. Corregia's letter.

A HUMBLE REMONSTRANCE

With a sincerity that bespeaks concern, Louis and Maria Corregia have addressed a letter to us which raises disturbing questions and gives all thoughtful men cause to reflect. There have been widely divergent views by psychologists on the causal or causative effects of violently oriented reading matter on human behavior. Some contend that it can trigger abnormal behavior, others that it serves as a release, a safety valve. It has been suggested that the federal government undertake a scientific study to determine the effect of violence on the human mind, and that scientific data measuring the effect be developed. But even if the results show (as we suspect they would) no harmful effect upon the average person, lack of proof of harmfulness is not proof of harmlessness.

When Alfred Hitchcock was interviewed upon the appearance of his film, *Frenzy,* a few years ago, he was asked if he thought explicit scenes of sexual murder might cause a viewer to commit criminal sexual acts. He was reminded by the interviewer that a young man, after viewing *Psycho,* had assaulted and fatally stabbed a woman who was taking a shower. Hitchcock concluded that the artist cannot be responsible for, or even concerned with, the moral consequences of his art. If the artist isn't, then perhaps society has to be.

A few years ago, *Encounter* reported that in Los Angeles, "Police have charged a college student with killing two men after reading a novel by the late French author Albert Camus." The novel, *The Outsider,* was required reading for one of the student's first-year college courses. There is an account in the book of the slaying of a man on a lonely beach. The student admitted that he selected two men whom he did not know to try out the slaying depicted in the novel.

These examples, along with those the Corregias cite, force us to conclude that it may be folly not to allow for the possible link between viewing and reading violent material and overt action of a violent and antisocial nature. We are reminded that during wars, armies are shown training films that are designed to get soldiers in a mood for killing. They are reported to be effective.

We had our own tragedy in this city a few weeks ago, which the Corregias refer to. You will recall that the bodies of four young women in their late teens and early twenties were found in a section of Vallins. Each had been assaulted, brutally tortured, and then strangled with her own stockings. The man charged with the murders, Walter Berle, a factory worker of seventeen, finally confessed to committing the crimes. Upon investigating Berle's life-style, the police reported that he owned an extensive collection of sado-masochistic books and photographs. Berle lived by himself in a one-room apartment and worked as a lathe operator in a furniture manufacturing plant. His employers said he was a responsible employee and that his work was satisfactory. It seems, however, that he did not have any close friends at work and that he always stayed by himself. His father was dead, and his mother lived with two other children in a neighboring city.

We recognize that censorship is an evil, but we are forced to ask if the endless outpouring of uncurbed violence in books, films, and magazines has not reached a point where society must declare surcease. We would agree with the Corregias that some form of restraint has become necessary if society is to remain decent and orderly.

As a result of the Corregias' letter, this newspaper has decided to prohibit lurid advertising of films in our entertainment section. From now on, films rated R and X will merely be listed by title. (We might point out to those cynics who look upon this as a token and meaningless gesture that we do so at a considerable loss of advertising revenue.) We will attempt to find other ways, too, of exercising reasonable restraint and we call upon everyone else—publishers, librarians, theater owners—to do likewise. Our goal is not to put shackles on art and literature, or eliminate free expression, but to get less pleasant representations out of sight. Perhaps our society needs to reconsider the merits of the old "Hicklin" rule.

Melanie Pym, director of the Vallins Public Library, read the letter and the editorial before leaving for work, and decided to clip both so she could discuss them with her staff. Upon arriving at the library, she immediately instructed her secretary to route the clippings to her three assistant directors. "Attach a note," she directed, "and ask Neil, Esther, and Sean if they can meet with me a week from today to discuss these articles."

Three days later, she received the following letter from Mr. and Ms. Corregia; it contained a copy of their original letter to the editor and the editorial.

Dear Ms. Pym:

We don't know whether you have seen these, but we have been most heartened by the response of the *Sentinel.* We are writing to ask you to consider some thoughts we have in regard to libraries.

We recognize that libraries have an obligation to make something of everything available and to present different points of view. We used to feel that libraries could not be held responsible for what people do with the information obtained from library materials, but lately we have been wondering if this is an easy way out and whether you shouldn't be judging material for your collection on the basis of its effect not upon the normal or average person, but rather upon the abnormal person—someone like Walter Berle, for example—in the interest of the welfare of others.

We are not suggesting that a library collection should be reduced to the level of pap, but would that necessarily happen if books and periodicals of the kind Berle read were eliminated? We do not have a list of specific titles we would like to see removed—you would know better than we what they are—but we would ask you to examine your collection and discard books that depict violent crimes and are thus potentially dangerous.

Please don't write us and say that no one knows the effects of reading upon people and try to excuse yourself by rationalizing that by having examples of all kinds of writing you are just doing your job. Hitler's followers said that they were just doing their job, and members of Nixon's Committee to Re-elect the President thought the same. If books can be a force for good, as educators have believed since time immemorial, then does it not follow that they can also be a force for evil? It just doesn't make sense to acknowledge the ennobling effect of certain books and deny the harmful effects of others.

We are asking you to consider our views and asking you how you can justify keeping material that depicts violence in your collection.

Yours truly,
Louis and Maria Corregia

The library director made copies of this letter and took them personally to her assistants. "I'd like to respond to these people," she said, "but I'd like to do so after we've had a chance to discuss their letters and the editorial. Perhaps you three could get reactions from some of the staff on what we should say and do. Mr. and Ms. Corregia and the editorial make some good points. Perhaps we *should* stop buying certain materials. Perhaps the quality of life *is* deteriorating because of what people read and see on TV and in the movies. Anyway, I'd like to talk with you about this."

Almost immediately, letters to the editor started appearing in the *Sentinel* supporting the views expressed by the parents of the dead girl and applauding the paper for refusing to advertise R and X rated films. Two letters raised specific questions about what actions were contemplated by the library in reviewing its collections. Ms. Pym clipped these as well.

Vallins is a large manufacturing and commercial city of 400,000 in a southern state. The Vallins Public Library has a collection of close to 1,000,000 volumes, which are located in the central library and its six branches. Everything in the collection circulates, with the exception of rare books and books in the reference collections. Periodicals, recordings, art reproductions, films, filmstrips, and other forms of media also go out for specified periods of time.

Melanie Pym has been director of the library for five years. Looked upon as an able administrator by the trustees and the staff, she has delegated the responsibility for the selection of material to her three assistants and the branch librarians. The branch librarians in selecting material for their collections do not have to clear their selections with anyone at the central library. Most of Ms. Pym's time is given over to administrative matters such as budgeting, controlling, and planning.

•   •   •   •   •

Evaluate the arguments raised by the Corregias and the editorial and determine how you would respond if you were asked to do so by the director or her assistants. What do you advise Ms. Pym to do at this point?

2.
And Gladly Teach
· · · · · · · · · · · ·

Eugene Farrell Kennedy was considered to be a truly excellent teacher—at least by most of the seniors at Claxton High School. A twenty-four-year-old alumnus of one of the nation's best graduate schools of education, he was a humane and sensitive individual who took his teaching responsibilities seriously. His classes were reported to be exciting; in fact, in the opinion of many students, he was the first person at Claxton who had been able to make twentieth-century American history—his subject—come to life. Mr. Kennedy attempted in his courses to use the method of synthetic history, in which he and the class studied all phases of a people's life, work, and culture in their simultaneous operation; and he supplemented the classroom scene by taking his students on frequent visits to places where contemporary history was being made—to the state house, the city hall, and wherever men were hammering out new codes by which other men would live. He encouraged his students to read newspapers and journals, watch television documentaries and news shows, attend and take part in local affairs, and then report back to the class what they had discovered and learned. Sometimes, he brought books and magazines into class which he knew were somewhat advanced for his seniors, and from these he would quote pertinent passages that he hoped would be thought-provoking. Lincoln Moore, the media specialist at Claxton High, found that of all the teachers, Gene Kennedy made the greatest use of the center's materials.

Maureen K. Black, the principal of Claxton High, and Sidney J. Dubnitsky, the head of the history department, prided themselves on having had the good judgment to add Gene Kennedy to the staff. They had heard nothing but favorable reports from students and parents during the young teacher's first year.

Not everyone was happy with Mr. Kennedy, however. His unbridled enthusiasm, unflagging energy, and great popularity had embarrassed some of the other members of the faculty. Seemingly resentful of his success, a few of them attempted to undermine the confidence that Ms. Black and Mr. Dubnitsky displayed in him, but they had little effect.

Claxton is a wealthy suburb of a large city in the western part of the country. Its high school has a comparatively strong tradition of excellence, and the annual cost-per-pupil of educating its 2,000 students is among the highest in the nation. The people of Claxton share a desire to see their children receive the best education possible, and they are willing to skimp in other places in order that the school system be well supported.

The building known as Claxton High is relatively new. When the school committee identified the need for a new high school a few years ago, the community went along with the request willingly; the old high school became a junior high, and the junior high became an elementary school. The town officials interpreted the lack of opposition to the new school as a mandate from the community that they were to go ahead with their emphasis on quality education.

One day, Mr. Kennedy was dealing with the question of political revolutionaries—the shapers of a new history, he called them—and in the course of the discussion, he quoted frequently from Robert Jay Lifton's book *History and Human Survival,* which he had borrowed from the school media center; the book was not in the curriculum. Lifton says that mockery is a basic component of modern-day political rebels. In the course of illustrating the author's meaning, Mr. Kennedy traced, as Lifton does in the book, the history of the classic slogan, "Up against the wall, mother-fucker!" Mr. Kennedy felt slightly uncomfortable with the expression, but he was sure all his students had heard it many times—if not used it. He felt that he could not have a meaningful discussion on the question of revolution if he ignored certain things that modern revolutionaries say and do.

That particular class had not gone as well as most, but the young teacher put it down to the fact that many students in the mixed class felt somewhat uneasy hearing the expression used in the classroom. There were no snickers, but there was some obvious shock on the part of some of the students.

On Wednesday morning, two days later, Mr. Dubnitsky came into Mr. Kennedy's home room during the latter's free period.

"Gene," he said, "I've just been in with Ms. Black. Apparently we've got a problem on our hands."

"What is it, Sid?" inquired Mr. Kennedy.

"Well, from what I can gather you used the word 'mother-fucker' in one of your classes. Is that true?"

Mr. Kennedy proceeded to explain how it had been introduced, stating that it seemed very logical and necessary for purposes of the discussion. Mr. Dubnitsky listened. "I can see your line of reasoning," he said. "But frankly, I don't think you should have done it. I think you should have alluded to the expression, without actually saying it."

The two men discussed the matter at some length, but Mr. Kennedy could not convince Mr. Dubnitsky that it was the right thing to do. He asked his department head how he had heard about it. Mr. Dubnitsky revealed that one of the boys in the class had told his parents about the discussion, and the parents had come to see Ms. Black. They said that a teacher who used language like that in the classroom should be dismissed, and they referred to Mr. Kennedy as a "corrupt person, unfit to teach young people." They were also planning to attend the school committee meeting next week, at which time they intended to press for Mr. Kennedy's dismissal. "Apparently they're mounting a campaign against you and have enlisted the support of several other parents in the community," he added.

Mr. Kennedy grew pale. "It looks as if you're not behind me, Sid," he said. "How about Ms. Black? How does she feel?"

"Let me clear up my position first," Mr. Dubnitsky retorted. "I think you made a mistake, but that doesn't mean I'm not behind you. I chalk the whole thing up to your inexperience. If you had been around longer, you'd have realized that it was not the thing to do."

"Are you telling me that after you've been around a while, you don't deal with things as they are?" Mr. Kennedy asked.

"You do, but you're more cautious," Mr. Dubnitsky replied.

Mr. Kennedy asked again where Ms. Black stood. "This is of such serious proportions," Mr. Dubnitsky replied, "that she wants us both to go down to her office now. I gather though, to answer your question, that she's not pleased with what you did."

When Mr. Dubnitsky and Mr. Kennedy arrived at the principal's office, Ms. Black, the superintendent of schools, and the chairman of the school committee were there. The chairman stated that he hoped they could resolve the situation satisfactorily. He invited the young teacher to tell his version of the story, asking him if he *had* used the expression in the classroom. Mr. Kennedy admitted he had, explaining the context in which it was used and his purpose in using it. The chairman reiterated what Mr. Dubnitsky had already mentioned—that some parents were going to demand the teacher be dismissed. He had heard they were circulating a petition calling upon the school committee to take immediate action, and that the petition would be presented to the committee at its next regularly scheduled meeting, that Thursday night. He assured Mr. Kennedy that the school committee would consider the issue carefully and make what it hoped would be the wisest decision. In the meantime, he thought it would be in the best interests of everyone concerned if the teacher maintained a low profile for the next few days, and did nothing that would stir up any further trouble. Their decision would be communicated to him on Friday.

At about eleven-thirty Thursday night, Mr. Kennedy got a telephone call from Ms. Black. She apologized for calling so late, but said she was sure he would want to know what the school committee had decided. The principal told him that the members were unanimous in deciding to ask for his resignation. She said she was sorry to have to report such bad news, but that she concurred with the decision; she went on to say that he could come to the school the next morning to gather up his belongings and bring in his letter of resignation.

After spending a sleepless night, Mr. Kennedy drove to Claxton High as usual. He went to his home room, to be greeted by Mr. Dubnitsky. "Gee, Gene, I'm really sorry about the decision," he said.

"I'm going to fight it, Sid," Mr. Kennedy replied. "If I don't, it'll look as if I've done something wrong—and I haven't. I told it like it was, and I was right in doing so. I'm going to get some support. Will you back me?"

"Look, Gene, I'd love to, but the word is out that anyone on the faculty who comes to your defense might lose his job too."

"God! That means Lincoln Moore might be in trouble. I got the book from the media center. I better warn him. He's the one who brought the book to may attention."

"He'd better get rid of it," Mr. Dubnitsky said quickly. "I'm sure sorry to see you go and I wish there were something I could do."

"Never mind, Sid. I'm going to prepare a strong case. I'm going to take this to the Civil Liberties Union and the Teacher's Association, and I'm not going to resign. No siree! They're not going to get off that easy. Talk about academic freedom! Talk about a progressive community! Ha! I didn't even get a formal hearing."

"Don't do anything foolish, Gene," Mr. Dubnitsky said as he was leaving. "Good luck."

Mr. Kennedy then proceeded down the hall to the media center. He was on good terms with the media specialist, whom he regarded as one of his best friends at the school. Lincoln Moore, a young, single man who had been at Claxton two years, and who was also very well regarded, had heard of his friend's dismissal, and he offered his sympathies. Mr. Kennedy asked the media specialist if, because of the latter's expressed commitment to intellectual freedom, he would help prepare some arguments which could be used in preparing a defense—an amicus curiae brief—and if he could obtain any help from the American Library Association. He then warned Mr. Moore that he might be the next target of attack, since the book was in the media center's collection. "I mentioned it unintentionally to Sid Dubnitsky," he added, "and he'll probably tell Black."

Mr. Moore assured his friend that someone would have discovered it sooner or later, and not to feel badly. "I bought it because I felt it complemented the curriculum," he said. "It was a good purchase. I've been meaning to write up a selection policy statement to cover me when materials are challenged. This is my first censorship case, by the way," he added impishly.

Just then, Ms. Black appeared. She saw the two men talking, but came over anyway and asked if she could speak to the media specialist privately. Mr. Kennedy left. Ms. Black said she wanted Robert Jay Lifton's book *History and Human Survival* removed from the collection. "I took it out of the media center last night and skimmed through it. I'm returning it now but I want you to remove it from the collection. You've probably heard that Gene Kennedy has been dismissed because he quoted a certain expression from it. Its presence in the collection could be a source of embarrassment to us. I'd feel obligated to inform the superintendent and the school committee that we have it. Anyway, they'd probably ask whether we did, and they'd want us to get rid of it. It wouldn't surprise me if some of the kids or their parents checked to see if we had it. I want to be able to tell them that it's gone."

• • • • •

What advice would you give Mr. Kennedy? How would you respond to his request that you help him? Is this the type of case the Civil Liberties Union would be interested in? Did Mr. Kennedy show poor judgment in openly quoting the controversial term in the classroom? How would you respond to the principal's injunction that the book be removed from the collection? How would you resolve the apparent conflict between loyalty to the school system and a commitment to intellectual freedom?

3.
The Art of Self-Defense
· · · · · · · · · · · · · · · · · · ·

The Shady Hills Branch, the newest of six branches of the public library in Lansdowne, a city of some 300,000 people, is located in the fastest-growing section of town. There are many families with children in this rather exclusive area, and the library has several programs designed to appeal to young people and children particularly.

Harvey L. Baxter has been in charge of the branch since it was constructed three years ago. When he was opening his mail one morning, he found this letter:

Dear Mr. Baxter:

The other day my ten-year-old son came home crying. He and two of his playmates had been beaten up by a gang of older boys. I asked him who the older boys were but he said he didn't know. I called up the mothers of the other two boys, and one of them knew more about what had happened. All three of our children were black and blue.

It seems some older boys, around fourteen or fifteen years of age, in our neighborhood have been borrowing karate and judo books from your branch of the library and have been trying out their newly learned jabs on younger children.

I have been wondering if you would be good enough to put your karate and judo books out of circulation for a while until the older boys lose interest in them, which I am sure will happen.

Yours truly,
(Ms.) Anna Whitmore

When Mr. Baxter had finished reading the letter, he went to the card catalog to see how many karate and judo books the library owned. On his way there, he met the children's librarian and told her about the letter. "The mother doesn't want them taken off the shelf forever," the children's librarian asked, "she just wants them taken off for a while? That's an unusual request, isn't it? What are you going to do?"

"I'll write her a reply, of course, but I'm not going to take the books off the shelves," Mr. Baxter replied. "That would be censorship. Say, would you check in the children's catalog and see if we have any karate books there?" The children's librarian said she would and that she would let him know right away. (She reported later that there weren't any.) Mr. Baxter continued on his way to the combined adult and young adult catalog. He took out a note pad and wrote down the authors' names and the titles of six books on karate and judo.

His list looked like this:

Freudenberg, Karl. *Natural Weapons: A Manual of Karate, Judo and Jujitso Techniques.*
Masters, Robert V. *The Complete Book of Self-Defense.*
Mattson, George E. *The Way of Karate.*
Otaki, Tadeo, and Donn F. Draeger. *Judo for Young Men.*
Oyama, Masutata. *Advanced Karate.*
Trias, Robert A. *The Hand is My Sword: A Karate Handbook.*

On his way back to his office, he stopped by the circulation desk to inquire whether karate and judo books were charged out very often. The clerk said they passed through her hands quite frequently.

Mr. Baxter decided that he might as well reply to Ms. Whitmore right away. He wrote:

Dear Ms. Whitmore:

I was sorry to hear about your son being beaten up by older boys, and hope that he is all right now and that it doesn't happen again.

I have given some thought to your request that we put our karate and judo books out of circulation for a while, and find that I cannot in good conscience do it. We librarians cannot be responsible for what people do with the material they take from the library. Supposing a man borrows a book on home electrical repairs and electrocutes himself—could the library be blamed? Or if someone borrows a book which gives the formularies for manufacturing poison, because he wants to get rid of insects, and one of his young children swallows some and dies—can the library be held responsible? Likewise, if someone takes out a book on the manufacture of explosives and blows up his house, can the library be held responsible?

I am sure you see my reasoning. We in the library wouldn't want these things to happen, but we can't keep them from happening. And even if we removed books on karate and judo, poisons, and explosives, people could still get the books in bookstores.

I am also afraid of the idea of taking something off the shelves for one person, because then we might have to do it for another person and another, and another, until perhaps we were left with nothing. I am sure that almost everyone has something he would like to see removed from a library's collection.

I am truly sorry that I can't go along with your request.

Yours truly,
Harvey L. Baxter
Branch Librarian

After Mr. Baxter sent off his reply, he promptly forgot about the whole matter.

He was going through his mail about a week later when he noticed another envelope from Ms. Whitmore. He opened it and was quite shocked to see a copy of a letter addressed to the Director of the Lansdowne Public Library, Emily Suzzallo. The letter read:

Dear Ms. Suzzallo:

I am sending along a copy of a letter which I wrote to Mr. Harvey L. Baxter at your Shady Hills Branch and a copy of his reply to my letter. I want you to know that I am not at all satisfied with his reply.

After you have read both letters, which I would like you to do before going on with my letter to you, I am sure you will agree that my request is not extreme. I am not asking much.

I am asking *you* to remove for a period of time the karate and judo books that the Shady Hills Branch owns. When I received Mr. Baxter's reply, I immediately got in touch with the chief instructor of judo and karate at the Lansdowne YMCA to ask him if serious harm could result from using a karate book without the benefit of a competent instructor, and he said certainly. He is strongly against a person teaching himself karate and trying out on others techniques which have not been demonstrated by competent trainers, and he said I could quote him. I think that he plans to discuss the matter with you or Mr. Baxter. Do you not consider the opinions of experts at all, or do librarians think that they know more than experts? If a member of the medical profession told you a book was dangerous, would you ignore him?

Mr. Baxter seems to worry that if he removes a few karate books from the shelves, everybody in Lansdowne is going to descend upon him demanding that books they consider harmful or don't like be removed. Is there any evidence that this would happen? Is there any precedent for this? Surely some librarians have obliged some patrons from time to time. Have they gone out of business? Are librarians impervious to reason? Don't librarians feel any sense of responsibility to their communities?

It seems to me that we have a "clear and present danger" situation here, and I hope *you* at least will recognize it.

I am asking you, therefore, if you would remove the karate and judo books from the shelves of the Shady Hills Branch temporarily at least.

I shall look forward to hearing from you.

Yours truly,
(Ms.) Anna Whitmore

When he had finished reading the letter, Mr. Baxter thought of calling Ms. Suzzallo. He decided not to, however, thinking that he would wait to see what she would do.

• • • • •

What would you do if you were Ms. Suzzallo? How would you feel about Ms. Whitmore's request? What do you think of Mr. Baxter's reply to Ms. Whitmore? Would you have done anything differently? What do you think of the arguments that Ms. Whitmore gives to justify her request?

4.
Those Sunday Afternoon Festivals
· ·

It was a cool Tuesday evening in late October, and Jane Reynolds, the director of the Temora Public Library, fidgeted as she waited for the members of the board of trustees to arrive. The October meeting of the board had been called for the regular time and place—seven-thirty at the Trustees Room of the library—but it was now a quarter of eight and they were still waiting for one member, Herbert Boutwell, to arrive.

Bertha Wilcox, who had requested that her name be placed on the agenda of the meeting, had arrived promptly at seven-thirty. She had been mysteriously secretive about her reasons for wanting to meet with the trustees, and when she had asked her long-time friend, George Tomlinson, who was the chairman of the board, if she could speak at the meeting, she implored him not to ask her why. Mr. Tomlinson had respected her unusual request and had decided, along with Ms. Reynolds, who always attended the meetings and who helped to draw up the agendas, that the normal order of business should be reversed and that Ms. Wilcox should be the first item of business that night. Finally, by eight o'clock, the tardy member of the five-member board scurried in, apologizing profusely. Ms. Reynolds sighed with relief when she saw him. The time spent in idle chatter while they waited for Mr. Boutwell to arrive had been painful, since everyone was terribly curious to know what Ms. Wilcox wanted.

After taking a good-natured jibe at Mr. Boutwell for arriving late, the chairman called the meeting to order. He welcomed Ms. Wilcox and then asked the secretary of the board, Emily Warburg, to read the minutes of the last meeting. The formalities over, he proceeded immediately to the first item of business—Ms. Bertha Wilcox.

Ms. Wilcox was a widow of about sixty-five. She had lived all of her life in

Temora and had been very active in the affairs of the town over the years, having served as president of the League of Women Voters and having held positions on several boards, including a twelve-year stint on the school committee. She was well-known and respected in the community, and when she spoke, most people, particularly the older citizens, listened to her. Her only child, a son, lived in Temora with his wife and their two teenage children.

"Thank you, George," Ms. Wilcox began eagerly. "Ladies and gentlemen, you are no doubt wondering why I am here and why I have not revealed my reasons for wanting to meet with this group. I am sorry for the suspense, but I did not want any of what I have to say to leak out. You see, my son and daughter-in-law didn't want me to come here and so I haven't told them I was meeting with you."

"The suspense is killing, Ms. Wilcox!" Ms. Warburg said with a chuckle.

"When you realize what is going on, I'm sure you'll want to settle everything right here, tonight, and that there'll not be any need for anyone to know I've met with you. Although," she added as an afterthought, "maybe other people have spoken to you about this matter already."

"What matter, Bertha?" the chairman asked.

"The Sunday afternoon programs. Your library has been inviting teenagers to the library on Sunday afternoons to listen to music and dance in the main reading room. I gather the library has been building up quite a collection of their kind of music to attract teenagers into the library."

"That's right," Ms. Reynolds said, somewhat nervously. "The Sunday afternoon festivals, as we call them, are very successful. We're getting lots of kids into the library."

"Well, I'm terribly disturbed by them," Ms. Wilcox continued. "You've been inviting parents to see what's going on, and two Sundays ago I came with my two grandchildren. What I heard was shocking. Some of the songs being played were—I don't even like to mention the titles, but I must—some of the titles were 'Lay, Lady, Lay,' 'Draft Dodger Rag,' 'We Can Get Together,' 'Mr. Tambourine Man,' 'Let It Bleed,' and 'You Can't Always Get What You Want.' The only reason I know those titles, and that's just a few of them, is because I asked my grandchildren what they were. I was appalled to discover that our library has been spending our tax money on music of this sort. Don't you know what this music advocates? It advocates drug use and sexual promiscuity and resistence to war and the government. I saw young children under twelve years of age listening. How can they grow up to have respect for all the decent things in life if they hear this kind of music? I feel I must do something for the good of the community. My son and his wife said they didn't want me to make a fuss and that they'd just keep their children away from now on."

Ms. Wilcox paused for a moment to catch her breath. Neither Ms. Reynolds nor the board members said anything; they merely looked back and forth at each other and at Ms. Wilcox.

"These songs are disgraceful," she continued. "They encourage sexual intercourse between teenagers. I just can't accept the fact that they're being played in our public library. I thought libraries were places where people went for knowledge and education and inspiration. Songs like these turn our young people against the military and the government. According to the words, it's smart to take drugs. And the language that's used in some of them! I tell you it's absolutely disgusting. I couldn't believe my ears. Our public library encouraging children to hear things like this! Do you know what these songs are saying? How can you do it? What on earth are you trying to accomplish? What possible good can come from youngsters listening to this kind of thing? No wonder we have a generation gap, and by playing music of this sort you're contributing to it. I'm sick with the thought that the library is doing this. Young people have susceptible minds. What's this music doing to them? You've got to stop permitting the young people to play this kind of song, or stop these Sunday afternoon programs."

Ms. Wilcox paused again, only this time Mr. Tomlinson spoke up. "Bertha, we can see you're upset," he ventured, fumbling for something to say. "I have to admit that I'm not familiar with the songs you mentioned. Is this right, Jane?" he continued, turning to Ms. Reynolds. "Are the songs as bad as Ms. Wilcox describes them?"

Mr. Tomlinson was about the same age as Ms. Wilcox, and he too had lived all of his life in Temora. He worked as a professional engineer in a large utility firm in a neighboring city. An easy-going and likable man, he had been involved in only a few minor controversies as a board member over the years, but always the controversies had been settled to everyone's satisfaction. Jane Reynolds was thirty-four and this was her first directorship. She had graduated from library school nine years ago. John Bayley, the former director, had paved the way well for Ms. Reynolds. He had been able to get the board of trustees to endorse the *Library Bill of Rights* and to agree that its principles should guide the selection of material for the library. The board felt that no other selection policy statement was necessary.

It was Mr. Bayley who had started to build up a collection of contemporary music, and Ms. Reynolds continued to buy extensively in that area, adding two new stereos, which she was anxious to see used more.

The first Sunday festival took place at the end of the first week of school. Ms. Reynolds, Mr. Tomlinson, and the young adult librarian attended and were very encouraged by the turnout. Approximately fifty teenagers showed up at various times during the afternoon to play records, talk, and dance. Everyone seemed to have a good time. The young adult librarian rearranged her schedule so that she could be there every Sunday afternoon, and Ms. Reynolds continued to drop in occasionally.

A few parents came from time to time and seemed pleased with what they saw. The library was noisy, but there was never any trouble. Ms. Reynolds was able to give the trustees a favorable report at their September meeting.

When Mr. Tomlinson asked Ms. Reynolds if the recordings were as bad as Ms. Wilcox had said they were, the director took a few seconds to gather her thoughts.

"I don't want to belittle the issues that Ms. Wilcox raises," she said, "but I'm not sure they're as clearcut as she makes them out to be. I must say, I'd hate to close down on Sundays. This is one of the most successful programs we've ever had. We're getting anywhere from seventy-five to a hundred kids dropping in. Several parents have thanked us for what we're doing because they're glad the kids are here and not out on the streets or in other places. I won't exaggerate and say that lots of parents have come, but there have been quite a few. I'd really hate to see us turn away our youth. We can't let the kids down. I really feel. . . ."

"How can you approve of what those songs are saying, Ms. Reynolds?" Ms. Wilcox intercepted. "They're unpatriotic, and obscene, and just plain disgusting."

"How are the records that the kids listen to selected, Jane?" inquired the treasurer.

"I'd like to know that too," Ms. Wilcox added.

"The kids select them themselves from our collection or bring in their own," Ms. Reynolds answered. "They play anything they want. Ms. Wilcox must have been there on a day when they were playing songs that were popular in the late 1960s and early 1970s. On other days, they might play other records. We don't control what they listen to."

"I have to admit to you, Bertha," one board member confessed, "I don't know any of the songs you mentioned. I think I've heard 'Lay, Lady, Lay,' but that's the only one I know."

"If you don't mind my saying so, I'm quite surprised to hear you say that," Ms. Wilcox declared. "I would've thought all of you would know what's going on. Don't you have any policies or guidelines that you follow when you're deciding what to buy? How can you justify having songs like that in your collection?"

"I'd like to try to answer some of your questions," Ms. Reynolds ventured. "We have the *Library Bill of Rights* which we use as our guideline in selection."

"We endorsed the *Library Bill of Rights* when Mr. Bayley was here quite a few years ago, Bertha," Mr. Tomlinson commented.

"What does it say?" Ms. Wilcox asked.

"I have a copy downstairs which I'd be happy to get for you," Ms. Reynolds said. "It's very short and only takes a minute or so to read. I'll run down and get it."

"I warn you all, I'm not going to be talked into giving my approval to what teenagers are being exposed to in this library. I don't really care what your bill of rights says. There's such a thing as common sense and that takes precedence over everything else. What possible good can come from the youngsters hearing what I heard in this very library? What do the rest of you think? Only three of you have spoken up. Am I right or am I wrong? Can you sit there and tell me that these records are not harmful?"

One member, who had not said anything, stated that she had great confidence in Ms. Reynolds' ability and that the board had given the director and her staff total responsibility for selection of materials. Mr. Boutwell remarked that he was sure many young people had these records at home and that they could hear them in other places. He said that he didn't think the library could shield children against the realities of the world. Just as he was beginning to say something about the library trying to be relevant to all members of Temora, Ms. Reynolds returned.

"Here's the *Library Bill of Rights*," she said, interrrupting Mr. Boutwell and handing a copy of the document to Ms. Wilcox, who read it. She put the sheet down and declared, "I don't see any reference here to music. Quite frankly, I don't think this justifies your Sunday afternoon festivals. In fact, I think this is a pretty poor statement to use as your guiding principle. I'm beginning to wonder what else there is in the library that shouldn't be there, if this is your guideline."

"Now, don't get carried away, Bertha," Mr. Tomlinson said firmly. "We're doing a good job here and we're very proud of our staff. Under Ms. Reynolds' direction we have seen a continuation—and even furtherance—of many of the fine things that Bayley started. Our circulation is up and we offer a wider variety of programs. We have more things for more people."

"Well, I don't want to get into that," the older woman rejoined. "I'm concerned about the Sunday afternoon programs. They must stop, or you must not permit songs of the kind that I heard to be played."

"I have to resist both suggestions, Ms. Wilcox," the director said, somewhat nervously. "I hope the board will back me when I say that I think these Sunday programs are extremely important. I can't see stopping them. And I don't want to censor what the kids want to hear."

"There's plenty of nice music around," Ms. Wilcox interjected. "Why can't you play some of it?"

"As we said earlier, the kids play what *they* want to hear. We don't interfere with their choices. In reference to the point you made earlier about the generation gap, I find I cannot agree with you. Drugs and revolution and the changing sexual mores are part of the songs you mentioned. But there have been no definitive, authoritative studies proving a cause and effect relationship between music and action. I feel this music is of extreme social value. In one way or another, all the songs you mentioned are social commentary. This generation has to come to terms with war, drugs, and sex. In music, the kids are expressing their fears artistically in the hope that their fears and observations will make a difference."

"Balderdash!" Ms. Wilcox exclaimed. "The people who write this music are doing it for the money."

"I don't know about that," Ms. Reynolds returned, brushing aside the comment. "Anyway, we're fooling ourselves if we think we can keep this kind of music away from kids. Take it out of the library and they'll get it somewhere else. I think the sentiments expressed in the songs are not the cause of the generation gap, but indicative of it. Perhaps in our small way we at the library are doing something to bridge the generation gap. I don't want to seem emotional about this, but we can't turn the kids away."

"You're not on trial here, Jane," Mr. Tomlinson said reassuringly.

"Well, it seems that my appeal to common sense has not worked," Ms. Wilcox concluded. "I had hoped that you would be willing to listen to reason and that you would put an end to these programs; but it seems you won't. I have no alternative but to bring this to the attention of other people in town."

"What are you saying exactly?" Mr. Boutwell asked.

"I'm saying that I will take this matter to the mayor, to the press, and to concerned citizens in town. I'll tell them about the songs being played in the library. They can't know, otherwise they'd want to do something about it."

At this point, she got up and headed for the door. Mr. Tomlinson stood up and asked her if she wouldn't stay and talk longer.

"I'm not going to be talked into accepting these programs," she declared. "That's my position. If you stop playing the records, I won't do anything."

"We can't just say we're going to stop playing these records," Ms. Reynolds insisted. "That's censorship and we're opposed to censorship."

"I don't care what you call it," Ms. Wilcox replied. "I call it common sense."

"We have to think this whole thing through, Bertha," Mr. Tomlinson said. "Surely you can see that."

"We're beginning to say the same things over and over, and we're getting nowhere," sighed Ms. Wilcox wearily. "I'll state my position once more. In my opinion, the programs can continue if—I repeat, if—songs of the kind I heard are not played. I am not going to compromise. If you persist, I'll speak to Mayor Pritchard. I'll write letters to the editor of *The Weekly Courier*. And I'll get support from various agencies and groups in town. You'll see that there are many people besides myself who are disturbed by what's going on."

"Are you threatening us?" the chairman asked.

"I suppose it looks that way. If the programs don't stop or you don't stop playing those songs, then just wait until next March at the town meeting when you want to get your budget approved. I tell you, I'll load the auditorium with people who think like I do, and we'll see to it that your budget doesn't get approved, or we'll cut it so badly that you won't have money to stay open on Sunday at all. If you're not willing to listen to common sense, then perhaps you'll listen to the threat of less money to operate on."

With that, she left the room. The chairman, who was seated again, got up and started down the stairs after her. The rest of the group could hear words being exchanged from the landing below. In a few minutes, Mr. Tomlinson returned alone. "Well, she seems to mean what she says," he said. "What do we do now?"

• • • • •

If you were one of the trustees, what would you do now? How would you react to Ms. Wilcox's comments? Are censorship and common sense compatible, as Ms. Wilcox says they are? Do you agree with Ms. Reynolds' contention that there is no causal relationship between music and action? Do you think Ms. Reynolds is being unreasonable by insisting that the music continue to be played? In this instance, is the *Library Bill of Rights* an adequate selection policy statement?

5.
Remember Dewey Stroud

· · · · · · · · · · · · · · · · · ·

DEWEY STROUD DID NOT DIE IN VAIN

Dewey Stroud was shot and killed in Gilmore during an occupation by 1,000 students of the administration building a year ago.

Remember Dewey on Thursday, October 9, a year after he was so brutally gunned down.

Dewey was one of 1,000 students demanding the dismissal of Professor Suter, who taught Arthur Jensen's theories that blacks are genetically inferior to whites. Students were warned to leave the building, but they refused to until Professor Suter was dismissed. One of the trigger-happy white security guards fired his service revolver into the crowd and Dewey was killed.

The progressive forces of Jackson State, Kent State, and Attica have seen their basic rights denied by a racist political structure that is trying to keep the oppressed from attaining power.

Everyone who is opposed to barbarism is urged to turn out on the quad in front of the library on October 9 to show that the ruling class of America cannot be allowed to continue the wanton murder of freedom-loving people in America. The ruling class must be shown that freedom lives!

Remember Dewey Stroud on October 9!

Michael Logan, Director of the Library at Gilmore College, finished reading the flyer that one of the three students who were in his office had handed him.

"You want me to have the library staff insert one of these in every book that is checked out of the library?" he asked.

"Yes," one of the students replied.

"Well, you know, we have a 'give-away' table in the foyer as you come into the library," Mr. Logan said. "How would it be if we put the handbills there, and people can take them if they want to?"

"That's not good enough," the second student said. "We want people to see these, and they might miss them on the table."

Michael Logan thought about the request for a moment, and then consented to it. He told the students that the only time the staff tucked flyers into books was when the library was sponsoring some activity it wanted to publicize, but that he would make an exception in their case. The three students looked at each other with obvious satisfaction.

"Now, we have another request," the first student said. "We want you to lower the flag to half-staff on October 9 to commemorate Dewey Stroud's death. We found out from the business manager that your staff looks after the raising and lowering of the flag."

"We want the people who will be in the quad that day to see that Gilmore remembers Dewey the way it does other distinguished faculty and alumni and national figures," the second student said.

"We're hoping that the whole college will turn out that day," the third student said, "and we want to be able to point to the lowered flag and show that the college regrets what it did to Dewey Stroud."

"It is true our staff looks after the flag," Mr. Logan said, "but that's only because it's right in front of the library. It's not ours, it's the college's. Frankly, I've never paid much attention to it. Why don't you take this up with someone else?"

"We were told you looked after it, and we're leaving it with you," the first student said.

The director looked at his calendar and realized that October 9 was exactly a week away. That meant he had only a few days to consider their appeal and discuss it with his immediate supervisor, the vice president for academic affairs.

He told the students that he would give their request serious consideration, adding that he was still not sure the decision was his to make. One of the students said he hoped the college would consent to their request. "All eyes will be on the flag-pole on October 9," he added. Mr. Logan said again that he would look into it. The students thanked the director for agreeing to insert the handbills in the books; handing him several hundred, they left.

Gilmore University is a private, independent, coeducational institution on the outskirts of Gilmore, an industrial, commercial, and transportation center of 300,000 people in one of the southern states. Gilmore has been quite successful in efforts to recruit blacks and other minorities into its programs; at the present time well over 600 of its 2,000 students are members of minority races. Dewey Stroud, who died during the student uprising a year ago, was a black student.

Michael Logan is thirty-five years old. He has been the director of the library for four years, having moved into the position from the assistant directorship when the previous director retired. He, like others on the faculty and staff, had hoped that the incident which precipitated Dewey Stroud's death had been forgotten—but apparently it hadn't been. As he sat in his office and reflected on the decision he had made to hand out the flyers, and mulled over the request to lower the flag, his thoughts flashed back to the events that led to young Stroud's death.

He remembered vividly the day he heard that Dr. Gloria Suter had undertaken to present to one of her classes Arthur Jensen's thesis that genes were largely responsible for the average 15-point IQ difference found between American blacks and whites. From the reports he got, the students in the class accused her of being a white supremacist. They indicated in no uncertain terms that they greatly resented her having introduced the Jensen theory into the discussion, and they challenged her to the point where she finally called off the class well before the end of the period. Immediately after the class broke up, several students rushed over to the library to see if there were any books by Jensen in the collection. There weren't, which fact the students related gleefully to one of the reference librarians. They also told the librarian what had happened in class, and she, in turn, reported the story to Mr. Logan.

The appointment at Gilmore was Dr. Suter's first teaching position. She had come to Gilmore directly from postgraduate studies in anthropology and sociology at a distinguished northern university.

Classes got underway the third week in September at Gilmore; it was during the first week of October that Dr. Suter introduced the subject of genes into her Personality and Culture course. According to several faculty members, Dr. Suter had merely mentioned Jensen's theories to her class, neither accepting nor denying their validity. But after being challenged for having done so, she decided that her academic freedom was being denied and she resolved to continue to talk about Jensen in subsequent classes. She had not planned on spending any time at all on the controversial psychologist, but after this episode she became determined to show the students that they had no right to deny her the opportunity to explore any theory she wanted to. Many students fought back, urging that her classes be boycotted. Life became quite difficult for Dr. Suter; she received unpleasant telephone calls, was hissed and booed when she passed in front of groups of students on the campus, and was called a racist.

Finally one day, a large group of students—some people estimated there were as many as a thousand—occupied the administration building, demanding that Dr. Suter be fired. The leaders of the movement were in the president's office, while the remainder of the students occupied the corridors. According to some eye-witnesses, a melee broke out in one of the halls between some of the students and one of the security guards. The guard was apparently trying to control the somewhat unruly crowd, and in attempting to do so brandished his revolver. In taking it out of his holster, according to this version, it discharged into the crowd, and Dewey Stroud was left lying on the floor. Students went directly to his aid, only to find he was dead. According to other witnesses, however, the crowd was peaceful, and the security guard shot Stroud deliberately.

The student leaders, upon hearing of the shooting, were able to get the students outside and calm them down. They told the gathering that they did not want the National Guard or the Gilmore city police to be called in, and they implored the students not to precipitate further violence. The students dispersed, and the leaders retrenched to consider what they should do next.

When Dr. Suter heard of the incident, she contacted the president immediately and informed him that she was resigning. He tried to talk her into staying, but she was adamant; she said she would be leaving the campus the next day. When the students heard of her decision, they decided that no further action was necessary.

The weeks that followed the shooting were unpleasant, but a surface calm did prevail on the campus. But now, a year later, the students had not forgotten the shooting. In fact, they wanted everyone to remember it, and they were planning a massive rally on the quad.

Michael Logan decided to call his boss and discuss the matter with her. He got the vice president for academic affairs, Alice Lentz, on the phone and told her of his visit from the three students and the requests they made. Ms. Lentz said she had already seen one of the flyers, adding that she was sorry Mr. Logan had agreed to break with precedent and insert copies in library materials. Mr. Logan defended his decision, pointing out that he thought that denying their request might cause trouble.

"Don't you see," Ms. Lentz said, "they're testing us to see how far we'll go. I would have said 'no' and let them make the next move. How about just putting them on the 'give-away' table, and if they say anything, telling them you were told to?"

"I can't go back on my word," Mr. Logan said.

"You could if you were ordered to," Ms. Lentz said. "I'm afraid that they'll think we're agreeing with their demonstration if we agree to hand out the flyers. Did you tell them we haven't done this for other people?"

"Well, uh, yes," Mr. Logan replied.

"Don't do anything with them until you hear from me," Ms. Lentz said. "Now about the matter of the flag. Who on your staff takes care of the flag?"

"Our custodian," Mr. Logan replied. "He checks a special calendar which we keep at the circulation desk every day to see if he should put it at half-staff for anybody. You know, I wish we could get rid of looking after the flag, just as I wish we didn't have to look after the copying machines. But you already know my feeling on the copying machines. For now, the darn flag is our responsibility, but we don't decide who it's lowered for. We just do it. By the way, I checked the calendar and it's not scheduled to be flown at half-mast for anybody else on October 9."

"That's too bad," Ms. Lentz said. "But I would appreciate your thoughts on whether we should lower it for Stroud. We don't have to decide right away, and in the meantime I'm going to discuss it with the president and others to see what they think. I'm afraid it will look as if we're agreeing that Jensen's theories should not be taught here if we agree to lower it. The flag is symbolic, you know. By the way, did you ever buy Jensen's book *Educability and Group Differences?*"

"No. I can't accept his theory and I didn't want to get students upset."

"Good. I think you showed good judgment. Well, let me know what you think about the flag."

• • • • •

What suggestion would you give Ms. Lentz? Do you think Mr. Logan should have agreed to pass out flyers? How would you have handled the students who made the request? Since the students equate lowering the flag with an expression of wrongdoing on the part of the college, would you lower it? How would you proceed at this stage? Would you buy Jensen's book for this library?

6.
"The Way It Is"

· · · · · · · · · · · · ·

When Clara diZangotti started working at the Howick Public Library two days ago, it was understood that she would spend most of her time at the general reference desk in addition to being young adult librarian—the first person to be so designated in the eighty-four-year history of the library. She was to have no more than eight hours a week away from the reference desk to plan activities and programs for her teenage clients, and she was to use the quiet times at the desk to select material for purchase appropriate to the interests of young people. This was the only basis upon which the head librarian, Irma Katz, a woman of thirty-six with eight years service, had been able to sell the new position, which she had been wanting for years, to the town manager—even though she and the trustees were convinced of the need for the public library to offer more services to young people in town. It was the manager's opinion that since the town had a recreation department ("which does nothing," Ms. Katz said) and "excellent library facilities at the high school and the two junior highs," to use his words, there was no need for a person to spend any time on young adult work at the public library. He has been disturbed by the amount of duplication in the collections of the schools and the public library, and was agitating for closer cooperation in buying. "If I had my way," he commented, "the schools would look after the school-age children and the public library, the adults and preschoolers." Fortunately for Ms. Katz, however, the trustees did not share the manager's opinion on this matter—and several other matters as well—for they backed her completely.

Howick is a pleasant, rather old-fashioned and conservative community, with tree-lined streets and many substantial frame houses on spacious lawns, a few small industries, and two modern shopping centers. It is located on the outskirts of a large east-coast city, and is inhabited almost entirely by com-

muters. The town has grown steadily, but not spectacularly, since it was settled a few years after the Revolutionary War, reaching a population of
29,000. The Howick Public Library building, constructed just two years ago,
is an attractive modern structure of brick trimmed with marble; it is built to
hold 125,000 volumes—the present collection is 75,000 volumes—and has
many interesting features, including both a listening room and an auditorium
equipped with a movie projector. The original public library was housed in a
small building given to the town by Andrew Carnegie; it had so outgrown its
quarters that the town had no choice but to approve a new library.

One of Ms. Katz's fondest hopes since the new building was constructed
has been to establish a regular film series, which would be held in the auditorium, and which might entice more of the town's younger population into the
library. She mentioned this to Ms. diZangotti during the latter's interview for
the job, and was heartened to learn that the young applicant had taken several
film and media courses at library school and seemed to have many good ideas
on how to make such a program work.

The staff of the Howick Public Library consists of four other professional
librarians besides the director and the new young adult librarian—two reference librarians, a children's librarian, and a head of technical services. The
five trustees have been very supportive of Ms. Katz's efforts to make the library "an instrument of education and enlightenment, spreading before
people of all ages materials which will stretch their minds and help them realize their potentials," as they phrased it in one of their annual reports. While
Ms. Katz and the trustees believe in the library's obligation to represent many
viewpoints, and have tried to do so, they have never ventured far enough into
the realm of unconventional thought or expression to alienate anyone in the
community; not once have they had a serious censorship problem or been involved in a controversy.

Late in the afternoon of her third day on the job, Ms. diZangotti was sitting
at the reference desk when she looked up to see a young man and a young
woman standing in front of her.

"Are you the new young adult librarian?" the boy asked. "The lady at the
charge-out desk sent us over."

Ms. diZangotti acknowledged that she was. "How can I help you?" she
said cheerfully.

"Have you got a few minutes?" the girl said. "We've got something we'd
like to discuss with you."

Ms. diZangotti invited them to sit down. The boy spoke first. "We have a
course at the high school on film-making," he began. "The school has the
equipment to make films, and many of us have cameras, and we fool around
making films. Last year we had a film festival in the school auditorium. The
parents came and everything. We're going to have another festival this year.
It's going to be an annual event."

"And that's why we came to see you," added the girl. "Some of us made a film and the principal won't let us show it at the festival."

"Why not?"

"Well," responded the boy, "the principal has to see the films before he agrees to invite parents in to see them. He thinks ours is obscene or something."

"It's crazy, really," the girl said. "I mean, we have a scene in the movie where this girl is in bed—she has no clothes on—and she holds up her hand and invites this boy to climb under the covers with her. He does. And then the scene fades out. In another place, we have some kids passing pot to other kids."

"The film—it's called *The Way It Is*—is trying to show what it's like to be a high school kid," the boy ventured. "And high school boys do climb into bed with high school girls—whether the principal likes it or not. And kids do smoke pot. The principal said it's too suggestive—that's the word he used— and that it'd give a false image to parents and give ideas to kids."

Ms. diZangotti smiled. "That's very interesting. But why did you want to see me?"

"Well," answered the girl, "we were wondering if you would let us show it at this library—in the auditorium."

"Since the word is out that it's banned," said the boy, with a knowing smile, "everyone wants to see it. Even lots of parents want to. And we can't show it at school."

"This library has the only other auditorium big enough to hold a crowd," said the girl. "It's not a dirty film. It's telling it like it is. I mean that bed scene is only a small part of the film. We've got all kinds of scenes in other places, like the school, kids' homes, the deli, the bandstand. We've even got a shot of the library in it—some kids walking up the front steps!"

The boy nodded as the girl spoke. "The other films that are okay with the principal have lots of the same stuff—kids at home, in school, on the street— only they don't have anybody in bed or passing pot."

"When are the other films being shown?" Ms. diZangotti asked.

"This Friday night," responded the boy.

"When would you like to show your film here?"

"You mean, you'll show it?" the girl said excitedly.

"Not necessarily," Ms. diZangotti replied quickly. "I just wanted to find out what your plans were."

The girl looked slightly dejected. "Any time that would be convenient would be fine with us."

"Let me mull this over," Ms. diZangotti said. "I just started working here a couple of days ago and I'm not sure what our policies are on a lot of things. Give me your names and telephone numbers and I'll get in touch with you. Who teaches the film course, by the way?"

The two students wrote down their names and addresses and the name of the teacher. They left, thanking the new librarian for listening and reiterating how much it would mean to them to show the film.

The next morning, Ms. diZangotti told Ms. Katz about the request. Ms. Katz complimented her new librarian for not having committed herself, adding that she thought it would be a good idea for Ms. diZangotti to contact the teacher to see what his thoughts were. "You two should know each other anyway," she said. "But before you do, let me fill you in on the situation here—it might have a bearing on our decision. In fact," she added, as an afterthought, "I'd like you to gather all the facts you can and tell me what *you* think we should do. It would be good training for you. I don't guarantee I'll go along with your advice, but I promise I'll listen to it!"

Ms. diZangotti said she thought that was a fine idea.

"First of all," Ms. Katz commenced, "we've never had a serious censorship problem in the library. I don't know, perhaps we've played it too safe or something. I guess I've always been able to find reasons for not getting really controversial things, and no one has ever pushed the matter with me. It could be, too, that the community has been willing to accept what we get—we do keep up with current fiction, much of which is repulsive to many people, and we buy sex education books and a number of other things that are considered controversial by some people. The trustees have supported everything I've proposed to them—sometimes after much discussion—and the city manager has usually gone along, sometimes grudgingly, I might add. I really don't know how the trustees would react to this request, but before I went to them I'd be well prepared. They've given me a free rein to run the library the way I see fit, but then I haven't really done anything very startling. I guess I'd expect them to back me if I decided to go ahead with the showing, and would consider it a vote of nonconfidence if they didn't. However, there are many things to consider here. If the principal has turned the kids down, then how would he feel if *we* were to show the film? Would it jeopardize our relations with him and the schools? I know him well, and he tends to be somewhat conservative. I'm sure, too, that if he doesn't want the film shown, many others, including teachers and parents, wouldn't. However, there are probably lots of others who would."

Ms. diZangotti listened intently while Ms. Katz spoke. "What if the trustees objected?" she asked. "Shouldn't we clear it with them first? If they say no, then our decision is made for us."

"They'd expect me to prepare a case for showing it," Ms. Katz responded. "I know them well enough to know they like to have all the facts before they decide on something."

"Good. I'll see what I can find out," the young librarian said confidently.

"Perhaps you should ask the kids if you can preview the film," Ms. Katz suggested. "And again, perhaps you should speak with the teacher."

When Ms. diZangotti arrived at the high school, she noticed a sign on the front door, which read: "All visitors must report to the principal's office." As she entered the principal's office a man who was standing behind a counter talking to another man glanced over, smiled, and asked if he could be of help. She introduced herself and told him who she was looking for.

"I'm Harris Cooper," the man said, "principal of the school. I'm pleased to meet you. I didn't realize they had a specialist in young adult work at the public library. I'm glad to hear it. Perhaps you could drop in on me before you leave today and we could have a chat."

Ms. diZangotti said she would be delighted to. The principal then directed her to the film teacher, who was able to tell her a bit more about the controversial film. He said it was typical of many underground movies in that it was elliptical in meaning and disjointed in continuity of theme. At the same time, he described it as quite interesting—extraordinary considering of the age and experience of the boys and girls who produced it. He admitted there was a suggestive scene, but said it was not inserted for sensationalism. "As a matter of fact," he said, "it seems quite natural and is not overdone at all. All in all, this is one of the best films I've seen a group of high school students produce." He confirmed that Mr. Cooper had refused to let it be shown at the festival because he thought it was too suggestive, adding that the principal thought it might incur the anger of some parents.

On her way out, Ms. diZangotti stopped in to see the principal. During their discussion, she revealed the nature of her visit. The principal was taken by surprise. He told her he hoped she and Ms. Katz would not oblige the students. "This is a conservative town," he said firmly. "And the school committee is conservative, too. It took us ages to get that course in film-making approved. The school committee frowns on experimentation. If they find out that the film was made as a project for the film course—and they would, of course—then it could mean the end of film-making for all students. I realize the choice is yours to make, but I'd like you to understand my position." He admitted that he did not like the episodes where the boy gets into bed with the girl and where students are seen handing drugs to each other. "Those scenes are bound to shock and disturb parents, and many of them will be over here trying to find out if these things really happen."

The young librarian was silent while the principal spoke. "I hope you and Ms. Katz will be practical and consider the larger good," he continued. "What I'm saying is that if you consent to the request, you could put an end to a very useful course, and you could damage relations between the high school and the public library, which have been very good in the past." As she left, Ms. diZangotti assured the principal that they would consider everything carefully before making a decision; she was extremely cautious not to commit herself even tentatively.

Later in the day, Ms. DiZangotti asked the two students if she could preview the film, which she did, with them present, the next day in the library auditorium. It was, she explained to Ms. Katz later, just as it had been described—quite extraordinary. The bedroom scene, she said, was a little more graphic than it had been described to her; before the scene fades, the boy is seen to be undressing under the blankets.

When Ms. Katz asked the young librarian if she was ready to make a recommendation, Ms. diZangotti asked for a day or two to think it over.

• • • • •

What would you recommend to the director of the library? What arguments would you offer in support of your recommendation in this instance? If you were a member of the board of trustees, how might you respond to the question of the library's screening *The Way It Is* publicly? What reaction might be anticipated from the city manager?

7.
The Trial of Richard Wetzel
· ·

"Have you decided who you're voting for this year, Dick?" Wilbur Ellis asked his assistant nonchalantly as they sipped coffee.

Richard Wetzel hesitated before answering. "I think I know you well enough to tell you this, Wilbur. I hope you won't tell anyone else, though. I think it better that it not get out. I'm a member of the Communist party, USA."

Wilbur Ellis is the director of the Schenley State College Library. A man of about fifty, who has been at Schenley as director for twenty years, he hired twenty-five-year-old Richard Wetzel six months ago to serve as assistant director.

Schenley is a publicly supported four-year college for men and women. It occupies the summit of a hill at the edge of a peaceful southern town—Holstertown—in the midst of a fertile, rolling agricultural section. The thirty-acre campus is rectangular in shape, with all of the buildings placed along the outer edges. With an average enrollment of 2,200 students and a full-time equivalent faculty of 200, it offers degrees in arts, agriculture, science, education, and business administration. Although it is primarily residential, Holstertown, with its population of 2,900, has a few industries, chiefly apple-product plants. The people of Holstertown are racially homogenous—90 percent white and native born—but the students at Schenley are of all races.

The college library, which is located next to the administration building at the west end of the grounds, contains 180,000 volumes and seats 320 students. There are, in addition to Mr. Ellis and Mr. Wetzel, three other professional librarians on the staff—a cataloger and two reference librarians. Mr. Ellis reports directly to the president of the college, Dr. Daniel Benns.

When Mr. Wetzel said he was a member of the Communist party, a suspicion of Mr. Ellis' was confirmed. "Are you fooling me, Dick?"

"No, I'm serious," Mr. Wetzel replied. "I joined the party in my last year at college. I didn't say anything about it to anyone—except my closest friends—while I spent my year at library school. And since you didn't ask me anything about my political beliefs when you interviewed me, and I didn't have to take a loyalty oath to get the job, I didn't bring it up. Does it make a difference?"

Mr. Ellis paused before speaking. "I don't know whether it does or doesn't, quite frankly. I'm just terribly surprised. And I guess I don't see how you can be. How does your wife feel about it? And what about your kids?"

Mr. Wetzel smiled at the questions. "My kids are only two and one! And Sarah feels the way I do."

"How could you have come here?" the director interrupted. "I mean to the heart of the South. The people in this area don't take kindly to communists. They cherish a traditional set of values. They're proud of the past. They loath communists and all they stand for. I have to admit I'm stunned by the news. What do you do as a Communist? Do you have any designs on the students here, or the faculty, or the community?" Before Mr. Wetzel could answer the series of questions, the director continued. "The real reason I asked you about the elections and who you were voting for is that I needed a lead-in to try to find out what you were up to."

"What do you mean?" Mr. Wetzel asked.

"Well, two or three faculty members told me some of their students have mentioned that you have been going to student meetings and using some interesting language, like proletariat, imperialist warmongers, bourgeois reformists, hirelings of capitalism, and things like that. Apparently, you've roused suspicions by some of the things you've said."

"I'm not a real hell-raising radical. I'm anxious for people to see the good in communism and the failures in capitalism. I hope to be able to establish contact with students who are anti-establishment and who may have attached themselves to various doctrines of anarchism, nihilism, or Marxism."

The director looked at his assistant with amazement. "Do you people really advocate overthrowing the United States government?"

"I'm speaking in the strictest confidence to you," Mr. Wetzel said. "You asked me, and I'll tell you, but on a confidential basis. If I thought you would make a fuss over it, I'd have lied when you asked me who I was voting for. I feel that the American system is racist, capitalist, and imperialist. The wealth of this nation is in the hands of a small minority of privileged men. The people of this country are merely tools being exploited by giant corporations—hirelings of capitalism, that's what they are. We want people to live and grow in peace, in love and happiness. We're trying to gain respectability, to secure our acceptance as a legitimate political party. We want to secure more power for the people. Our approach is a soft-sell one. We want to make friends for the CPUSA."

Mr. Ellis had the look of one who has seen a ghost. "I'm stunned by this news. I don't know what to say or do."

"What is there to say, Wilbur?" the young man asked. "As librarians, we have academic freedom, don't we? And academic freedom means the freedom to inquire, discover, and teach the truth as we see it without fear of hindrance, loss of position, or any other form of reprisal. I'm not violating any law by being a member of the Communist party. Some anticommunists may find our doctrine outrageous; but unpopular and dangerous as it seems to some people, we still have the right to make it known. I think the university has a duty to act as the critic of society. You asked earlier whether I have any designs on the students or others here. Well, yes, I do. As a Communist in an educational institution, I accept an obligation. If I were a teacher I would probably exploit the classroom to indoctrinate the students in the Marxist-Leninist philosophy. I have some plans as a librarian along those lines."

"It sounds to me, then, as if you are disqualified as a discoverer of truth under your own definition of academic freedom," the library director said. "You're committed to communist beliefs and aren't searching for truth. You feel you've got the truth. But how do you plan to operate as a librarian?"

"I think I can help to slant the collection, for one thing," replied Mr. Wetzel. "I think we should subscribe to the *Daily World* and the *People's World* for another. But that's not my main objective. I'm more interested in nonacademic possibilities—attending meetings, helping to form groups, appearing at rallies, things of that sort. Again, I must remind you that I am taking you into my confidence. I've grown very fond of you, and I trust you. I realize that you may not agree with my philosophy, but as long as you don't have any complaints about my work—and you have mentioned on several occasions that you're very satisfied—then there's no reason for anyone to know that I'm a Communist. I would prefer that it not get out. You won't mention it to anyone, will you?"

"You put me in a tough spot," Mr. Ellis replied. "I don't know what to do, quite frankly."

"I've told you this in confidence. As a professional librarian, you can't tell anyone."

"Look, Dick, I'm too surprised to think straight right now. Let me think it all over. I'm sure there must be some Communists on the faculties of other universities. I know Angela Davis was a Communist, but they fired her in California."

"She was fired because she was black," Mr. Wetzel rebutted.

"Well, I don't know the full story in her case," the director responded cautiously. "I'd rather not get into that right now. I have some hard thinking to do in regard to what you've told me and what you've asked me to do—to keep it quiet, that is."

They left the cafeteria and walked back to the library offices in silence.

Mr. Ellis spent the better part of two days thinking about whether or not to tell the president about his assistant's Communist party membership. Finally, he decided to mention it. Dr. Benns was just as surprised as Mr. Ellis, but there was no equivocation on his part. "He must go. I'm sure the trustees will back me. We can't have a Communist on the staff. This is shocking news."

"Wetzel asked me not to tell you," the librarian said. "He told me he was telling me in confidence. But I decided it was more important that you know than that I honor his request."

"I think you did the right thing in telling me," the president stated reassuringly. "This man is a sworn enemy of the United States. He should be exposed. Let's see, he's been here six months, and he has a contract that's good for a year. We'll let him stay till the year is up."

"He said he feels he has the right to engage in extramural activities," Mr. Ellis said. "To be fair to him, he has done fine work so far, and there's no indication that he has done anything on the job for which he should be punished. I've been extremely pleased with his work."

"I think it's very fortunate that you were able to find this out before he comes up for tenure. We can still get rid of him easily."

"From the way he spoke," the librarian continued, "I got the impression that he thinks a man's right to employment must be based exclusively on how he performs professionally, and not on his beliefs, his private thoughts, or his associations."

"It's all very well for him to say that," said Dr. Benns. "But a man's beliefs may be highly germaine to his tasks. I remember something Sidney Hook wrote in this regard. He asked if the Civil Liberties Union would hire as its director a man who had declared his strong opposition to civil rights. It's a good question. Or supposing it were discovered that a candidate for the superintendency of a home for the aged and infirm was a fanatical believer in enforced euthanasia. Wouldn't that belief be relevant to his eligibility for the position? Can a person who applies for a job whose qualifications call for an absence of racial prejudice express racist ideas? A man's beliefs *are* relevant."

Mr. Ellis pondered for a moment before speaking. "I think you've got a good point. But doesn't this criterion justify getting rid of anti-Nazi teachers in Germany during the thirties if their opinions were different from the schools which employed them? I'm wondering what remains of the concept of academic freedom if we apply that test. Wetzel feels he is justified in being a Communist under the rubric of academic freedom."

"I find that amusing," Dr. Benns said with a laugh. "He's appealing to academic freedom in his defense when his goal as a Communist is the destruction of that freedom and others. I don't think a Communist even today is free from party discipline. I don't think he can be independent. I go back to my original question. Should a Communist be permitted to teach or work at an institution that is supported by taxpayers? The taxpayers are being asked to support financially and encourage those who are working for society's destruction. It seems to me Wetzel is like the Trojan Horse. He's making friends, but then he's hoping to destroy them. I'm going to discuss this with the trustees, but I know damn well they'll be furious that we hired him in the first place. They're violently anticommunist. You almost can't mention the word in their presence. They'll demand we get rid of him right away."

The librarian heard nothing from the president for a few weeks. In the meantime, Mr. Wetzel continued to be an exemplary employee. He was efficient, helpful, tactful, and fair. Neither Mr. Ellis nor his assistant brought up the subject of communism after their initial talk, both acting as if nothing had ever happened.

Finally, the president asked Mr. Ellis to come to his office to discuss Mr. Wetzel. "I met with the board, and we came to a decision about Wetzel," he started. "It was their unanimous opinion that the man must go. They were anxious that he be discharged right away; however, I was able to convince them that we should let him finish out his year. They say he is not to participate in any activities on the campus. It will be your job—an ugly one, I admit—to inform him of the decision."

"I'm not looking forward to that," the library director commented. "Can you tell me the gist of what was said?"

"In essence," Dr. Benns began, "they feel that no one who advocates the overthrow of the government of the United States is wanted here. They don't want any trouble on the campus. They feel there's a difference between academic freedom and academic license. I told them about some of the expressions he is reported to have used, and one labelled that 'inflammatory rhetoric.' They said that if he were to stay, several graduates would probably stop contributing to the alumni fund. And we need all the financial help we can get."

"So you've decided he can finish out his year," Mr. Ellis said. "And I'm to tell him that."

The president said that the board had the right to establish its own policies, and one of the policies it was going to establish as a result of this was that Communists not be hired. He pointed out that they wanted to protect themselves from further occurrences of a similar nature. The president added that Mr. Wetzel should be informed at once that his contract was not being renewed.

When Mr. Ellis got back to his office, he called his assistant in. "Dick," he began, "I have some bad news. I've been instructed by the president and the trustees to inform you that your contract will not be renewed when it expires at the end of this academic year."

"How come?" the young man asked with an expression of amazement. "I thought you were very satisfied with my work."

"I am. But it's because of your membership in the Communist party."

"You told them!" Mr. Wetzel said sharply. "You told them! I'm really surprised and shocked that you would have. I thought I could trust you. I feel sick to think you betrayed my confidence."

"Calm down, Dick," Mr. Ellis said, quietly. "I had to decide what was best for the school, and in my opinion I did the right thing. I couldn't live with what you told me. Maybe they would've said it was all right. I didn't know."

"I'm disgusted," Mr. Wetzel went on, fixing his eye on his boss. "I thought you would have subscribed to the statement in the AAUP *Statement of Principles on Academic Freedom and Tenure.* The one which says that the teacher is both a citizen and an officer of an educational institution and that when he speaks or writes as a citizen, he should be free from institutional censorship or discipline. You're telling me that you give up these rights as a librarian? The 1964 AAUP *Committee Statement on Extramural Utterances* says that a faculty member cannot be dismissed for an expression of opinion unless that expression clearly demonstrates the faculty member's unfitness for his position. You've had nothing but praise for my work, so it would seem that my expression of opinion hasn't made me unfit for the job."

As Mr. Wetzel was speaking, Mr. Ellis reached for his copy of the college bulletin and began to look for a statement on freedom of expression. He found one and read it aloud. "Outside the fields of instruction, artistic expression, research and professional publication, the faculty member, as a private citizen, enjoys the same freedoms of speech and expression as any private citizen, and shall be free from institutional discipline in the exercise of these rights. The conduct of the faculty shall be in accordance with standards dictated by law."

"You have justified my actions by that statement," Mr. Wetzel said. "I'm sure the ACLU will take up my case, and I'm sure I can enlist support from the students. You're not going to get rid of me that easily. Do you mean to tell me that you can be unbiased as a capitalist librarian? I'm going to fight this."

• • • • •

Do you think Mr. Wetzel has a case? Do you think a person's beliefs, political or otherwise, should be a factor in his hiring? Are loyalty oaths desirable? Should Mr. Ellis have told the president? What do you think of the arguments of Mr. Wetzel, Mr. Ellis, and Dr. Benns? What is the position of the American Library Association with respect to situations of this kind?

8.
After the Ball Is Over

· · · · · · · · · · · · · · · · ·

Claudia Martindale hung up the phone. Her worst fears had been realized. Charles Stringer had been elected to the board of trustees.

"Were the results in, dear?" her mother asked.

"Yes. Charles Stringer won," Claudia said dejectedly. "I wish I hadn't called. Now I'm going to have a miserable night. I could have waited until tomorrow morning to get the bad news."

Claudia Martindale has been the director of the Rowell Public Library for three years. It is generally agreed that during her short time with the library, she has accomplished a great deal. For one thing, she was able to get the library board to adopt the *Library Bill of Rights*; for another she believes that she has made the collection far more "relevant" to larger segments of the community, including young people.

Three members of the community had run for the one vacant trustee position. This was the first year, as far as anyone could remember, that three people were interested in becoming a library trustee. As a rule there were two candidates at the most, and often only one. The board consists of five members who serve for seven-year terms. When a vacancy occurred by virtue of the retirement this year of an aged trustee, three people, a housewife, a young doctor, and Charles Stringer had sought election. Mr. Stringer owned a small sporting goods store in town and was very active in local affairs. He had run twice for the school committee, but was defeated both times. This time he tried for trustee of the library, and, to the chagrin of the director, he won.

Claudia Martindale was upset at his victory because he was suspected to be a member of the John Birch Society. Whenever he had spoken on behalf of his candidacy at various coffees that were sponsored for him around town, and at the League of Women Voters' Meet the Candidates night, he had always said that he felt the library should be "cleaned up." He said he was tired of the trash the library was buying and that someone ought to be elected who would stand up to the librarian and who could restore the balance of the board, which he felt had gone "too far to the left." He had been careful to avoid any talk of personalities; when he was asked his opinion of Ms. Martindale, he pointed out that he was not directing his comments at any one person. He merely stated that the board needed a better balance, and that he could provide it.

The advertisements he took out in the local paper prior to the election— and he was the only one who did this—invariably mentioned his concern for the "profane, indecent, and obscene" material that was finding its way into the library, and consequently into the hands of the town's young citizens, who he felt were in danger of being corrupted. His appeal was on a very emotional level, and it seemed to have reached many people.

When Ms. Martindale got to the library the next morning, she tried not to reveal her feelings to the staff. However, many members knew her well enough to see how disappointed she was. "I'm at the stage where I'm wondering if this is the community's way of telling me that they don't approve of what I've been doing," she said to her assistant, Judith Saul, as they analyzed the election results. Ms. Saul said she didn't feel that was so, pointing out that Mr. Stringer had had a very well-organized campaign. "Let's face it, Claudia," she said, "who gives a damn about the position of library trustee? People just remembered his name when they voted. It was bound to turn out this way."

The phone rang as they were talking. It was Monica Paivio, the chairwoman of the board. She called to ask if Ms. Martindale had heard the election results and to speculate on what it would mean to have Mr. Stringer as a member; they concluded that it boded ill for both the board and the library. The chairman said she had called the new member at his sporting goods store to welcome him to the board and to give him the date of the next meeting. The librarian said she would call right away to congratulate him and invite him to the library for a tour and a chat.

The newly elected board member said he would be delighted to come over and get acquainted. The librarian mentioned that she would put together a packet of readings on the responsibilities of library trustees, adding good-naturedly that there were one or two entitled "How to Be a Good Trustee." They established ten o'clock on Thursday morning as the time for him to be there. After she hung up, Ms. Martindale told her assistant that he didn't sound like the ogre she thought he would be.

On Thursday, Mr. Stringer arrived at the library at the appointed time. Ms. Martindale took him around and introduced him to the staff, explaining the operations as she went. When they returned to her office, she handed him the brochures on the role of the trustee and a set of documents on intellectual freedom, which included the *Library Bill of Rights*, the *Freedom to Read*

Statement, and the *Statement on Labelling.* Mr. Stringer was particularly interested in these documents. He looked through them slowly and deliberately, emitting an occasional "hmmmm" and making pencil notations on the margins.

Ms. Martindale waited uneasily while he read; she was the first to break the silence. "The trustees endorsed these documents about three years ago," she said. "We're guided in our selection of material and in our programs by them."

"I notice these statements have been adopted by the American Library Association and a few other organizations," Mr. Stringer said. "But there's no law that says we have to do what they say, is there?"

"I'm not sure I know what you mean."

"Who says we in *this* library have to express all points of view? Who says any library has to express all points of view?"

"In endorsing the *Library Bill of Rights* our board has said, in effect, that they want all points of view and all forms of expression represented in this library," the director ventured.

"Perhaps I'm not making myself clear. Let me put it to you this way. The Constitution and the Bill of Rights—not the *Library Bill of Rights* but the first ten amendments to the Constitution—don't say that libraries have to represent all points of view, do they?"

"Well, no," Ms. Martindale answered hesitatingly. "But one of the basic tenets of a democracy is that all points of view have a right to be uttered."

"But this is not a democracy," the trustee fired back. "It's a republic, and there's a big difference between the two."

Ms. Martindale could feel herself being drawn further into the discussion than she wanted to go. She felt the new trustee was far more able to handle himself in a discussion of this sort than she was. "I contend," he went on, "that we have no obligation whatsoever to present all points of view in this library and that in attempting to do so are putting ourselves in an indefensible position. I do not see how anyone could prove otherwise to me. Look," he continued, his voice becoming quite stentorian, "if someone in this community says, as I am saying, what right have you to purchase books that I find offensive, and you say because the *Library Bill of Rights* says we should, what does that mean to me? Your position is indefensible. The *Library Bill of Rights* is not a law; it doesn't *have* to be obeyed. Librarians and trustees and the American Library Association obey it because they choose to, not because they *must*. By saying you feel an obligation to represent all points of view, you are assuming a responsibility you have no legal right to assume. I intend to challenge the board's decision to ratify the *Library Bill of Rights,* and I intend to see to it that only the right and proper points of view are expressed in this library."

"Are you advocating that we censor certain materials?" Ms. Martindale asked nervously. "I've always believed that any piece of material that hasn't been banned by the courts has a right to representation on the shelves of our collection. There's not a book on our shelves that's been banned by the courts."

"That just confirms my original argument. We don't have to buy certain things even if the courts have not banned them. Who says we do? Nobody, except the American Library Association. And who are they to tell us what we will do in our library?"

"The First Amendment says that Congress shall make no law abridging freedom of speech," the librarian said.

"But there's more than one interpretation of the First Amendment," the trustee rejoined quickly. "You should know that. Haven't you read Thomas Emerson's book *Toward a General Theory of the First Amendment?*"

"Yes, and I think we've been trying to subscribe to the 'absolute' interpretation in this library," Ms. Martindale said.

"Well, that's where we disagree. I subscribe to any of the other tests, but particularly to the 'bad tendency' test. Anyway, how can you use the First Amendment as a guide when there are so many tests? How can you single out one over the others? What right do you have to do it? And I mean what legal right? I think you and the board have taken on more responsibility than you're entitled to."

"I think we'd better continue this discussion at the board meeting next Tuesday night."

"Good. I want to. And one other thing. I have here a list of books that I don't think we should have in this library. I've been gathering this list off and on for the past two weeks. I've checked all of them out in my name and I intend to tell the board on Tuesday night that they will have to convince me that I should return them. Somebody has to clean up this library and I intend to be the one to do it. I object vigorously to having these books in the library. Doesn't anybody on the board recognize the community standards test for determining whether something is deemed objectionable?"

Mr. Stringer handed over his list of books. There were six titles on it: *Manchild in the Promised Land; Do It!; Soul on Ice; The Sensuous Woman; The Sensuous Man;* and *The Inner City Mother Goose.* "Where's the so-called 'socially redeeming value' in these?" he asked.

"I think this is a matter for the board to discuss," the librarian said. "I'll bring this list with me to the meeting."

With that, Mr. Stringer got up, said he would see Ms. Martindale at the trustees' meeting, and left.

Rowell is a modern industrial city in the western part of the country, with a population of 41,000. Downtown Rowell is composed of office buildings and shops; conspicuous among these is the public library, a two-story red brick structure of Romanesque design, surrounded by trees and covered with vines.

With the exception of Charles Stringer, the present board members, all of whom have served no less than two consecutive terms, have tended to be somewhat complacent in their attitude to the library, accepting whatever leadership the librarian has provided. Ms. Martindale got them to endorse the *Library Bill of Rights* with very little trouble; they probably would have done it sooner had the former director brought it to their attention. In addition to Mr. Stringer and Ms. Paivio, who is a housewife, the board consists of a retired social studies teacher, a pharmacist, and an architect.

• • • • •

What do you think of Mr. Stringer's arguments? Does the library have a legal basis for presenting all points of view and all forms of expression? If you were in Ms. Martindale's place, what would you do before or at the board meeting?

9.
The Joseph Carver Company

The Joseph Carver Company, located in a large metropolitan area in the Midwest, employs approximately 3,000 workers, and is engaged in the manufacture of electronic products. Although the company has many large and small competitors, it has managed to maintain its position as one of the leaders in the electrical equipment industry because of its emphasis on research and because it provides excellent service to its customers.

The Carver Company was one of the first to recognize the important role a library could play in its operations, for it has had a library for twenty years. The most recent librarian retired a year ago. She was replaced by Joyce Gardner, a young graduate of a library school in the area.

Ms. Gardner was recommended by a member of the library school faculty as "one of the brightest and most promising students to come along in some time." She had a good academic record and possessed a certain natural charm which endeared her to everyone. She had no difficulty convincing Craig Phillips, the Assistant Director of Research and Development (to whom the librarian reports), that she was the right person for the job.

Ms. Gardner was hired and placed in charge of the company library. She is a willing worker, an imaginative and thorough researcher, and she has made many valuable contributions to the work of the engineers who are engaged in research. The officers and staff of the company have been most pleased in their choice of a new librarian.

One day, after Ms. Gardner had been on the job for six months, she received, as did all employees, a written announcement that the company, because of its pre-eminent reputation in electronics, had just secured a long-term government contract to manufacture delicate and secret components for radar systems. The president was delighted to impart the news, which meant that several hundred new jobs would be created in the somewhat economically depressed region. The announcement also said that most employees engaged in research activities (including the librarian) would have to gain security clearance. Ms. Gardner applied for and received clearance at the "secret" level.

It happened that Joseph Carver, Jr., the president of the firm, lived in a town that was served by the same newspaper—*The Sun-Courier*—that served Ms. Gardner's home town. While it was not possible for him to know all employees personally, he had met the new librarian on several occasions, and had been quite taken with her cheerfulness and helpful manner. He began to notice that the name Joyce Gardner appeared at the end of letters to the editor of *The Sun-Courier* at the rate of about one a month. He wondered whether this was the same Joyce Gardner who worked in the company library; and one day when he thought of it at work, he had his secretary check Ms. Gardner's address to see if she was writing the letters. The secretary reported that the addresses were the same. He then began to read her letters with more interest. It amused him to see how she had an opinion on almost every topic—education, fluoridation, zoning, landfill—and he often found himself agreeing with her point of view.

One day, after Ms. Gardner had been with the firm a year, he read a letter which disturbed him. In it, the young librarian bitterly excoriated the military and firms that produce armaments of war for the government. She suggested that the only way to achieve world peace was for the large powers to abolish their standing armies and to cease manufacturing war equipment of all sorts. His immediate reaction was to haul Ms. Gardner on the carpet. He thought better of that, however, and decided instead to discuss her views with her immediate supervisor. He asked Mr. Phillips, who had not seen the letter, to inform the librarian that she should not deal with this theme again—or, if she felt she must, to use a fictitious name, or request that her name be withheld. He instructed his assistant to remind her that the government contracts which she had in effect denounced paid a good portion of her salary, and that if the company did not have its government business, several hundred employees would have to be laid off—including possibly the library staff.

When Mr. Phillips got back to his office, he invited the librarian to drop in to see him. He tried to put her at ease by talking about how the job was going generally, and then said, casually, "By the way, Joyce, I read a recent letter which you wrote to the editor of *The Sun-Courier*. It dealt with your views on how to achieve world peace. Mr. Carver read it, too, and he wanted me to speak to you. I think he feels that someone who works for the government— as we do, in effect—shouldn't criticize its policies publicly."

Ms. Gardner told her supervisor that she felt very strongly about the opinions she had expressed, and that she felt equally strongly that she had the right to express them. She talked about people in a democracy being free to use their intelligence, express their opinions, and challenge their leaders. She also doubted whether her opinions, as expressed in the letter, would have any effect. "I'm sure the Carver Company will continue to make military equipment regardless of what I say," she jeered.

Mr. Phillips claimed he understood what she was saying, but that he had gotten the distinct impression from the president that she was to omit this topic from her letters. "You'd better not write any more letters like this, Joyce," he urged. "The image of the company will be harmed, and it won't do you any good either."

"Mr. Carver can't stop me from writing what I want, when I want, in my newspaper, can he?" exclaimed Ms. Gardner, indignantly. "What I do as a private citizen is—to put it bluntly—none of his business or the company's."

"I can understand your getting worked up over this, Joyce, but what's more important to you—the opinions you think should be expressed or using your name? I don't think Mr. Carver's request that you use another name or leave your letters unsigned is too much."

"Are you and he telling me that I give up certain rights as a citizen when I work for a company that does work for the government?"

"No, we just want you to use better judgment. You know, none of these radical views came up when you got security clearance," said the supervisor pettishly.

"I don't think my views should be labelled radical," Ms. Gardner shot back defensively. "And anyway, when I got clearance several months ago, I didn't have the views I now have."

Obviously distressed, the young librarian asked if she could have a little time to think things over. Mr. Phillips agreed willingly.

• • • • •

What would you do if you were Ms. Gardner? Should Ms. Gardner have used "better judgment"? Is it unreasonable to ask her to sign a fictitious name or withhold it altogether? What considerations of professional ethics, if any, impinge upon this case?

10.
The Nudes
· · · · · · · · ·

Cynthia Barbagallo settled back in her chair and opened the evening paper. The first thing that caught her eye was a headline, which read: "Addington Artist Holds One-Man Show in Birchfield." The article told of Edward Blake, a local resident, who had been painting for several years and who was considered good enough to have his paintings—mostly watercolors of familiar scenes in Addington and the surrounding countryside—exhibited in the famous Worthington Museum in nearby Birchfield.

"Did you see where Ed Blake exhibited some of his paintings in Birchfield, Sally?" she called to her roommate. "You know him quite well, don't you?"

Ms. Barbagallo's roommate, Sally Carlson, said yes to both questions, adding that she thought it was a remarkable accomplishment for a person who had only been painting seven years. "Say, Cynthia," she said excitedly, "why don't you ask him if he'd like to exhibit his paintings in the library when they come back from Birchfield? Or, if you like, I could ask him. I'm sure he would say yes. You know, you could hang them in the wide hallway that connects the children's room with the main part of the library. At least for a while you could get rid of some of that crap you have there now!"

Cynthia Barbagallo, the director of the Addington Public Library, said, "That's a good idea. I'm sure the trustees wouldn't object, if Ed Blake would be happy to do it. Thanks for the idea."

"Can't you ever do anything without asking those old fuddy-duddy trustees if they approve?" Ms. Carlson asked. "Why do you have to check with them?"

"It's really a matter of keeping them informed," Ms. Barbagallo replied. "And besides, they're not so bad. They get upset if they hear we're doing things they don't know about. I tell them everything so they can't come back to me and say I didn't tell them. That's not strictly true," she said, as it occurred to her. "Sometimes I don't tell them things that aren't worth discussing, or things they would feel obliged to discuss when I don't need their opinions."

"I'm not with you, Cynthia. What do you mean?"

"Well, I don't tell them if we decide to buy a new kind of masking tape, or if we make some minor rearrangements in the shelving areas. Things like that."

"But you would tell them about exhibiting Ed Blake's paintings?"

"Sure. Because someone might mention it to them," Ms. Barbagallo replied. "And I wouldn't want them to be taken by surprise."

"Now, I get you," Ms. Carlson said. "Do you want me to speak to Ed?"

"Hold off on it for now, Sally. We have a trustees' meeting coming up next Tuesday night. I'll broach the subject with them then."

The board met as scheduled. After the usual business was dispensed with, Ms. Barbagallo asked if anyone had seen the news of Edward Blake's exhibit. Everyone had. She then mentioned that she would like to invite Mr. Blake to exhibit his paintings at the library—in the hallway, which, as she pointed out, was the only place they could go. They all agreed it was a fine idea, expressing their hopes that Mr. Blake would consent.

Ms. Barbagallo telephoned Mr. Blake on Wednesday and outlined the idea to him; to her delight, he consented readily. He told her the paintings would be coming back in three weeks, and that the Addington library could have them for a month when they arrived.

With great enthusiasm, Ms. Barbagallo told the staff about the exhibit; she also asked the member who looked after publicity if he would get something in the local paper. "Give it a big buildup—photos, the works," she directed.

After the paintings were hung, several people came to the library for no other reason than to see them, and many who came to use the library or borrow material took a special trip through the hallway to view the exhibit.

As Ms. Barbagallo was walking through the hallway one day on her way to the Children's Room, she spotted Ann Levy, one of the library's regular patrons, looking at the exhibit. "The boy certainly is talented," Ms. Levy commented wistfully. "No detail is slighted. Look at *After the Storm*. The lowering sky is so melancholy, and the wet, reflecting streets so haunting. How accurate! It is exquisite."

"The paintings are magnificent," Ms. Barbagallo replied. "We've had many fine comments about them."

"I dabble in painting, and how I wish I could capture the emotion he captures," Ms. Levy said, meditatively.

"I didn't know you painted, Ann."

"I'm just a Sunday painter, but I enjoy it," Ms. Levy announced.

"I wish we could have exhibits of this sort all the time, but unfortunately we don't have that many artists around," Ms. Barbagallo commented. "I'm thinking of asking people who make things with their hands, or who have collections of rare and precious items, if they'd be willing to display them in the library."

"Good idea," Ms. Levy answered. "Good luck with it. I've got to run now."

About a week after this discussion took place, Ms. Barbagallo looked up from her desk to see a young woman standing in the doorway of her office.

"Could I see you for a moment, Ms. Barbagallo?" the young woman asked, timidly. "I'm Rebecca Levy, Ann Levy's daughter."

"Oh, yes. I thought I recognized you. Please come in and sit down. How can I help you?"

"Well, I don't know how to put this exactly," Ms. Levy began. "But the other day my mother was in admiring the paintings of Edward Blake."

"Yes, I remember."

"Well, when she got home, she told us you had said you wished there were more talented artists in town whose paintings you could display. I think she was saying to us that she wished you had invited her to display *her* paintings. You know, she's not bad—no Rembrandt or Tintoretto, mind you, but not bad. She'd kill me if she knew I was here, but I thought there was no harm in sounding you out in an idea I have, which could involve my mother."

"You know, Ms. Levy," Ms. Barbagallo said with a smile, "I have a feeling . I know what you're going to ask! And I think it's not a bad idea."

"You read my mind all right. But I wanted to suggest that you might want to display not only my mother's paintings but those of others in town. I think it would be a great publicity gimmick, and it would win a lot of friends for the library. Not only that, the people whose work is exhibited would probably be thrilled to death."

"I have to admit to you," Ms. Barbagallo said, "it has always bothered me that one has to be great to get some recognition. I'm sure there must be dozens of people in town who have paintings they would like to exhibit here. I'm all for giving it a whirl. Let me mull it over for a while, and don't be surprised if your mother announces one day that she's exhibiting her artwork at the library!"

"Thanks very much for being so understanding, Ms. Barbagallo," said Ms. Levy. "If you do call her—or should I say when—please don't mention that I spoke to you."

"Don't worry, if the idea succeeds, I'll probably pass it off as my own anyway!"

At the next board meeting, Ms. Barbagallo reported that the exhibit of Edward Blake's paintings had been very well attended and that the comments had been most favorable. She then suggested inviting other artists in town, with or without talent, to exhibit their artwork in the hallway. At first, some of the trustees snickered, as if to indicate they didn't believe the proposal was to be taken seriously. Ignoring the skeptics, the director went on to explain that she thought it would be good publicity, would win friends for the library, and that—equally important—it was a nice thing to do.

The trustees agreed to try it, but stipulated that members of the library staff were not to act as art critics—which none of them were qualified to do—accepting some people's painting and not others'. Since the primary motivation for displaying the paintings was to make friends for the library, everyone's paintings, no matter how bad, would have to be accepted.

The offer was made to the people of Addington through the newspaper and by word of mouth, and the response was excellent: eight people, including three teenagers, appeared at the library or telephoned to say they wanted to take advantage of the library's offer. Ms. Barbagallo drew up a schedule to accommodate the town's "artists," assigning each person a different month. Ms. Levy was first on the list. Her paintings, which were mainly townscapes and seascapes, turned out to be surprisingly good. At the end of the first month, Ms. Levy's canvases came down and the next person's went up. The second person specialized in still-lifes of flowers, hunting trophies, and fruit pieces; and they too were quite good. Ms. Barbagallo was always on hand to help unpack the paintings and help with the hanging. After five townspeople had displayed their artwork—which had consisted of landscapes, still-lifes, animals, and abstracts—the director was able to give a highly favorable report to the trustees.

One day, she went to help a young man named Milton Dorf unpack his paintings. She introduced herself and started to unwrap a painting. Suddenly, to her surprise, she found herself looking at a painting of a nude. She glanced over at those he had already unpacked, and saw that they were all nudes. "These nudes are really nude, aren't they?" she said with a look of surprise.

"That's my specialty," Mr. Dorf said.

"This may present a problem," she said nervously.

"Why?"

"Well, this passageway is the main thoroughfare between the children's room and the main library. I can see some parents becoming very upset when they see them."

"Your announcement that you wanted to exhibit people's artwork didn't say anything about not exhibiting nudes," Mr. Dorf said.

"Well, frankly, it didn't occur to us that someone might bring in a collection like this."

"Some of the finest painters in the world have painted nudes," Mr. Dorf said. "Rembrandt, Boucher, Ingres, Courbet, Manet—you name them. What's wrong with them? Do you think they're dirty?"

"Well, no," Ms. Barbagallo said, quickly. "I'm just taken aback at the thought of these hanging in the library. I know people are going to scream when they see them. They're very detailed."

"I've used the painters of the New Realism as my mentors, particularly Pearlstein," Mr. Dorf said. "Have you seen any of his paintings? His *Reclin-*

ing Nude on Green Couch hangs in the Corcoran Gallery in Washington, and his *Reclining Nudes on Red and Blue Drapes* is in the Allan Fromkin Gallery in New York. There are reproductions in the September and October, 1971, issues of *Art in America*, if you want to look them up."

"I will. But your paintings are so explicit that I'm sure people will object."

"You're treating the paintings as if they're pornographic or something. Nothing in nature is beyond the artist's range. Do you consider nudes to be erotic art? Are you worried that some harm will come to grownups and children if they look at them? These are works of art, not sleazy photographs of men and women baring their bodies."

"I'm not quarreling with them as art, but I'm thinking of the reaction when people see them."

"Are you telling me you don't want to hang them?"

"No. Not really. You must know that some people are offended by paintings of this sort. I'm not telling you anything you don't know, surely."

"People with dirty minds might be offended, I suppose. But others will see them as works of art. Are you going to deprive them of the right to see them because of the others? Is that fair? Is it right? I thought you librarians were concerned with freedom of expression. I'm expressing myself artistically, and you're thinking of stopping me. It was your idea to invite people to exhibit their paintings. Somebody doesn't do a tree, or a horse's head, or a banana and an apple and a bunch of grapes, and you don't want to exhibit their work. I resent very much the fact that you would hesitate in my case. I look upon my paintings as works of art, just as the other exhibitors did."

The director was silent for a moment. "Okay. Let's put them up. The trustees might order me to take them down, but I'm willing to put them up."

"I suppose I could make it easy for you by saying forget it," Mr. Dorf said. "But unless you come out flatly and say you won't exhibit them, I'd like to see them up there."

Ms. Barbagallo said again that she was willing to hang the paintings, which she and Mr. Dorf then proceeded to do.

After the artist left, several staff members came into the director's office to express their astonishment, pointing out that there would be numerous complaints. Ms. Barbagallo said she felt she had no choice but to put them up, since the board had endorsed the principle of the *Library Bill of Rights* and since they had agreed to exhibit the townspeople's artwork. The librarian instructed the staff to refer any complaints to her.

A woman with a child entered her office shortly after the staff members left. "Ms. Barbagallo," said the woman, "I don't think I'm a prude, but those paintings you have up in the hall are absolutely disgusting. I rushed my daughter through the corridor so she wouldn't see them. How can you have them up there where children are always passing by? The person who painted them must have a filthy mind. How can the library pander to such filth? Art is one thing, but this is degrading."

The director explained the program and attempted to offer a rationale for hanging Dorf's nudes. The woman was not satisfied; she said she was not going to come to the library again until the exhibit was removed. A circulation clerk suddenly appeared in the office. "I'm getting all sorts of negative comments about the paintings," the clerk said. "People are outraged. They're all asking how you could have agreed to put them up. I've never seen such a negative reaction to anything."

The director decided to call the chairwoman of the board to tell her about the reaction. The chairwoman was home at the time, and she agreed to come to the library immediately. When she arrived, she went right to the hallway. Then, she went to Ms. Barbagallo's office. "Those paintings took my breath away," she said. "We simply can't leave them up."

Before Ms. Barbagallo could speak, a reporter from the local paper went by her door. "I think I saw Jake Ingram from the *Standard* go by with his photographer," she said. "I'd better find out what they're up to." The librarian and the chairwoman followed the men from the paper, catching up with them in the hallway.

"Quite an exhibit you've got there, Cynthia," Mr. Ingram said wryly. "I was going to come to see you after we get a few pictures. Snap a few, Joe," he said to the photographer.

"What do you plan to do, Jake?" Ms. Barbagallo inquired.

"I don't know yet, but you know we took a few pictures of the other exhibitions. I thought we'd get a few of this one."

"How did you happen to hear about this one so quickly?" Ms. Barbagallo asked.

"Someone called us and said there was an exhibit we might be interested in at the library," he answered. "Boy, were they right. This will make some story."

"Do you have to print it, Mr. Ingram?" the chairwoman inquired. "We're not sure it's going to be staying up."

"Hum, censorhip, huh?" Mr. Ingram said with a sardonic smile. "And prior restraint on the newspaper, too?"

"Look, Jake, we haven't decided whether the exhibit will stay up yet," the director said firmly. "So do us a favor, will you? Don't publish anything yet."

"The mere fact that it's been up for an hour or two is news, and we're in the news business," Mr. Ingram responded. "You must have known what you were doing when you agreed to exhibit the paintings. But okay. I won't do anything until I hear from you. But I might interview this guy Dorf in the meantime."

The director and the chairwoman went back to the director's office. The chairwoman said the paintings would have to be taken down right away.

"Much as I respect your opinion," Ms. Barbagallo said, "I think we should discuss this with the board. I don't want to rush into anything. Could we call an emergency meeting of the board for tonight or tomorrow night?"

"I think you're making a big mistake leaving them up there, Cynthia. And as chairwoman, I'm directing you to take them down."

"I can't do it, because other board members might feel differently. I think we have to think this through carefully and coolly. Don't think I like the paintings, but they are expression and we're here to champion freedom of expression."

"Well, okay, then, let's see what the other members say," the chairwoman said. "Try to set up a meeting for tonight."

All but two of the seven trustees said they could attend the meeting. Ms. Barbagallo began to think of how she could justify keeping the paintings up.

•   •   •   •   •

What would you do at this point if you were Ms. Barbagallo? Comment on the manner in which the exhibits program has been handled by the librarian and trustees generally. Would you have agreed to hang the paintings of the nudes in the first place? How would you handle a meeting with the board? What arguments might be advanced to justify continuing the exhibit?

11.
As the Twig Is Bent

Lying not far from the geographic center of the country is Herndonville, a city of 500,000. A leading industrial center in the area, it is a place of interesting contrasts. In the western part of the city are the best homes, set amid trees, lawns, and shrubbery, and occupied largely by successful business and professional people; to the north is a string of residential suburbs with comparatively modern bungalows and apartment buildings, built within the last thirty or forty years and still being constructed, which house the transient middle class and people economically able to move out of the poorer areas of the city; to the south and east are the contrasting lower-middle and low income areas, whose dwellings are largely frame houses and straight-fronted tenement buildings. Many large office buildings, warehouses, factories, and mercantile establishments also occupy the south and east sections of the city. In the early days of Herndonville's industrial development, many foreign-born groups—Germans, Italians, Poles, Russians, Greeks, and Syrians—were attracted to the city. Through the years, these national groups have continued to observe their own cultural activities and festivals, which the Herndonville Public Library helps to commemorate.

The main library, a large yellow brick building of neoclassic design, stands next to the city hall in the heart of the busy downtown section; it forms the core of a city-wide system of fourteen branches and several sub-branches. The director of the Herndonville Public Library is a woman of fifty-five. Reporting to her are two assistant directors—one who looks after branch operations and another responsible for the operation of the main library. The assistant director in charge of branches is Kenneth Storey, a man of fifty who has held this position for fifteen years. Since each of the branches scattered throughout the city attempts to fit the particular needs of the people it serves, they vary considerably one from another in collections, programs, and services. The city's racial and economic diversity has presented an interesting challenge to the staff of the library.

The Moss Bluff branch is located in one of the low-rent, high-crime areas in the eastern section of town. Under the direction of branch librarian Amy Gerstenberger, who has been there six years, a study was recently undertaken to determine the composition of the community served by the branch. It was found that 45,000 people live in the area; that the vast majority are unskilled or semiskilled laborers; and that the population is 30 percent immigrant or first and second generation. Ms. Gerstenberger has had the good fortune recently to hire a number of resourceful young librarians, all of whom have a sincere interest in the problems facing the people of the Moss Bluff area— race, unemployment, crime, delinquency, social change—and have tried to assemble programs of service which will help with their solution.

One of the newest members of Ms. Gerstenberger's staff is Dana Gonzales, a very recent library school graduate. Ms. Gonzales, who specializes in work with young adults, has contacted the leaders in the community, the teachers and principals, the members of the clergy, and the young people themselves to find out what the branch can do for its teenage population. She noticed, as she spoke with young people, that they frequently had comic books with them, which they would read even in the library. In her discussions, she found that comic books were the favorite reading material of many young people in the area. In her desire to invite use of the library, she asked the comic book readers if they would like to see the library subscribe to a few comic books, which could circulate for a specified period of time. "The response was overwhelmingly favorable," she said when she presented the idea to Ms. Gerstenberger, who also endorsed it heartily.

The branch librarians in Herndonville have relative freedom in the selection of materials, within a prescribed budget, except that the assistant director and the director have the right to veto requested purchases. Since Ms. Gerstenberger routinely clears any new services or new approaches with Mr. Storey, she called him to say she would be putting in an order for some comic books. He remarked that he "didn't particularly like the idea," but if it encouraged use of some of the branch's other materials he was willing to "give it a try." He said he would go along with the suggestion for another reason as well: he did not want to discourage Ms. Gonzales in her efforts to promote greater use of the library. He did not ask how many subscriptions they planned to place, nor which comic books in particular, apparently leaving the decision to Ms. Gerstenberger and Ms. Gonzales.

Since neither the branch librarian nor her young adult specialist knew very much about comic books, and since they didn't want "to fall into the trap of getting what *we* think is best" (as Ms. Gonzales expressed it), they agreed to ask the potential users which titles they would like to see in the library. Several young people made suggestions, all of which Ms. Gonzales wrote down.

She then checked in Katz's *Magazines for Libraries* to see where they could be ordered and what Katz had to say about them. Both women were a bit surprised to find that most of the requests fell into the categories of "counter-culture" and "underground comix"—*Bijou Funnies, Fabulous Furry Freak Brothers, Feds 'n' Heads Comics, Moondog, Up From the Deep, Zap Comix,* and such. There were a few requests, but not nearly as many, for the more traditional comic books— *Lois Lane, Wonder Woman, Batman, Superman, Thor*—but none for *Walt Disney, Bugs Bunny, Archie, Casper,* and the like.

Ms. Gerstenberger had her order clerk send for several counter-culture comics, which, when they arrived, were placed on the magazine shelves; all but the current issues circulated. Many young people were delighted when the first few arrived, but after a while they began to complain that there were never any in. One day, as Ms. Gonzales was listening to three boys discussing this common complaint, it occurred to her that they might set up a comic book exchange table in the lobby of the library. This suggestion, too, was greeted with great enthusiasm. Ms. Gonzales proposed the idea to Ms. Gerstenberger, who consented readily. "It'll take some pressure off us to subscribe to more of them," she said jokingly when she mentioned it to Mr. Storey, who gave his consent reluctantly. The custodian found a table in the basement which he placed in the entranceway, and Ms. Gonzales made a poster which she tacked to the side of it. Some young people brought comics to trade, and others just took some without leaving any in exchange, but there were no complaints; all who took advantage of the new service seemed pleased with it.

Mr. Storey often said that he didn't get around to the branches as often as he would like—most of his dealings with the branch librarians were conducted by phone—and now, with a new branch being constructed, he got around even less. However, he did come to the Moss Bluff branch about three months after the comic book exchange table was set up. As he walked into the library, he stopped by the table to look at some of the comic books. He gathered up several and went into Ms. Gerstenberger's office.

After discussing some personnel matters and a few changes in accounting procedures, he placed the sample comic books in front of the branch librarian. "I took a look at some of the comics on your exchange table as I came in," he said, "and I have to admit they aren't the kind of thing I had in mind when I approved the exchange idea. Is this the kind of comic book we're subscribing to as well?"

Ms. Gerstenberger glanced at copies of *Moondog, God Nose, Trashman, Wonder Wart-Hog,* and *Mr. Natural,* and said yes. "The kids call them 'head comix,' and they love them," she said. "I don't see how they can read them, but they do."

"I didn't realize they were even printing things like this," Mr. Storey confessed. "Good Lord! They're nauseating. Is nothing sacred?"

"The kids want them, and we've had no complaints from their parents. I haven't kept any statistics—because they would be hard to gather—but I know kids are coming in just to borrow and swap comics. We're reaching a lot of kids whom we wouldn't reach otherwise."

"I find it hard to believe that this kind of comic book can't do some harm," Mr. Storey said, thumbing through a copy of a Robert Crumb comic. "You know, when I see these I have to ask if we're not becoming some sort of cafeteria rather than a library? Surely we don't have to cater to *all* tastes. If I recall correctly, Fredric Wertham has dealt with the subject of comic books in a book called—what's the title?—*Seduction of the Innocent.* He contends that comic books don't help children get rid of their aggressions, the way some people think, but of their inhibitions. He comes down hard on comic books, suggesting, if I remember his phrase, that they can bring about some sort of moral disarmament. That book was written in the early fifties, but he has since corroborated his theory in a later book, *A Sign for Cain,* which deals with violence; it was written in 1966. He has a chapter in *A Sign for Cain* on comics, in which he reasserts his previous claim. He was instrumental in getting people to take a serious look at what their kids are reading."

"From my reading on violence," Ms. Gerstenberger said, "I've found that psychologists and sociologists cancel each other out. No one has been able to prove that someone who reads violent books is going to go right out and commit a violent act."

"You've fallen into the trap," Mr. Storey said, "of having to have something proven. Can't people act on feelings and suspicions and reactions? Does everything have to be proven? Is there no such thing as conscience which tells us what is right and wrong? Thoreau, Milton, Mill, and others spoke about men obeying their consciences. They said a man's conscience was higher than anything else. If a man's conscience tells him something is wrong, does he have to have statistical proof to confirm it?"

"I think the important thing here," Ms. Gerstenberger said, brushing aside her boss's comments on conscience, "is that the kids are using the library. That's all that matters in my opinion. We're here to be used. We're reaching a segment of the population we wouldn't be otherwise with these comic books, and I'm tickled we are."

"Well, are you trying to get them to take out other things as well?" Mr. Storey asked. "Shouldn't that also be one of our goals?"

"I don't think so," replied Ms. Gerstenberger. "I'm content that they merely use us for our comic books and for our swap table. We don't insist that little old ladies who come in to read light fiction take out other things, so why should we with kids who like comics?"

"I'm surprised to hear you talking like this," Mr. Storey retorted. "I thought we were always trying to put people in touch with other and better things."

"I'm convinced that many of the kids who read head comics will never read anything else. At least they're reading something."

Mr. Storey frowned. "I guess that's one way of looking at it. I'm still concerned that we're subscribing to this particular kind of comic book," he said, pointing to the batch on the desk.

Ms. Gerstenberger asked if he was suggesting they should cancel their subscriptions, or do away with the exchange table. He responded that he would like to think the matter over. Later in the day, after Mr. Storey had left, Ms. Gerstenberger relayed the conversation to Ms. Gonzales, who felt it would be unfortunate to have to disband such a successful venture.

A week after his visit to the Moss Bluff branch, Mr. Storey sent a letter—a kind of diary of his thoughts—to Ms. Gerstenberger.

Dear Amy:

While I appreciate your efforts, and those of Ms. Gonzales, to encourage greater use of the library by the younger population, and commend you for your sincerity and industriousness, I feel I must ask you to cancel your subscriptions to comic books and remove the exchange table from the lobby.

On the way out of the branch the other day, I checked to see if Fredric Wertham's books—the two I mentioned—were in your collection, because I was going to ask you to read them. They weren't. But when I got back here I looked them up and read them again. They convinced me more than ever that comic books, particularly the kind you are subscribing to and which appear on the exchange table, are catalysts for violence. I think they have gone too far, that they are too violent, too sexy, too condoning of immorality. I am convinced that in the marketplace of ideas not all ideas should have an equal place. We are treating everything the same, as if everything had equal merit. It doesn't. I don't think the library should spend its money on this sort of destructive material.

You know that the crime rate in your part of the city is higher than anywhere else. By having comic books of the counter-culture and underground type, we are sanctioning violence and perhaps contributing to a violent world. I know it is unfashionable to say things of this sort, and that one risks being labelled intellectually stunted, but they have to be said, and I am prepared to say them. To speak frankly, most of the children in the area you serve do not come from homes where their parents are great readers, or where they are likely to be exposed to culture and refinement. No one helps them interpret the material they read. I am not suggesting that comic books alone make a person violent, but I am suggesting that along with other things—poverty, frustration, the mass media, alcohol, drugs—they can. I think the harm is in too much exposure to the depiction of violence, which can have a cumulative effect and which needs some release—and the release is often in acts of violence. Why can't we make an effort to expose them to some of the good things of life? Surely no one in his right mind can believe that young people can be exposed only to violence—to pictures of muggings, killings, rapings, and maimings, to blood and gore—and not expect their sensibilities to become blunted. "Just as the twig is bent the tree's inclined." When we say that we are protecting the right of people to express themselves freely, aren't we being dupes, often fighting for their right to make money and exploit our baser instincts? Let's face it, we're being taken advantage of. Freedom without restraint becomes license, and if people aren't willing to exercise some self-restraint then maybe someone has to do it for them. You have to lose some freedom to gain some freedom. You lose the right to act irresponsibly by shouting fire in a crowded theater, but you gain the right to utter an honest opinion. But these comics are a clear case of abuse. They are taking advantage of freedom. When I was in library school, I read a piece by Ortega y Gasset entitled *The Mission of the Librarian.* I don't know if you were exposed to it at your library school, but its message has always stayed with me. He states that "liberty has not come upon the face of the earth to wring the neck of common sense," and then he goes on to suggest that the librarian should be a "filter interposed between man and the torrent of books." Quite frankly, we're acting like a funnel rather than a filter. There are no unmixed goods in this world: every virtue becomes a vice through excess.

I have rambled on at some length, as you can see, but I felt you deserved to know why I feel the way I do. Again, I appreciate what you are trying to do, but I can't accept your method. I have had my secretary transcribe some pertinent quotations from Dr. Wertham's books, which I would like you and Ms. Gonzales to consider. Please discuss my letter and the attached quotes with Ms. Gonzales, and let me know what you think."

Sincerely,
Kenneth Storey
Assistant Director

Attachment
SEDUCTION OF THE INNOCENT

Slowly, and at first reluctantly, I have come to the conclusion that this chronic stimulation, temptation and seduction by comic books, both their content and their alluring advertisements of knives and guns, are contributing factors to many children's maladjustment. (p. 10)

Many adults think that the crimes described in comic books are so far removed from the child's life that for children they are merely something imaginative or fantastic. But we have found this to be a great error. Comic books and life are connected. A bank robbery is easily translated into the rifling of a candy store. Delinquencies formerly restricted to adults are increasingly committed by young people and children. (p. 25)

The general lesson we have deduced from our large case material is that the bad effects of crime comic books exist potentially for all children and may be exerted along these lines:

1. The comic-book format is an invitation to illiteracy.
2. Crime comic books create an atmosphere of cruelty and deceit.
3. They create a readiness for temptation.
4. They stimulate unwholesome fantasies.
5. They suggest criminal or sexually abnormal ideas.
6. They furnish the rationalization for them, which may be ethically even more harmful than the impulse.
7. They suggest the forms a delinquent impulse may take and supply details of technique.
8. They may tip the scales toward maladjustment or delinquency.

Crime comics are an agent with harmful potentialities. They bring about a mass conditioning of children, with different effects in the individual case. A child is not a simple unit which exists outside of its living social ties. Comic books themselves may be the virus, or the cause of a lack of resistance to the social virus of a harmful environment. (p. 118)

The average parent has no idea that every imaginable crime is described in detail in comic books. That is their main stock in trade. When questioned more closely even experts who have defended the industry did not know what an endless variety of crimes is described in detail in story after story, picture after picture. If one were to set out to show children how to steal, rob, lie, cheat, assault and break into houses, no better method could be devised. It is of course easy and natural for the child to translate these crimes into a minor key: stealing from a candy store instead of breaking into a bank; stabbing and hurting a little girl with a sharp pen if a knife is not handy; beating and threatening younger children, following the Superman formula of winning by force. (p. 157)

When I first announced my findings that these comic books are primers for crime, I was greeted with these arguments:

1. It is not true. Only the rarest comic book does that.
2. It is not true any more, though it may have been true in the past. Now that is all changed.
3. If true, it was always thus.
4. Crime comic books have no effect at all on children's behavior.
5. Crime comic books are a major force in preventing juvenile delinquency.
6. Crime comic books are not read by children, but only by adults.
7. Comic books affect only "emotionally unstable" or "insecure" children and not the average child.

All these arguments have influenced the public. That they are self-contradictory was evidently overlooked or forgiven.

What is the relationship of crime comic books to juvenile delinquency? If they would prevent juvenile delinquency, there would be very little of it left. And if they were the outlet for children's primitive aggressions, this would be a generation of very subdued and controlled children.

Our researches have proved that there is a significant correlation between crime-comics reading and the more serious forms of juvenile delinquency. Many children read only few comics, read them for only a short time, read the better type (to the extent that there is a better type) and do not become imbued with the whole crime-comics atmosphere. Those children, on the other hand, who commit the more serious types of delinquency nowadays, read a lot of comic books, go in for the worst type of crime comics, read them for a long time and live in thought in the crime-comics world. The whole publicity-stunt claim that crime comics prevent juvenile delinquency is a hoax. I have not seen a single crime comic book that would have any such effect, nor have I ever seen a child or young adult who felt that he had been prevented from anything wrong by a comic book. Supposing you wanted to prevent promiscuous, illegitimate sexual relations, would you publish millions of books showing in detail where and how the man picks up the girl, where they go, the details of their relationships in bed and then how the next morning somebody breaks into their room and tosses them out of bed? A comic-book defender would say this teaches that "Sex does not pay."

The role of comic books in delinquency is not the whole nor by any means the worst harm they do to children. It is just one part of it. Many children who never become delinquent or conspicuously disturbed have been adversely affected by them. Pouring sordid stories into the minds of children is not the same as pouring water over a duck's back. One would think that this would be the most elementary lesson in child guidance. But child experts have overlooked this for years without really studying children's comic-book reading.

How can a doctor discover that a man's diet is a contributing factor to his illness when he omits to ask the man what he eats, approves of what he is eating (without looking into what it really is) and does not know what these foodstuffs contain? This type of guidance has been practiced on children for years.

In 1951, *Harper's* magazine, in a piece attempting to refute my comic-book conclusions, quoted triumphantly the statement of a judge that he "never came across a single case where the delinquent or criminal act would be attributable to the reading of comic books." Should not such a statement carry tremendous weight in my investigations? How could I disregard it if I wanted to be thoroughly scientific?

So I did look into it. I checked. How many juvenile delinquents had come into this judge's court, altogether? *One single case!* Could he really defend the millions of crime comic books as they are? He had this to say,

"I am firmly convinced that children should not be.permitted to read the more lurid type of comic magazines, those which portray crime, violence, killing and sex situations. I am opposed to those books which are sadistic in tone. An unrelieved diet of violence and crime can do no good even to those children who are well-adjusted. Some children might readily obtain ideas of violence from comic books. Many children lack in maturity and judgment to control their actions after reading such books." (pp. 163–165)

The experts say children do not imitate what they see in comic books. As Governor Smith used to say, let us look at the record:

1. A boy of six wrapped himself in an old sheet and jumped from a rafter. He said he saw that in a comic book.
2. A twelve-year-old boy was found hanged by a clothesline tossed over a rafter. His mother told the jury that she thought he re-enacted a scene from comic books which he read incessantly. The jury returned a verdict of accidental death and scored comic books.
3. A boy was found dead in the bathroom, wearing a Superman costume. He had accidentally strangled himself while trying to walk on the walls of the room like his hero.
4. A boy of ten accidentally hanged himself while playing "hanging."
5. A fourteen-year-old boy was found hanging from a clothesline fastened over a hot-water heating pipe on the ceiling. Beside him was a comic book open to a page showing the hanging of a man. The chief of police said, "I think the comic-book problem can't be solved by just a local police ban. It will require something bigger."
6. A ten-year-old boy was found hanging from a door hook, suspended by his bathrobe cord. On the floor under his open hand lay a comic book with this cover: a girl on a horse with a noose around her neck, the rope tied to a tree. A man was leading the horse away, tightening the noose as he did so. The grief-stricken father said, "The boy was happy when I saw him last. So help me God, I'll be d----- if I ever allow another comic book in the house for the kids to read!"
7. A boy of eleven was found hanged from a rope in the bathroom. He had the habit of acting out stories he had read in comic books.
8. A boy of thirteen was found hanged in the garage. On the floor was a comic book showing a hanging.
9. A boy of twelve was found hanging from a clothesline in a woodshed. On the floor was a stack of comic books.
10. A ten-year-old boy was found unconscious, hanging from a second story balcony. He got the idea from a comic book he had been reading.

11. A boy died after swinging in a noose from a tree. He had tried to show another boy "how people hang themselves." The City Council denounced the "mind-warping" influence of comic books.
12. An eight-year-old boy jumped from a second-floor fire escape "like Superman" and broke both his wrists. (pp. 231–232)

The most insidious thesis of the experts is that comic books "serve as a release for children's feelings of aggression." Children, so the stereotyped argument runs, need vicarious violence to overcome frustration through aggression. If comic books make people get rid of their aggressions, why are millions of them given to young soldiers at the front whom we want to be aggressive? Comic books help people to get rid not of their aggressions, but of their inhibitions. (p. 246)

Suppose a child comes to me with a gastrointestinal disorder. I examine him carefully and come to the conclusion that the cause of the trouble is an impure well. I give some medication for the child and tell him not to drink that water any more. A little while later another child comes to me with the same condition, and after that still another. In each case my clinical judgment traces the trouble to the same well. What under such circumstances is the doctor's job? Should I wait until more and more children from this neighborhood come to me? Should I listen to those who say that after all there are children who have drunk water from this well and not got sick? Or to those who say it is good for children to get sick to the stomach occasionally, to "adjust them to reality"? Or should I listen to the owners of the well who claim first that children do not drink from their well, secondly that the well water is good for them and thirdly that interfering with the owners' right to use the well in any way they please is against their constitutional liberties?

I should certainly not be influenced by the child's opinion that he likes this well, nor by the assertions of those in the pay of the well-owners who claim that this particular well satisfies a "need" in children. It seems to me that my duty as a doctor is to make sure in the first place that these children *have* been drinking from this well. And then to be guided by an expert determination whether this well is sufficiently contaminated to have caused the trouble.

That is exactly what I did with comic books.

My conclusion as to the harmfulness of crime comic books got an ever larger foundation as my case material increased over the years. In the Lafargue Clinic, in the psychiatric service and the mental hygiene clinic of Queens General Hospital, in the Quaker Emergency Service Readjustment Center, in practice and in consultation, some five hundred children a year came to my attention. In the clinics I built up an intimate relationship with the community so that I had frequent contact with practically every public and private agency in New York that deals with mental-hygiene problems of children and young people. My associates and I gained a survey of children of all classes and dealt both practically and scientifically with all factors known to influence children adversely, from physical to mental.

At the beginning of our comic-book studies, crime comic books were not recognized as a pathogenic factor. As we went along we had the advantage that we could study them in the setting of an all-inclusive mental-hygiene approach and in their interaction with all other psychological and environmental factors. Comic books transcend all class lines, all intelligence levels, all differences in home conditions. But there is no doubt that the long-range harm is greater and more insidious in all those children less well-endowed materially, intellectually, educationally and socially. The much-abused concept of the predisposed child is misleading in any such study. It is far more scientific to use the concept we worked out at Lafargue, of the *endangered* child.

I have testified six times under oath on the harmfulness of comic books. On only three of these occasions were comic books the original issue. On all six occasions comic books and/or photostats of comic-book pictures were received and filed as evidence by the court or the legislators. In all but one case (in which I testified in affidavit form), I was subject to searching cross-examination. In all six cases the issue was decided in accordance with my testimony, and for the side for which I testified. This sounds very optimistic, but that is not how it turned out in the long run.

At a Post Office hearing in Washington I had to give a psychiatric analysis of what constitutes obscenity. By way of comparison with nudity in art and photography, I introduced comic books which I called obscene. I pointed out that the picture of a nude girl *per se* may be the opposite of obscene, as compared to one of a girl in brassiere and panties about to be tied up, gagged, tortured, set on fire, sold as a slave, chained, whipped, choked, raped, thrown to wild animals or crocodiles, forced to her knees, strangled, torn apart and so on. (pp. 296–298)

Whenever there is any court action stemming from comic books the question of *what is in comic books* does not come up at all. The industry relies then on the constitutional guarantee of free speech. It draws people's attention away from the real issue and veils the business in an idealistic haze. The framers of the Constitution and its amendments would certainly be surprised if they knew that these guarantees are used to sell to children stories with pictures in which men prowl the streets and dismember beautiful girls. The industry regards selling books to children as its prerogative, that is to say as a right to be exercised without external control. To use constitutional rights against progressive legislation is of course an old story. Theodore Roosevelt encountered it when he campaigned for pure food laws.

In these assertions of freedom in the case of comic books, just the opposite is concealed. "We are allowing ourselves," said Virgilia Peterson, "in the name of free speech (oh, fatal misuse of a high principle) to be bamboozled into buying or letting our children buy the worst propaganda on the market. It is a tyranny by a handful of unscrupulous people. It is as much a tyranny as any other on the face of the earth."

What is censorship? The industry has obscured that by claiming that the publisher exercises a censorship over himself. That is not what censorship means. It means control of one agency by another. When Freud speaks of an internal censor in the human mind, he does not mean that instinctive behavior can control itself. He specifically postulates another agency, the superego, which functions as censor. The social fact is that radio, books, movies, stage plays, translations, do function under a censorship. So do newspaper comic strips, which all have to pass the censorship of the editor, who sometimes—as in the case of the Newark *News*—rejects advance proofs. Comic books for children have no censorship. The contrast between censorship for adults and the lack of it for children leads to such fantastic incongruities as the arrest of a girl in a nightclub for obscenity because she wrestles with a stuffed gorilla, when any six-year-old, for ten cents, can pore for hours or days over jungle books where real gorillas do much more exciting things with half-undressed girls than just wrestling.

It is a widely held fallacy that civil liberties are endangered or could be curtailed via children's books. But freedom to publish crime comics has nothing to do with civil liberties. It is a perversion of the very idea of civil liberties. It has been said that if comic books for children were censored on account of their violence "you couldn't have a picture of Lincoln's assassination in a textbook." Would that be such a calamity? There are many other pictures of Lincoln's time and life that would be far more instructive. But the whole inference is wrong, in any case. A picture of Lincoln's assassination would be incidental to a book expounding larger themes. In crime comic books, murder, violence and rape *are* the theme.

There seems to be a widely held belief that democracy demands leaving the regulation of children's reading to the individual. Leaving everything to the individual is actually *not* democracy; it is anarchy. And it is a pity that children should suffer from the anarchistic trends in our society.

When closely scrutinized, the objections to some form of control of comic books turn out to be what are psychologically called *rationalizations*. They rationalize the desire to leave everything as it is. The very newspaper, the New York *Herald Tribune*, which pioneered in comic-book critique, said editorially later: "Censorship cannot be set up in this one field without undermining essential safeguards in other fields." The example of Canada alone, and of Sweden and other countries, has shown how spurious this argument is. A committee set up by comic-book publishers stated at their first meeting that censorship is an "illegal method." That certainly confuses things. An editorial in the New York *Times* entitled "Comic Book Censorship" says on the one hand: "We think the comic books have, on the whole, had an injurious effect on children and in various ways"; but goes on to say: "Public opinion will succeed in making the reforms needed. To wait for that to happen is far less dangerous than to abridge freedom of the right to publish." How long are we supposed to wait? We have now waited for over a decade—and right now there are more and worse crime comic books then ever before. And would the forbidding of mad killers and rapers and torturers for children abridge the freedom of the *Times* to publish anything it wants to? Why should a newspaper that stands for the principle of publishing what is "fit to print" make itself the champion of those who publish what is unfit to print? (pp. 325–327)

A Sign for Cain

When those who carry out content analyses of crime comics record conventional methods of murder, the industry and its defenders reply that this is part of life and that children should learn about it. When they refer to particularly outlandish ways of homicide, the reply is that these are just wild fantasies which every child knows cannot be true and real— like the slaying of the dragon in the fairy tale. One such cruel method is to drag a person to death by tying him to an automobile and then driving off. Crime comics call it "erasing faces." Millions of children have read about that. It is a visual object lesson of a particularly cruel and exciting method of killing. When I pointed out that this is described and illustrated in many comic books (and illustrated it in my book *Seduction of the Innocent*), I was told that this was only fantasy and never really occurs. Students of criminology and of pathology know better. Such an idea should not be planted in the minds of young children; but adults should know that it has happened, and how and where it can happen. In the beginning of the Fascist regime in Italy, a workman, the secretary of the metalworkers' union in Turin, was dragged behind a truck in just this way, and his unrecognizable body was left in the street. In Sikeston, Missouri, a young Negro millworker, accused of attempting to attack a white woman, was tied by the feet to an automobile. Then the car sped at seventy miles an hour through the streets of the Negro section of the city and the man was dragged to his death. A pretty Negro girl, Gloria La Verne Floyd, aged nine, was lassoed and dragged behind a car by white youths in Jackson, Mississippi. She received multiple injuries. (This case even reached the *Congressional Record* of 1963.)

How carefully the violence is calculated to go to the limits of what parents might stand for is proved by the instructions given to those who write the text and draw the pictures. For instance, a "Note to Writers and Artists" from the editor of one of the biggest comic-book publishers has a list of taboos, *i.e.,* things to be avoided. The memorandum shows clearly that these comics are directed to children (which is frequently denied by apologists for the comics). The editor writes that if the list is followed, the product "will not offend the mothers and fathers of our readers." What are these taboos? Item No. 7: "We must not roast anybody alive." Item No. 12: "We must not chop limbs off characters."

In addition to the depiction of violence, there are auxiliary characteristics which reinforce the lesson. Race prejudice is all-pervasive. The clean-cut, tall, white, Arrow-collar Nordic is contrasted with all others, who are inferior, criminals, or menaces. Negroes are depicted as slaves, savages, or fit subjects to be hanged. Indians, Mexicans, Mediterranean people are downgraded. Oriental people are shown as ugly, brutal and threatening, even as subhuman. This is a veritable hate literature. Even before children can think for themselves, they are taught to hate. It is an automatic hate. Those interested in civil rights have neglected this long racist indoctrination of children. (pp. 196–197)

12.
"Whodunit?"

· · · · · · · · · · ·

Chamberlain College is a small, state-supported residential liberal arts college with an enrollment of 600 men and women. It is located in Merrymont, a quiet, secluded town in the southwest corner of one of the less populated states. The 1,800 permanent residents of Merrymont are either members of the staff of the college, farmers, or commuters to jobs in larger cities and towns in this and surrounding states. The town is administered by part-time officials, but most of the service departments—police, fire, public works, and such—have full-time employees, although, understandably, they are few in number. The police department, for example, consists of a chief of police, Rodney Lancaster, and five officers. The college has its own security force, administered by the business manager of the college.

Ms. Marie Bales is the director of the Sorell Memorial Library at the college. She has held that post for seven years. An efficient administrator, she enjoys an excellent working relationship with the long-time college president, Dr. Warren J. Corbin, to whom she reports directly. Dr. Corbin has been supportive of the library in many ways, not the least of which is financial, because he believes that a good library is vitally important in a small, isolated community. The town public library is tiny and open only three afternoons a week; it is staffed by volunteers.

Over the years of their association, Ms. Bales has not had occasion to bring many problems to Dr. Corbin, but when she has, he has always listened attentively and offered advice which she has usually found helpful.

Yesterday, about 1:30 P.M., the president received a call from Ms. Bales. She stated that something urgent had come up and that she had to see him as soon as possible. Dr. Corbin invited her to come to his office at 3:00 that afternoon.

When Ms. Bales arrived, Dr. Corbin remarked that she appeared to be somewhat nervous; then, settling back in his leather chair, he invited her to outline the problem.

"This morning, around eleven o'clock," she began, "I had a visit from Police Chief Lancaster and one of his officers. Chief Lancaster told me that his department had received a call late yesterday afternoon from a man in town who said his car had been stolen from in front of Barrett's drugstore. The police found the abandoned car early this morning. It was smashed into a tree two miles down the road on the way to Asheton.

"According to Chief Lancaster, the person or persons who had been in the car had been drinking heavily, because there were several empty liquor bottles on the floor of the car. He said that the bottles didn't belong to the owner of the car. But—and this is where we come in—there were also three of our library books on the back seat of the car.

"Chief Lancaster returned the books to me this morning and asked, very matter-of-factly, if I would tell him who had checked them out. He said that neither the owner of the car nor anyone in his family has ever borrowed books from our library, so he suspects that the person who checked them out might be able to lead him to the thief. He was very nice at first, feeling, I'm sure, that I wouldn't hesitate to cooperate with him. With our charging system, it's very easy to check and see who has borrowed books, and he knew this. I told him—nicely, I think—that I didn't feel I had the right to give out information of that sort to anyone not connected with the college. When he saw that I was reluctant to concur with his request, he was very surprised. I told him I would have to discuss this with you before I did anything. He became a bit irritated with me, saying this was his only lead. He was really dismayed that I wouldn't help him. I began to get the feeling he suspected that the person who had borrowed the books had also stolen the car. He then asked me what our policy was in matters of this sort. I told him we didn't have a written policy covering an incident like this, and that such a thing had never come up before. I told him that I would call him back after I had spoken to you. This didn't satisfy him, but he and the other officer finally did leave. Before he left, however, he said he was going to speak with the chairman of the Merrymont board of selectmen about my reluctance to cooperate. He muttered something else as he left—something about a court order, which I didn't quite catch.

"After he left, I did check to see who had borrowed the books and found that it was one of our freshmen—a Robert Lodge, who comes from Chicago. He lives in Loren Hall. I have come to you to ask if you think I should give them Lodge's name."

• • • • •

Do you think Ms. Bales was right in not turning over the student's name to the police? What advice do you think Dr. Corbin should give her? Are library records confidential? Can legal steps be taken to produce the names of library borrowers? In a professional–client relationship, is the professional obligated to protect the client in spite of the circumstances?

13.
The Old Order Changeth

• • • • • • • • • • • • • • • • • • • •

When Alberta Talmudge and Elizabeth Lyall announced to the board of trustees that they would be retiring, the members where aghast. As far as everyone in Lewisville was concerned, Ms. Talmudge and Ms. Lyall were the library.

Ms. Talmudge, a native of the town, had become head librarian forty-four years ago, when she was twenty-one. A graduate of a four-year liberal arts college, she did not go on to take a library science degree, nor did she take any library courses along the way. She had "just picked things up from my predecessor," as she put it, and she continued running the library, until the day of her retirement, much as it had been run since it was founded in 1897. Neither she nor Ms. Lyall, who joined the staff only three years after Ms. Talmudge and who was her assistant (in name only, however, not in title), ever married, saying always, when the subject came up, that they were "married to the library." Ms. Talmudge had hired over the years a number of women from the community (mostly elderly, single women and widows) for the other positions—circulation clerks and library assistants, who pasted in pockets, lettered Dewey numbers on books, shelved material, and so forth—who became intensely loyal to their employer. Innovation in the way things were done was exceedingly rare, which was the way everyone on the staff preferred it. The orthodox library programs were unspectacular, to say the least.

Lewisville is a residential community, with a population of 14,000. Nestled in the foothills of a prominent mountain range in the mid-Atlantic states, it is only ten miles from Lydham, the dominant city in the area with a population of 150,000. Lydham, with its bustling activity and traffic-filled streets, offers a variety of recreational and shopping facilities, which the people of Lewisville use. The larger city has two newspapers—a daily and a weekly, with sections devoted to Lewisville activities—two radio stations, and one television station. Interest in music is expressed in the support of a symphony orchestra; art exhibits, lectures, and city-sponsored courses of study provide for participation in other cultural activities.

Lewisville, on the other hand, remains aloof from the soot and din of industry and is purely residential; its shady streets, bordered by many handsome houses with spreading lawns and gardens, make it a charmingly picturesque town. In its early days, Lewisville was the home of rarefied aristocrats who traced their lineage back to the original Mayflower pilgrims. Many of these people linger on, gazing wistfully toward the old and looking suspiciously upon the new; however, some younger families, who have no pride of ancestry and no concern with tradition, have moved into town. This group is wealthy but liberal in its outlook; it is interested in reform and progress. The older gentry have only very reluctantly welcomed this newer crowd into their hallowed ground.

The town has one high school, one junior high, and three elementary schools. There is a League of Women's Voters group, a Daughters of the American Revolution Sisterhood, a veterans' organization, numerous garden clubs, and several churches representing most denominations. There are the usual rows of businesses and stores—restaurants, drugstores, shoe stores, banks, insurance offices—along Main Street, and there is one shopping center, consisting of a grocery store, a women's shop, a hardware store, and a five-and-ten, on the outskirts of the town.

When Ms. Talmudge announced that she and Ms. Lyall were retiring, all five members of the board tried to talk them into staying. Ms. Talmudge was sixty-five, however, and she felt it was time for some "new blood in the library," as she expressed it; Ms. Lyall, who was a few years younger, said she did not "want to stay on under anyone but Ms. Talmudge." Most of the other staff members decided to wait and see what it would be like to work under someone else; although they were reluctant to admit it, some of them needed the money their jobs provided.

The trustees accepted the two resignations under protest, and started what they considered the onerous task of finding a new library director. Before she left, Ms. Talmudge made a few recommendations to the board and the mayor, who served as board chairman ex-officio, which they followed. She recommended (1) that the board hire a professionally trained librarian to replace her, and that they advertise the position in a professional library journal; (2) that they give the new head librarian an official assistant, whom the new head would select; and (3) that salaries be improved so that librarians would be interested in coming to Lewisville.

Olive Lauder was hired in November. A library school graduate, she came to Lewisville after three years as a reference librarian—her first library job—in a public library thirty miles away. She made a favorable impression upon the trustees and Ms. Talmudge; even though she had little experience as an administrator, the board felt she was the right person for the job. She thought it interesting, she later told a friend, that the board did not ask her views on controversial materials, nor did she offer them. She wanted the job badly, she said, so she had "turned on the charm and told the board what they wanted to hear."

Upon arriving at the Lewisville Public Library, the new director found that her predecessor, who had been responsible for the selection of material (consisting exclusively of books and periodicals), had avoided anything even remotely controversial. Ms. Lauder knew from the interview, which Ms. Talmudge had sat in on, that the librarian and the board were conservative in their approach to selection of materials, but, as she confessed to another librarian after she had been on the job for a short while, "I didn't know *how* conservative."

The first thing she did in her new position was contact her library school to find an assistant. Grace Humbert, who had just graduated and was looking for her first job, was hired. The board had raised salaries somewhat, as the departing librarian had suggested, but not enough to interest anyone but a very recent graduate in the position.

The new director found herself with a budget already approved for the next year, which meant she had to live with the figures that had been agreed upon. She asked Marcus Chase, mayor of Lewisville, if she could increase the budget at all, and he said no, reminding her that she would have the opportunity to prepare her own budget for the year following. "Once the budget has been reviewed by me and the finance committee in the fall," he said, "it's never adjusted upward after that! We told you that during the interview, remember?"

"Yes, I do," replied Ms. Lauder, smiling, "but I thought I would try to get more anyway!"

The library operated on funds supplied by the town and a few endowment gifts and bequests, which the trustees administered; the latter were used only for materials. The year's budget is shown in Table 1.

The staff consists of eight people: head librarian Olive Lauder; assistant librarian Grace Humbert; circulation clerks Virginia Nelson and Esther Peshkin; library assistants Florence Most, Rita Butler, and Jennifer Broughton; custodian (part-time) Richard Huston.

The board and Ms. Talmudge had informed Ms. Lauder when they interviewed her that she and her assistant would have to work every other Saturday, help staff the reference desk, do the cataloging, handle their own correspondence, and even spend some time, if necessary, at the circulation desk. Ms. Lauder agreed to this, and she was able to get Ms. Humbert's consent as well. The library was open from 10:00 A.M. to 9:00 P.M. Mondays to Fridays, and from 10:00 A.M. to 6:00 P.M. Saturdays.

The new director and her assistant worked well together, learning the procedures quickly. But they mentioned to each other on several occasions that they did not feel accepted by the staff. "I feel we're being watched to see if

Table 1

	Town Funds	Trustee Funds	Total
Salaries	$43,500		$43,500
Materials	8,000	$1,800	9,800
Other operating expenses			
Office supplies	100		
Library supplies	600		
Postage	80		
Buildings and ground maintenance	400		
Telephone	300		
Printing (booklists)	80		
Heat & light	2,800		4,360
		Total	$57,660

we'll attempt any changes," Ms. Lauder commented one day, "but we've got to inject some life into this collection before long. Have you realized that in selecting materials Ms. Talmudge ignored completely anything that might be considered even slightly controversial?"

"I have," Ms. Humbert replied. "It must have pained her to go through *Publishers Weekly* each week and see some of the things that are advertised there."

"Can you imagine what she would have done if she ever saw one of the underground newspapers?"

"It would have rocked her!"

"You know, Grace, I think it's about time we spiced up the collection a bit, made it more 'relevant,' if you'll pardon a hackneyed expression."

"Are you sure we should attempt it so soon?" Ms. Humbert asked. "I'm thinking we'd better prepare them for the shock. Ms. Nelson was saying the other day that she wondered 'how they could get away with publishing all the trash they publish.' She said she was glad this library didn't get any of those—what did she call them?—'disgusting sexy books.' She told me that Ms. Talmudge believed the library should make only the very best available to its public. Apparently, they sent a lot of books back after they arrived. Ms. Talmudge and Ms. Lyall looked them all over before they let them go on the shelves."

"Yes, I know," Ms. Lauder said. "She told me that when I was interviewed. You know, the board and the staff don't know about the *Library Bill of Rights*. I think it's something we should acquaint them with. But I want to do it without raising any suspicions."

"They don't have a book selection policy statement either, do they?" Ms. Humbert asked.

The director replied that they didn't. "I think I see what you're driving at. We could tell them we're in the process of drawing up a book selection statement, and that the *Library Bill of Rights* is the starting place. Good thinking."

"I'm not sure I said that," Ms. Humbert said laughingly. "But it *is* a good idea."

Since the library did not have a copying machine, Ms. Lauder ran off copies of the *Library Bill of Rights* at the Town Hall, making enough for each member of the staff and each trustee. She called a brief meeting of the staff one day, when everyone was at the library at the same time. She started out by saying that she wanted to have staff meetings as often as possible, so she could keep everyone informed of what she was doing, and so she could have the benefit of their thoughts and suggestions on matters affecting the library. She said she was genuinely interested in their reactions, and that she wanted them to share their suggestions with her at any time. After that short introduction, she told them that she and Ms. Humbert were anxious to draw up a materials selection statement, and they wanted the staff members to offer suggestions on how it should read. She then distributed copies of the *Library Bill of Rights*, stating that it would be necessary to endorse the urgings of that document as a prelude to drafting their own statement.

"Does this mean that we should buy something of everything?" one person asked.

"Not if we don't want to," replied the director.

"Well, then, why should we endorse it?" Ms. Most inquired.

"Well, it states that the library should present all points of view and resist abridgement of free expression," Ms. Lauder answered. "I feel that's the library's role."

"Then you're saying that everything goes, aren't you?" Ms. Butler said.

"Yes. I guess I am."

Ms. Humbert then offered her interpretation, which was very similar to Ms. Lauder's, but no one else said anything. Ms. Lauder thanked them for their thoughts, repeating that she would like to have frequent meetings. "The staff has not bought the Bill of Rights," the director said later, as she and her assistant talked. "I think they thought we were selling them a bill of goods!"

Two days later, as Ms. Lauder was drafting a letter to the trustees telling them of her desire to talk about the *Library Bill of Rights* at the next board meeting, she looked up to see Ms. Nelson standing in the doorway.

"Can I see you for a moment, Ms. Lauder?"

"Certainly. Please come in. Sit down. What can I do for you?"

"It's about the meeting the other day, and the Bill of Rights. Some of us feel that if we endorse that statement it will mean we'll start getting all sorts of books which we feel the library shouldn't have, all sorts of books by radicals and people with filthy minds. This library has the reputation of being a fine place; we wouldn't like to see it change."

Ms. Lauder explained again how she interpreted the *Library Bill of Rights*, stating that she felt the library should have something of everything for everyone, even, she added, "if it means getting a few books which we ourselves wouldn't like." She quoted from the *Intellectual Freedom Statement—An Interpretation of the Library Bill of Rights*, that librarians "will make available to everyone who needs or desires them the widest possible diversity of views and modes of expression, including those which are strange, unorthodox or unpopular."

"You said you wanted to hear our views," Ms. Nelson said, "and I'm giving them to you. Aren't you going to take our feelings into account when you establish your policies? It sounds to me as if you said you wanted our opinions but you really don't. I don't want to work in a place that gives out trash, and I'm sure the other women on the staff feel the same way. They've told me they do."

"We can't place a label on material," Ms. Lauder stated. "It may not be trash to other people. That's the point. Librarians don't have to endorse everything they hand out and they can't label it."

"You said you wanted us to speak freely, and I'm doing just that. If you start buying trash, and by that I mean cheap, sexy stuff and radical viewpoints written by weird people, then I'll have to quit. You'll be forcing me out of my job. And I'm not the only one who feels this way. We'll probably all go." The head librarian told the circulation clerk that she would think over what she had said.

Later, Ms. Lauder told her assistant of the discussion. "I'm prepared to see them all go if that's the way they feel."

Ms. Humbert agreed. "The staff has to be behind us in what we do or we don't have much chance of succeeding," she said.

"Well, that brings me to another point," Ms. Lauder said. "I feel we have to inform the community of what we're trying to do. That means we must prepare them for a change in our buying patterns, and we're going to start getting a few things that some of them might not like. What I'm saying is that we have to mount an effective campaign to inform the community that we intend to follow the dictates of the *Library Bill of Rights* and some of the other documents on intellectual freedom. I hope that by doing so we can stave off any attacks by censors. I'm going to attempt to clear this with the trustees."

"What do you have in mind, exactly?" Ms. Humbert asked.

"Letting the trustees and the people of the community know about the *Library Bill of Rights*, informing them about the role of the library as an institution for democratic living, that sort of thing. I feel the best defense is a good offense."

"Isn't there a danger of stirring people up by doing that?"

"I suppose so. But it seems to me that this way we're not doing anything sneaky. We're not trying to put anything over on our community. We should have them with us in what we do."

"Sounds great, Olive, but will it work?"

"Well, we'll see," the director said. "I'm going to talk with the trustees and see if they have any ideas on how we should proceed. I'd like your ideas too. I mean, should we broadcast the Bill of Rights over the radio stations, put up posters? Things of that sort."

"I'm kind of playing the Devil's Advocate role here," Ms. Humbert said. "But don't you think you're going to get the same reaction from the trustees that you got from Ms. Nelson?"

"That could be. But it has to be done. I guess I gave the trustees the impression I was going to continue doing things the way Ms. Talmudge did them. But I'm not. I want to be able to forestall any negative reactions to some of the things we'll be purchasing by preparing the community in advance."

The five trustees of the Lewisville Public Library are all representatives of old, established families, a sort of town gentry. One operates a real estate agency; another, before he retired, an insurance company; a third is a retired college professor; a fourth a wealthy housewife and widow; and the fifth, the mayor. They were content with the way Ms. Talmudge ran the library, hiring Ms. Lauder in the hope that she would maintain the same approach. They met once a month, except during the summer months, and spent most of their time talking about local events and people in town. Ms. Talmudge had customarily given them a monthly report, enumerating circulation figures, operating expenses, increases in registration, income from fines, and matters of that sort. There were rarely any meaningful discussions. Only very occasionally did the trustees offer any advice, and then only when someone in the community requested something of the librarian. For instance, the high school principal once asked Ms. Talmudge if she would consider adding films to the collection or at least joining the state film cooperative (under which cooperating libraries purchased one film a year that went into a collection which circulated from library to library), but they decided against it. Another time, librarians in the area spoke of establishing reciprocal borrowing privileges, but the board decided that Lewisville would not join such a plan—it would have meant, they felt, that "too many people from the outside would take advantage of Lewisville's fine collection." They were a friendly enough group, not unpleasant in any way, but rather parochial in attitude. They took a great deal of pride in their library and their community—as they were.

14.
To Catch a Pusher

• • • • • • • • • • • • • •

Mr. and Ms. Ronald Hulse thought it would never happen to them. They could not have imagined that one of their children might be on drugs.

Lisa Hulse had discovered some capsules in her teenage daughter's room, and suddenly the awful suspicion hit her. She slumped down in a chair, trying to think what she should do. She decided to wait until her husband got home and discuss it with him. As she sat there, she thought back over her daughter's behavior during the past two months. Christine's lack of interest in so many things. The long stretches of time alone in her room. The clandestine telephone conversations with new friends. The peevishness. The loss of appetite. The desperation for money. It was all falling into place now. Ms. Hulse managed to go about her regular chores for the rest of the day, but she walked around as one in a daze.

The family—Mr. and Ms. Hulse, Christine, and a younger son in grade school—had supper as usual. Ms. Hulse was so quiet and pensive during the meal that her husband and children remarked that she seemed to be in another world. After supper was over and the dishes were cleared from the table, the parents went to the TV room to watch the early evening news, as was their custom. Turning up the volume a little louder than usual so no one would hear them talk, Ms. Hulse told her husband what she had found. She handed the capsules over to him and spoke of Christine's recent behavior. The father felt they had better confront their daughter directly. He turned off the TV and asked Christine if they could see her.

He wasted no time in asking Christine to explain the capsules. Christine blushed. Realizing how difficult it would be to deceive her parents, she decided to admit that she was experimenting with marijuana, amphetamine, and barbiturates.

After the parents asked the customary "whys" and "what fors," they wanted to know where their daughter was getting her drugs. Christine was reluctant to say, but finally she admitted she was getting them at her high school. No amount of demanding and coaxing could draw forth the name or names of the pushers; the girl was not going to break the code by telling who they were. At one point, however, she did say that the pushers were fellow students and that the school media center and the girls' washrooms were where the contacts were being made. She went on to say that it was also possible to get LSD and harder drugs, including heroin, at the high school.

After a lengthy and painful discussion, during which Christine told how she first started smoking marijuana and taking "ups" and "downs," Mr. and Ms. Hulse said they were going to speak to the principal to see if something couldn't be done to stop the pushers from distributing drugs at the high school. Christine implored her parents not to go to the school, but they refused to listen to her pleas. Ms. Hulse said they had a perfect right to speak to the principal any time they wanted to, adding that they would be very careful not to implicate Christine in any way. They said it was illegal to peddle drugs and that they wanted to see if the authorities were attempting to catch the distributers.

The next day Ms. Hulse contacted the high school principal, Roger Podendorf, and asked for an appointment for her husband and herself. She told Mr. Podendorf that the purpose of the appointment was to talk about drugs. The appointment was set up for 8:30 the following morning.

The Hulses arrived at the school promptly. After the amenities were over, Mr. Hulse got to the purpose of their visit. He explained to the principal that he and his wife had learned that drugs were available at the high school, and that they wanted to know if some effort was being made to catch the pusher or pushers.

Mr. Podendorf admitted that they had a serious drug problem in the community and that he knew several students were experimenting with all types of drugs. The subject of drugs had been discussed at many school committee meetings, where it had been suggested that all school personnel remain constantly on the look-out for pushers. He spoke of the difficulty of proving in a court of law that a person was distributing drugs. Always, the principal said, the question boiled down to evidence, and he pointed out that teachers and school officials were very cautious about accusing someone without actual proof.

Mr. Podendorf went on to explain that students were very tight-mouthed about who the dealers were. The authorities had apprehended two pushers, he said, but he admitted that there were several others still around—and that he had a good idea who they were. He reminded the Hulses of the recent community survey, which showed that drug use was the number-two area of concern (after the tax rate) among people in the community. He said they were trying to deal with the problem through a program of drug education, which had been going on for several years.

Mr. Hulse said that his daughter had informed him and his wife that the school media center and the washrooms were being used as distribution places; he suggested that these areas should be supervised more carefully. Mr. Podendorf remarked that this news came as no surprise.

"If you know these places are being used to push drugs," the father asked, "why don't you step in and apprehend the pushers?"

The principal explained that to prosecute a dealer they need incontrovertible evidence. "We have to catch someone in the act of handing drugs to another person," he said, "but it is difficult to prove in a court of law that a person suspected of handing drugs to another person actually did so. It's one person's word against another's."

"Look," Mr. Hulse said. "Why don't you install two-way mirrors in the washrooms and the media center?"

Mr. Podendorf thought for a moment before speaking. "Not a bad idea," he said. "But even if we see them from behind the two-way mirrors, it will still be their word against ours."

At this point, Ms. Hulse asked if they could use the media center's video-tape equipment, which her daughter had told her about, to film the suspected pushers. "If you think you know who they are," she said, "why not keep tabs on *where* they are? When they go into the washrooms or the media center, start up the cameras."

Mr. Podendorf agreed they might be able to do something along this line, and he told the Hulses that he would take the suggestion to the superintendent and the school committee. After asking if the principal would give them a report on how the idea was accepted by the school committee, the Hulses left.

Before going to the superintendent and the school committee, however, Mr. Podendorf decided to discuss the suggestion with the media specialist, Agnes Ippolito, since she and her staff were the only ones who knew how to operate the equipment, and since the media center might be one of the places where the equipment would be installed. Ms. Ippolito was asked to come down to the principal's office.

After Ms. Ippolito arrived, Mr. Podendorf explained the proposal to her, saying that he thought the idea of using video equipment was a good one. He said they would knock out some cement blocks from behind the mirrors in the boys' and girls' washrooms, and set up the equipment in the custodian's closet, which was in between the washrooms. He then asked Ms. Ippolito where she thought they might install a two-way mirror in the media center, asking her at the same time how she felt about the idea, and reminding her that she and her staff were the only ones who knew how to operate the equipment.

• • • • •

What do you think of the proposal that the media specialist and her staff videotape suspicious activity in the washrooms and the media center? How would you react as a media specialist to a request that you participate in such a program? Is videotape gathered without one's knowledge admissible evidence in a court of law? Is there a question of invasion of privacy here? Do the school authorities have the legal right to do what is being proposed?

15.
It Can't Happen Here

Gerald Ferraro and Arnold Zottman met at library school and became good friends. Both men are in their early twenties. Upon graduation six months ago, Zottman became a reference librarian in a large public library on the east coast and Ferraro became director of a public library in Huntley, a small semirural town of 14,000 in a midwestern state.

Although they have not seen each other since graduation, they do correspond from time to time. One evening when he arrived home, Mr. Zottman found this letter from his friend.

Dear Arnold,

I want to tell you about a problem I've got in the hope that you can offer some advice on what I should do. As you know, I've always had great respect for your judgment and would welcome your views.

As I've told you, the job at Huntley has gone along quite well—until now. In telling my story I may go over some things I've already mentioned, but I want to make sure you have the full picture. When I came here, I was anxious to make the library a real bustling center of activity, but soon recognized I would have to move slowly. The staff seemed reluctant to go along with me on many things at first, so I realized I would have to spend some time discussing my ideas with them. When I was hired, the trustees said they wanted me to experiment and innovate, but they were actually far more conservative than I had been led to believe during my initial interview. Since I had the impression from library school that boards tend to be reactionary, I was not too disappointed or surprised. I planned my strategy for change carefully, I thought, and, to make this part of the story short, have been quite successful. Among other things, I convinced the staff that they have an obligation to greet library visitors cheerfully and serve them willingly. At several board meetings and gatherings, we discussed the *Library Bill of Rights* and the other documents on intellectual freedom—everyone accepted them in principle. With the board and the staff, we analyzed why we were reaching only a small percentage of the population of Huntley. We all agreed, finally, that in order to attract more people we would have to do things and buy materials that are different. We've bought toys, games, puzzles, and things of this sort for the children's room; we've increased our collection of recordings in the adult and young adult areas; we've deposited materials all over town; we've set up book return bins in prominent locations in town; we've mailed out books to people who have difficulty getting down to the library; we've matched up people in town by interests and started chess clubs, stamp clubs, and other clubs that meet regularly at the library; we've had various experts talk about their specialties and answer questions—tax authorities, doctors, lawyers, nutritionists, and others. After a while our circulation figures began to increase, and the number of registered borrowers has risen dramatically. We've tried to please people in every way we can.

I encouraged people to make requests and established the policy of purchasing everything they asked for without making judgments. I felt the board and staff agreed that since the townsfolk are paying the bills they should have a say in what we purchase. Actually, I wish more people would take advantage of this service, because it consumes only a small portion of our materials budget. Since we buy everything that's requested, I've delegated the responsibility for filling these requests to the people who worked at the reference desk; they don't have to clear the purchases with me, in other words.

Some of the requests have been for "controversial" material, but, true to our word, we fill them. About three months ago, however, we got three dandy requests at once. A request for *Evergreen Review*, one for *Down These Mean Streets*, and one for a girlie magazine. Can you imagine that? A girlie magazine! Well, the reference librarian ordered them, as she was supposed to, and we notified the patrons when they came in, about a month ago. *Evergreen Review*, being a periodical, did not circulate, so it went right on our periodical shelves, which are arranged alphabetically by title. *Down These Mean Streets* went out, and was returned at the end of the borrowing period; it was put on the open shelves, in its proper place. The girlie magazine we keep in the workroom, where people can't get it without asking for it. We got it because, as I said, we don't place any value judgments on people's tastes and because it was requested. I tell you, the things that can happen to a librarian! I had trouble convincing the staff that we should buy that magazine in the first place, and I haven't told the trustees about it at all. I reminded the staff that if somebody wants the latest Joyce Carol Oates or John Kenneth

Galbraith, we get it—no questions asked. But ask for something not considered regular library fare, and we find all sorts of reasons for not getting what's wanted. Do you see my reasoning?

Well, to continue with my story. Shortly after *Evergreen* appeared, I got my first complaint. It was from a woman who resented the magazine's being within easy reach of young people on the periodical shelves. She suggested it be placed on the top row, out of reach and out of sight. We pointed out to her that our periodicals were arranged alphabetically by title. (It happened that *Evergreen* was on the second from the bottom shelf under our arrangement.) Some young people are taller than many adults, we said, but she remained adamant. Again, we were anxious to please our users, not alienate them. The periodical was put on the top shelf as she suggested, and this seemed to please her. However, there were others who were not so easily satisfied. They wanted it removed altogether. It got back to the trustees that we had a "filthy" periodical on open display. They asked me about it, but we agreed that we should keep it—although some members would have been happier if we had dropped our subscription. That controversy died down.

Another problem occurred soon after, when a man found *Down These Mean Streets* on the shelves. He was outraged. He found it disgusting and offensive. He stormed into my office one day, saying he didn't see how we could make a book like that available. He wrote a blistering letter to the editor of the local paper in which he took me and the board to task for having such filthy material on the shelves. We had a censorship case on our hands—the kind we heard and read about in library school. Only it was happening to me! It *does* happen in real life!

The board and I met frequently to discuss our strategy, for we felt we should stand by the purchase. We had to choose, it seemed, between trying to please some of our patrons by having it and displeasing others by having it! You know, that's a tough problem. How do you defend the right of something to be in the library and at the same time defend the right of a person to object? If you're committed to the freedom of expression, then it seems to me you *have* to defend someone's right to object. How do you not put somebody down because he holds a different point of view than yours? I don't like this snooty attitude librarians have of shoving a form in people's faces and having them state specifically why they object to whatever they're objecting to. It seems to me we're always trying to find ways to put the would-be censor down, and bring him around to our point of view. Anyway, we took the stand that the book had a right to exist and be made available as long as the courts had not banned it. We answered his letter with a letter of our own, which stated that as long as the courts had said the book was protected under the First Amendment we would keep it. It was not an easy decision to make. I think deep down we would rather have let the book disappear mysteriously. We said we were going to be true to the *Library Bill of Rights*, come Hell or high water. We said that censorship is the way of unfree men, not free men, and we spoke of the difference between a totalitarian state and a free state. Oh, we waxed eloquent in that reply! We reminded him that democracy is a dangerous way of life, but that it is our way. We said we recognized that errors would be committed in a free society, but that was one of the prices we paid for being able to pursue the un-shackled dictates of our consciences.

Well, we left the book on the shelves and heard nothing more for a while. A couple of days ago, however, as I was opening my mail, I found an unsigned letter filled with obscenities telling me that if I know what was good for me I'd get rid of *Down These Mean Streets* and others like it. The next day, I answered my phone and someone who refused to iden-tify himself told me that my children would probably be beaten up one of these days unless *Down These Mean Streets* and *Evergreen Review* were removed. Naturally, I told the trustees about this, and they were terribly alarmed. To think of such a thing happening in Huntley! It couldn't hap-pen here, they said. They advised me to tell the police, which I did. The police said they would drive around my house from time to time to see if everything was all right. Of course, my wife was terrified. She pleaded with me to take the book and periodical off the shelves. I said I would wait and see whether the episode died down.

This morning, as I was on my way to the garage, I found our cat strung up by the neck on a tree. There was a note tied to her collar. It said, "Next time one of your kids might be strung up like this." God! What an experience. I went back in the house and called the police. They came about ten minutes later. They advised me to get rid of the books people were objecting to. I said I couldn't make that decision on my own, but that I would have to consult with the trustees. We had an emergency meeting of the board this afternoon. All five members agreed that every-thing has gotten completely out of hand. They've ordered me to remove the controversial book and magazine from the shelves, and they say I should ask the paper to announce that we've done so. They could not stand by and see this happen, they said. The police are working on the case, but they have no leads. The man who originally leveled the com-plaint against Thomas' book said he had had nothing to do with the threats. He was annoyed at us, he admitted, but said he would never fight us this way. I can't in good conscience surrender to these threats. If you surrender to violence or threats of violence, then fear of threats and threats themselves become your guiding principle in selection. What do you think?

By the way, I've never told the board about the girlie magazine. I know them well enough to be certain they'd say "get rid of it."

I'd appreciate your reaction to all this. Perhaps being removed from it, as you are, you can see it more objectively. What would you do if you were me? What would you do about the girlie magazine?

I'm looking forward to hearing from you soon. I hope *your* job is going well!

Sincerely,
Gerald

● ● ● ● ●

What advice would you give Mr. Ferraro at this point? How well do you think he and the board have handled the case thus far? Did they make any mistakes? Is the board right in advising the librarian to remove the material? What do you think of Mr. Ferraro's reasons for subscribing to the girlie magazine? Should he have told the trustees about it? Would you subscribe to a girlie magazine in a public library? If taxpayers have the right to determine what is bought, as Mr. Ferraro contends, should they have the right to determine what is not to be bought?

16.
Calories Don't Count

· · · · · · · · · · · · · · · · ·

Victor Malby was just getting up to leave the table in the college dining room when Margaret Stromberg passed by on her way to another table.

"Oh, Victor, I'm glad I caught you," she said. "One of my students informs me that your library has several books by Adelle Davis. I'd like to talk with you about this sometime soon."

"I'll be in my office all afternoon," Mr. Malby replied. "Drop around any time."

Victor Malby is director of the Lieberman Memorial Library at Hindley University, a major private university located on a campus in an urban setting. Approximately 4,000 students are enrolled in the six colleges and schools of the university. The Lieberman Library contains the general library collection, but the other colleges maintain collections in their specialized fields.

Associate Professor Margaret Stromberg is head of the home economics department at Hindley. She offers courses in Nutrition and Health, Management and Consumer Problems, and Food Accounting. Because she is so distinguished in her field, the president of Hindley was pleased that he was able to lure her away from another institution; she has been at Hindley three months.

When Victor Malby returned to his office after his noontime stroll around the campus, he called the reference desk and asked the librarian who answered if she would prepare a list of Adelle Davis books which the library owned, and if she would bring him the ones that were on the shelves.

In about a half an hour the librarian appeared with a list of three books— *Let's Get Well, Let's Eat Right to Keep Fit,* and *Let's Cook It Right.* She also brought along the first two books, saying that the third was charged out.

The library director skimmed through them for a few minutes, observing that they had been checked out frequently, and then set them aside and returned to some papers on his desk.

He was deeply engrossed in his work when Dr. Stromberg arrived. As soon as she entered his office, she noticed the two Davis books on the corner of his desk. "Ah! I see that you're ready for me!" she said with a smile.

"We have three of her books," Mr. Malby announced, returning her smile, "but one of them is checked out."

"Is the other one *Let's Cook It Right* or *Let's Have Healthy Children*?"

"Let me see," he said, consulting his list, "it's *Let's Cook It Right*."

Dr. Stromberg then stated that Davis was "a dangerous faddist and her books are teeming with mistakes, misconceptions, and irresponsible statements." She went on to say that some students might try to diagnose their own illnesses after reading Davis, and that they might try to cure themselves with vitamins instead of going to doctors. She alleged that it is extremely risky to take high dosages of vitamins without a doctor's recommendation, and that Davis recommends adding vitamins to the diet well beyond the normal level. "Americans enjoy a food supply that is unsurpassed in nutritional value," she said, "and our students deserve to be told only what is right. Nutrition quacks are only confusing people." It would be a good idea to remove the books from the shelves for these reasons, she said, adding that this could be justified because Davis' name does not appear in any lists of recommended books by recognized health authorities. She hastened to say that she was not suggesting any form of censorship. "There's nothing I can do about the books being available in the corner drugstore or bookshop, but I can't stand by and see a distinguished school like Hindley sanctioning—by owning —books like Davis'. A reputable institution such as Hindley shouldn't have books that aren't of sound factual authority and aren't recommended by health authorities. It makes no sense at all to have a renowned department of nutrition and then have books by irresponsible quacks on the shelves of the library." She went on to say that she wouldn't be surprised to see the government proscribe Davis' books as they did with Taller's *Calories Don't Count*. The librarian asked what she meant. The professor said that, as well as she could remember, the Food and Drug Administration had ordered the publisher to stop printing the book.

Dr. Stromberg again urged the librarian to withdraw the books. After a moment's reflection, the librarian decided, on the professor's advice, to remove the books from the collection. He asked his secretary to get the cataloger to pull the cards and make arrangements to have the circulation clerks bring him *Let's Cook It Right* when it came back. He then asked the professor, who was delighted with his decision, if she could furnish him with a list of recommended titles. She could think of two she had seen recently. One was compiled by Harvard University's department of nutrition and the other by *Today's Health*'s library panel. The library director said he was sure he could locate them, if Dr. Stromberg would send him the references, which she agreed to do. He said he would like to check the library's holdings against the lists and fill in the gaps where necessary.

About a month after this occurred, Mr. Malby left his job to accept the library directorship at another university. He was replaced by Louise Auerbach, who had been the director of a smaller academic library. She was quite satisfied with many of the procedures that her predecessor had established at Hindley, and continued many former practices, making changes only where she felt improvements would result.

One of the systems Mr. Malby had set up involved his personal review of purchase requests that came from students. The library committee had suggested that it would be a good practice to encourage students to make suggestions as to which materials the library should buy. Accordingly, a "student request" box had been placed in the main reference room and students were instructed to place their purchase recommendations in it. Mr. Malby's secretary, Melissa Russier, who stayed on under Ms. Auerbach, went through the box once a week and brought the suggestions to Mr. Malby for a decision. Mr. Malby had bought virtually everything the students requested in an effort to encourage them to show interest in the library. Ms. Auerbach liked the idea because it was a good way of knowing what students were interested in; consequently, she decided to continue the practice—although she was more selective in what she ordered from the suggestions.

One day, as Ms. Russier was going through the list of recommended purchases for that week (there were rarely more than two or three a week) she noticed a request for two of Adelle Davis' books—*Let's Eat Right to Keep Fit* and *Let's Get Well*. The student, Carolyn Collis, who filled out the request wrote that she had been told by one of the reference librarians that the books had been removed by the former director of the library. She also said she would like to discuss the books with Ms. Auerbach. The secretary brought the requests into Ms. Auerbach and explained that Mr. Malby had removed Davis' books from the collection on the advice of Dr. Stromberg. She told the new director that the books were in a storage area in the basement, along with other books that had been weeded from the collection.

Ms. Auerbach decided to call Dr. Stromberg to discuss the matter. The home economics professor repeated many of the things she had told the former director, re-emphasizing that they were not suitable material for the Lieberman Library. At one point, she asked Ms. Auerbach why she was making this inquiry. The library director said she had had a request that the books be made available again. Dr. Stromberg remarked that she thought "it would be a serious mistake to put them back in circulation." At the end of the conversation—Ms. Auerbach did not commit herself to a decision—Dr. Stromberg mentioned that Mr. Malby had left before she could send him lists of recommended books, but that she would send some to Ms. Auerbach, who said she would be glad to get them. Ms. Auerbach then instructed her secretary to invite Carolyn Collis to come and see her.

Ms. Collis appeared at the library director's office two days later. After a few preliminary remarks, Ms. Auerbach told Ms. Collis what Dr. Stromberg has said about Adelle Davis, pointing out that Davis' books apparently were not on the Harvard list of recommended books, or any others.

Ms. Collis, who was in her senior year at Hindley, said she knew that Davis' books were considered controversial, but that the message Davis is trying to communicate is that many food refiners and packagers are removing large quantities of essential natural vitamins and proteins from food, and that people need to take vitamins to supplement their diets. She added that many large and powerful food companies try to discredit Davis' credibility because "she comes down hard on their products." She cited a reference from Beatrice Trum Hunter's book, *Consumer Beware*, which tells of a grant of more than a million dollars by General Foods Corporation to Harvard's department of nutrition. "Anybody can see that a list Harvard would produce would be biased," she contended. "Some people are opposed to Ms. Davis, but others swear by her theories. Some experts are opposed to the findings of Linus Pauling on vitamin C, and the Shute brothers on vitamin E, too, but a lot of people have benefited tremendously by taking both these vitamins." The student urged Ms. Auerbach to put the books back on the shelves.

• • • • •

If you were in Ms. Auerbach's position, what would you do at this point? How would you handle the request? Does Dr. Stromberg's right to academic freedom extend to removing books from the shelves of the library? How should Mr. Malby have handled the situation?

17.
Biting the Hand That Feeds

To the visitor, Spencer City looks very like any other city on the prairie. Lying along the Gregory River and close to one of the main railroads, it derives its support chiefly from the livestock and packing industry. The Spencer City Stockyards Company, located on the bank of the river, is the largest employer in the area for nearly forty miles around; it also has what its president jokingly refers to as "the dubious distinction of being the largest single taxpayer in Spencer City." It might be said that the Spencer City Stockyards Company gives Spencer City and the surrounding area much of its livelihood, for not only does it employ more than 1,000 people directly but it uses great quantities of hay and alfalfa, which local farmers supply and which a local trucking firm picks up and delivers.

In spite of its reputation as a "workingman's town," this city of 26,000 is thought to have a tolerably good public library. Built in 1893, the two-story library building of modified Romanesque design houses a valuable collection of curios—Indian arrow and hammer heads, fossils, geological samples, and the like—as well as 64,000 volumes, The head librarian, who also serves as the reference librarian and the cataloger—she is the only professional on the staff—is Margaret Boyle, a library school graduate of five years. Ms. Boyle, a divorcée with two small children, came to Spencer City six months ago from a much smaller public library in a neighboring state, where she had also been head librarian.

The new director feels very strongly that the library has an obligation not only to provide books and other materials, but to actively encourage their use. Thus, she has spent much time out in the community—at the schools, at the various businesses and manufacturing plants, at club meetings—seeking ways to serve the people of Spencer City better. Inside the library, she has instituted film programs, forums, story hours, and discussion groups, many of which have been very successful and well attended. All those who know of her activities, particularly the trustees and the city manager, are amazed at how much she has been able to accomplish in the short time she has been at the library. "I am happy here," she frequently tells people, "and I feel I can do some good in the community."

On one of her trips from a neighboring library on the other side of the Gregory River, where she had gone to borrow some books for a patron, she made a wrong turn and found herself on a narrow, unpaved road directly across the river, at its narrowest point, from the Spencer City Stockyards. Glancing across the river as she drove, she noticed what appeared to be a reddish liquid being discharged into the river from a drainpipe in the basement of the abattoir. Her immediate suspicion was that it was animal blood. Finding her way back to the main road, she continued on to the library.

When she got there, she decided to tell the person on the staff with whom she had the closest relationship, Lucy Clift, what she had seen. Ms. Clift, an older woman and long-time resident of Spencer City, whose husband worked at the stockyard, was in charge of the children's room—a position she had held for eighteen years without having had any formal library training.

Ms. Clift confirmed that it probably was animal blood coming out of the pipe. "You must have passed by when the waste treatment facility wasn't working," she said. "Bert tells me that it breaks down every once in a while, and they have to go back to dumping in the river until it's fixed."

"Well, I'm sure glad to hear they don't do it all the time," Ms. Boyle said with a sigh of relief. "Still, they must be violating some pollution laws and acts when they do."

"I don't think it's worth worrying about, Maggie. It doesn't happen often."

"I wonder, though, if the Spencer City Citizens for the Protection of the Environment know about it," Ms. Boyle asked, almost to herself.

Ms. Clift looked Ms. Boyle directly in the eye. "Maggie, if I could offer you a word of advice, I'd say, leave it alone. The stockyard is the major employer in the area. So many people are dependent on it for their livings. It pays more taxes to Spencer City than anybody else. It pays a good portion of your salary and mine," she added.

"I know," Ms. Boyle said. "But I wonder if they have thought of a backup treatment facility?"

"Bert said the first one cost a small fortune," Ms. Clift said. "So I'm sure they don't want to spend money on another one, particularly if the one they have breaks down only once in a while."

"Did they dump in the river all the time, before they had that treatment facility?"

"I believe they did."

"Thanks for giving me the information, Lucy," Ms. Boyle said. "I'm sure glad to hear it doesn't happen all the time."

That evening, when a friend, a high school teacher in Spencer City, came over to see her, Ms. Boyle related to him what she had seen at the packing company and her discussion with Ms. Clift. He suggested that it probably didn't happen often, as Ms. Clift had said, and he saw what he called "the wisdom" in not challenging the city's largest and most powerful employer. When Ms. Boyle mentioned that she was going to discuss the matter with the environmental protection group in the city, he pointed out that the Spencer City Citizens for the Protection of the Environment was a small, unofficial group of ten or twelve people, mostly housewives, who had "no legal clout." In spite of his reservations, however, she decided that she was going to contact someone.

The next day, Ms. Boyle called an acquaintance who was a member of the group, who said that she and the other members were aware of the situation, but that they didn't feel there was very much they could do about it. "The stockyard is extremely important in Spencer City's economy," she said, "and there are many people who would resent our doing anything. Our group really is not very effective. We haven't accomplished very much. We got after the Algonia Paper Company for discharging fibers and other wood materials into the river, but we haven't done much else."

"What did you do in that case?" inquired Ms. Boyle.

"Well, we threatened them with a Citizen's Complaint. Actually, though, they were sympathetic because the president's son, who is one of our members, when he got back from college, was all hepped up about the environment and had an influence with his old man. The discharges were using up the oxygen in the water and destroying life. We pointed out that sludge was building up on the bottom of the river. They were quite reasonable and installed a treatment plant. We've also indicated the futility of spraying for caddis flies. Things like that."

Ms. Boyle and the woman agreed that the matter should be discussed again with the members of the environmental protection group, and they each volunteered to contact five or six people to invite them to a meeting, held a week later at Ms. Boyle's apartment. Eight people attended. It was mentioned during the discussion that some of the members had already sent a letter to the president of the Spencer City Stockyards Company, pointing out that on occasion the stockyard was discharging refuse into the Gregory River, thereby violating the Refuse Act of 1899. There was no reply to the letter. When this failed, some members made an appointment with the president, who denied that the company emptied blood into the river. According to him, the waste treatment equipment was only rarely inoperative; and when it was, he said, it was usually repaired in a day or two. When asked what was done in the meantime, he responded that they "made other arrangements." Ms. Boyle revealed that the husband of one of her staff members, Bert Clift, had admitted that they did empty blood into the river when the waste treatment equipment wasn't working. The various people assembled agreed that it would be difficult to expect Mr. Clift to contradict the president of his company, particularly if it meant jeopardizing his job. One person suggested that they might write another letter, this time a threatening one, demanding that the plant cease operation when the waste treatment equipment was not working. Another suggested that they also mention the possibility of taking this up with state and federal authorities. Another thought the letter should mention that an employee of the stockyard had confirmed the charge that the company dumped blood into the river, without naming the employee. Finally, Ms. Boyle offered to write a letter incorporating these thoughts, which they all signed and then sent to the president.

A few days after the letter was mailed, Ms. Boyle received a visit from the city manager and the chairman of the board of library trustees, who was president of the Spencer City Brick and Tile Plant. They told her that the president of the stockyards had informed them of the letter. The city manager said he thought Ms. Boyle had acted unwisely in signing the letter, and he reminded her that the stockyard was the principal taxpayer and employer in the area. The chairman of the board, who described himself as a personal friend of the president of the stockyard, said that the waste treatment equipment seldom failed to work, echoing the phrase she was beginning to hear frequently—"It isn't worth getting upset about."

Ms. Boyle felt nervous, but managed to tell the city manager and the chairman that she felt she had the right to act as a private citizen, which is what she said she was doing, and that she felt the matter should be discussed and a solution sought. The manager said that she was too closely identified with the library to take sides on an issue like this, adding that he felt she was "biting the hand that fed her." The chairman said the president told him they would not be taking any action on the letter, and that he could convey that to Ms. Boyle. The president wanted to know who had told Ms. Boyle they were discharging refuse into the river. The library director said she would not reveal the person's name. The chairman then said that if she wasn't prepared to identify her source, she shouldn't have put that statement in the letter.

It was obvious that both the chairman and the city manager were irritated with Ms. Boyle; for the first time since she had known them, they spoke harshly to her and said things which she was not accustomed to hearing from them.

"I advise you not to get involved with that kooky group of environmentalists," the manager added. "We don't want the federal and state authorities breathing down our necks over something that simply isn't that important." After repeating a few of their earlier comments, the two men left.

That night, as she was having dinner with her friend, Ms. Boyle related what had happened during the day. "I told you so," he said. "If you had listened to me it wouldn't have happened. Now why don't you forget about it, and go back to running the library?" Ms. Boyle said that sounded like capitulation—something she was not prepared to do. She pointed out that the decision as to whether the environmental group took any further action was not hers to make, adding that she would be giving the group a report on what had occurred. After her friend left—he was most unhappy with what she was doing—she began calling the members of the group to inform them of the reaction of the president of the stockyard company; she also mentioned what she called "the veiled threats" which she had gotten from the manager and the chairman of her board. It was decided that the group would meet again the next night at the library, to plan further action. When the six assembled— three housewives, a free-lance photographer, the son of the president of the Algonia Paper Company (who was not working), and Ms. Boyle—they decided to picket the stockyard during Ms. Boyle's lunch hour on Thursday. They were to carry placards and distribute handbills which identified the stockyard as a polluter. Ms. Boyle expressed her reservations about that course of action, attempting to get the group not to act precipitously. "What else can we do?" one member asked. "It's better for the company that we keep it within the community than to involve state and federal officials."

"They'll see we mean business if we do this," another person ventured.

During the discussion, one member suggested that the library might sponsor an open meeting at which people in town could hear about the problem. Another suggested that Ms. Boyle put together a booklist and set up exhibits which would present the environmentalists' point of view. "Up till now," Ms. Boyle said, "I've been acting as a private citizen, which I have a right to do. But when we start talking about involving the library through meetings and booklists and exhibits—I'm not sure I want to go that far. But I'll think it over. I'd like to confine myself to the march, which I'm still hesitant about." She pointed out that by going ahead with the march they would be inviting trouble from people in the community, who, she said, "seem to be willing to close their eyes to anything illegal that the stockyard does." The matter was debated at considerable length, but finally they decided—Ms. Boyle still reluctantly—to stage the picket march.

"If you pull out now," one of the group said to Ms. Boyle, "it will look as if you don't have the courage of your convictions."

"I didn't think you were the kind of person to get others to do your dirty work," said another.

The six assembled at noon on the following Thursday, and began to march up and down on the sidewalk in front of the main office building. Within minutes, a police car drove up, but the officers merely sat and observed. Soon, a reporter and a photographer from the local newspaper arrived, interviewing the picketers and taking pictures. One of the marchers told the reporter that if this demonstration failed, they would be holding meetings in the library and that the librarian would be preparing booklists and exhibits alerting the community to the threat to the environment.

When a sizable group of onlookers began to form, two policemen got out of the patrol car and went over to ask the picketers to disband.

"We don't want any trouble," one of the policemen said. A discussion ensued, during which the marchers protested that picketing on the sidewalk is an act protected by the constitutional right of free speech. By this time, some of the onlookers began to shout obscenities and epithets at the picketers. At this point, the group agreed to disband.

"We've accomplished our objective," one of them said. The police agreed to let them go, so the picketers climbed into their cars and drove off.

On the way back to the library, where they agreed to go after they left the stockyard, the marchers decided to wait and see what the reaction was before they attempted anything else. They convened in Ms. Boyle's office briefly and talked about what had happened. "I'm in for big trouble," Ms. Boyle said seriously. "The manager and the chairman are going to be furious."

"You have a right to express your own opinions, Maggie," one person said.

"Picketing and handing out handbills are protected by the constitution," claimed another, "and as a citizen you have the right to free speech."

The librarian wondered if the manager and the chairman were aware of that. She said she knew that what she did was legally right, but added that she wasn't sure it was politically right—meaning, as she rephrased it, "I don't think it was a move that is likely to endear me to the manager and the chairman."

The next morning when she arrived at the library, Ms. Boyle met Ms. Clift coming in at the same time. Ms. Boyle uttered a friendly hello, but got a very curt hello in return. She tried to make conversation with the staff members, but they merely responded in monosyllables. Word of the picketing had gotten around. Needing someone to talk to, she called a member of the environmental group, who reported that she too had had a few unfavorable reactions. Ms. Boyle agreed to go over to the member's house for lunch.

When she got back to the library after lunch, she knew the local paper would have arrived. Eagerly, she picked it up. There, on the front page, was a picture of the marchers—she was readily distinguishable—and a story of what had happened, which she read apprehensively. She felt an ache in the pit of her stomach as she read the comment about the library being used to hold meetings and preparing booklists and exhibits. She returned to her office, looking quite pallid. She did nothing all that day. Fortunately for her, she was not scheduled to work that Saturday. She asked her friend that evening if they could go away for the weekend, which he agreed to do willingly.

On Monday morning, she got to work at the usual time. Shortly after she arrived, the city manager appeared in her office.

"I must ask you for your resignation, Maggie," he said without any preliminaries. "The board and I met this weekend, and the six of us agreed that you can't stay on."

Ms. Boyle turned ghost white. "Without a hearing?"

"There is nothing to say," replied the manager. "You know and we know what you did, and we think you can no longer be effective here. The trustees and I had a slew of calls from people in town, demanding that you be let go. I am sorry to have to do this, because you were working out so well, but we warned you not to pursue this matter. Anyway, we wouldn't have permitted your group to have meetings in the library, or set up exhibits."

"I can't believe this is happening," said Ms. Boyle. "All because I exercised my right to free speech."

"Look Maggie," the manager said. "I don't want to get into it again. We've decided that you should leave right away, but we'll give you a month's severance pay. I would like to have your letter of resignation as soon as possible. If you choose not to write one, then I'll write you a letter of dismissal. Good luck to you in the future." The city manager turned on his heel and left.

• • • • •

What would be your comments about what Ms. Boyle did in this case? Do you think she acted wisely? What suggestions would you have made to her if she had asked for your advice?

18.
"Ask the Librarian"

· · · · · · · · · · · · · · · ·

"You know," June Young said to her husband as she glanced up from the morning paper, "I resent the fact that so many people write newspapers and ask them questions which we could answer very easily in the library."

June's husband looked up from his section of the *Draper Daily Star.* "What do you mean?" he asked.

"Well, every day somebody named Ted Hein answers a raft of questions that people write to the "Ask the Star" column. You've seen it, haven't you?" she asked, bending the paper over so that her husband could look at the page.

"Sure," he replied. "And I've found many of the answers very useful."

"They are useful, but I'll bet he gets much of his information from the library."

"So?"

"Well, I'd like to see people come to our library with questions of this sort."

"Well, why not start your own column in the Pemberton *Guardian*?" Ralph Young suggested playfully.

"You know, that's not a bad idea," Ms. Young replied, thoughtfully. "I think we *could* sponsor an "Ask the Librarian" column in the *Guardian*. And I and others on the staff could answer whatever questions are asked. I'm going to see if the trustees buy the idea and if I can sell it to the paper. The *Guardian* doesn't have a column of that sort."

"It sounds like it would be fun to do," said Mr. Young. "I'm sure the answers would be accurate. You know, I listen to the talk station on the radio when I'm driving to and from work, and it always irks me when people call up and ask some know-it-all ex-disc-jockey, who probably has only a dictionary and an almanac beside him, questions libraries could answer much better. Of course, as you've often said, maybe they wouldn't get as good an answer from the library! They'd be told to come down and check the card catalog," he added with a laugh.

As Ms. Young drove to work, she continued to think about the possibility of conducting an "Ask the Librarian" column in the local paper. She thought of the publicity it would generate for the library, of how it might encourage use of its resources, and of how people would realize that the library staff could answer their questions. She was very excited about the idea by the time she reached the Pemberton Public Library.

Pemberton, a town of 70,000, lies thirty-five miles south of Draper, a large metropolis and the focus of a vast complex of suburban and industrial cities and towns. Pemberton has a daily newspaper, the *Guardian*, but the people of Pemberton also have access to two Draper newspapers, one of which is the *Draper Daily Star*.

June Young has been the director of the Pemberton Public Library for eight years. She is active in a number of clubs and organizations in town, always being on the lookout for opportunities to foster library use. When her husband suggested, somewhat jokingly, that she conduct an "Ask the Librarian" column, she saw this as another good way of promoting the library.

Ms. Young mentioned the idea of the column to several members of the staff that day, and they all agreed that it was an excellent one. When she brought it up at the next board meeting, the members were unanimous in their endorsement—as long, they stipulated, as it did not become a "consumer protection" or "Dear Abby" column. She then broached the subject with the editor of the *Guardian*, who agreed it merited a trial.

It was decided that the questions would be sent to the library directly and that the staff would print those that seemed to be of widest interest. In the case of questions that weren't selected, the staff was to telephone the questioners with the answer or mail it to them. The editor and Ms. Young agreed that the column should appear once a week to start and more often if it proved successful—and if the staff could handle the additional work.

In order to engender interest, the paper ran a feature on the library, complete with pictures of the building and members of the staff, and, of course, it described the new feature. The first column was started with examples of questions people might ask and their answers, all of which were taken from various reference books that the library owned. After this sample appeared, legitimate questions from people in the community began to come in. In that first batch of mail, the staff was asked how many wives Clark Gable had had, and who they were; whether Americans spend more money on liquor or cigarettes; whether a person had to be a citizen to apply for a civil service job in the state; where the V-E Day surrender was signed; and how Valentine's Day originated.

When questions were printed in the paper, only the initials of the questioners were used—no address or any other identification was given. It was felt that names and addresses were needed if additional information was required to answer the question, or if the question was to be answered by phone or letter.

The editor of the *Guardian*, the board, and the library director were delighted with the public's response. Fifteen or so questions were received a week, of which anywhere from five to ten appeared in the paper.

One day, Ms. Young and two young staff members were going through the mail when they encountered the following letter.

Dear Librarian:

I am a widow with two children—a boy age fourteen and a girl age twelve. The other day as I was cleaning my son's room, I came across a pornographic magazine which was filled with color photographs of naked men and women engaging in various sex acts. I was alarmed to see this, to say the least. I left the magazine there, but I don't know what to do. I know your column is not a "Dear Abby" column, so I will not ask you what I should do, but rather I will ask you what effect viewing pornography can have on young people? I figure you should know this being in the library business and knowing something of the effects of viewing this kind of material. If you do have some suggestions, too, as to how I should proceed with my son, I would welcome them.

Yours truly,
(Ms.) Sylvia Helme

• • • • •

How would you respond to Ms. Helme? Would you select this letter for inclusion in the "Ask the Librarian" column, respond privately to it by letter or telephone, or deal with it in some other way? Do you think librarians should give their opinion on controversial questions of this sort? What are the effects of pornography on young people?

19.
Ours Not To Reason Why

• • • • • • • • • • • • • • • • • •

The Wheelis University Library was designated a regional depository for United States government publications by one of the state's Senators in 1932. It also collects all the official printed records of the United Nations.

Wheelis University is a small liberal arts institution, with a student body of approximately 1,500. It enjoys an historic and continuing relationship with a Protestant denomination, but commits itself to an ecumenical and ethnic openness in the conduct of programs, admission of students, and selection of faculty. The library has a total collection of 250,000 items, including books, periodicals, and most forms of media. In order to encourage the widest use of its resources, the library operates an open stack system.

One day a few years ago, Dorothy Malden, head of the order department, was sitting at her desk when the director of the library, Hazel Billington, approached her. It has been customary for the head of the order department to look after the depository function.

"Dottie," the director said, matter-of-factly; "I received this letter today from the Superintendent of Document's office telling us that they're recalling a document called *Boobytraps*. That's Defense Department Army Field Manual, number 5-31."

"What's their reason?"

"They say it was issued by mistake and that it's administrative in nature. Correct me if I'm wrong, but I think we can have all government publications except those that are intended for official use only, or have no interest to the public."

I think you're right. Do you plan to send it back?"

"Do we have any choice? Would you mind locating it, please, and then send it back."

"You don't think there's any censorship involved her, do you?"

"No. I'm sure they have a good reason, and I'm willing to go along with it. We've got enough to worry about without complicating our lives over something like this."

Ms. Malden decided not to pursue her line of questioning, and the Wheelis University Library returned its copy of *Boobytraps*.

A couple of years later, another document was recalled in the same way. This one was issued by the Treasury Department and entitled *Narcotics Identification Manual*. The form letter from the Superintendent of Documents stated that the manual had been prepared for administrative use only and that it was to be returned directly to the Customs Bureau.

Instead of taking the letter to the head of the order department, Ms. Billington routed it through the interdepartmental mail. She merely wrote a note on it which said: "Dottie. Please send this one back the way we did that other one a few years ago. Hazel."

Upon receiving the directive, Ms. Malden checked to see if the library had the document, which it did. She decided to look up the depository act (*Government Depository Libraries: The Present Law Governing Designated Depository Libraries*) to see if the Superintendent of Documents had the right to recall publications. She read the law, noting particularly the following passage: "The law requires that the Government publications, when forwarded to a depository, shall be made available for the free use of the general public, and must be retained permanently by all depository libraries not served by a regional depository, and by regional depositories themselves in either printed or microform copy." She also noted, with considerable interest, that the failure of the depository library to be "maintained so as to be accessible to the public" is one of the reasons a depository library can lose its status. It occurred to her to consult the *Freedom of Information Act* (5 USC 552) to see whether by recalling publications the government agencies were violating the safeguards of the act. She came to the conclusion that under the *Freedom of Information Act*, the library, as a citizen, could request the agency to allow it to make a photocopy of publications, which she interpreted to mean they would still have a copy of any recalled document.

Armed with this information, she walked into the director's office. Holding up the recall letter, she said, "Have you got a minute, Hazel, to talk about this request and your note? I'm concerned about giving up these documents, and I'd like to suggest a few courses of action which we could follow."

The director stated that she felt obligated to surrender the document; however, she invited Ms. Malden to proceed with her suggestions just the same.

"I think there are four possibilities open to us," the department head said. "We could send it back as directed. Second, we could ignore the request. Third, we could make a copy and return the original publication. And fourth, we could purchase another copy in microfilm."

"How could we follow your last suggestion?"

"Well, a microprint edition of all the publications listed in the *Monthly Catalog* is being published by a commercial firm. You know, of course, that the Depository Act allows us to replace our copies with microform. If we had the publication now on microfilm, would we be expected to cut the recalled publication out of the microprint set?"

"Well, we don't have to answer that, Dottie, since we don't have the publication on microfilm. I think I want to stick with the first alternative you suggested—that is, I want to return it. I think we have to have confidence that the various agencies know what they're doing."

"But as a depository library we're expected to retain at least one copy of all government publications, either in printed or microfacsimile edition."

"Why are you resisting their request?"

"Well, I'm disturbed that the government seems to want to restrict the free flow of information. I've become suspicious of the government lately, and look upon this as another attack upon our basic freedoms."

"Aren't you over-reacting a bit? They merely had second thoughts about this publication and have asked for it back. That's not unreasonable. I've listened to your arguments, but I still feel we should return it. And that's *my* suggestion. Don't forget, I'm in charge of the library and therefore responsible for the actions we take. I say we send it back."

The director's tone was clear: there was to be no further discussion. Ms. Malden said she would return it. "Well, I tried," she remarked as she left the office.

One day, about a year later, Ms. Billington looked up from her desk to find her secretary standing in the doorway with a man she had never seen before. The secretary introduced the library director to a Mr. Carl Ahern, who was identified as a Customs Bureau agent. Mr. Ahern explained that he was there to recall a document entitled *Customs Enforcement Manual*. He explained that the manual was needed by the bureau and that the bureau's budget was not large enough to furnish copies for both the bureau's use and the depository libraries. He said, too, that the manual had been printed for administrative use only, handing her a letter from the Superintendent of Documents authorizing him to collect it.

Ms. Billington said she would be glad to oblige, inviting the agent to meet the person who looked after the depository operation. He explained his mission to Ms. Malden, who remarked that they must have wanted the document badly to send someone in person to get it. "Sending you here is an expensive way to do things," she quipped. Mr. Ahern said he was just doing his job and could add nothing to what he said earlier. Ms. Billington asked her department head to give him the document, which she did.

After the agent left, Ms. Malden went to see Ms. Billington. "I'm not giving up any more of these documents for anybody, Hazel. I did it this time to save you embarrassment. I've given up my last one."

"Okay, Dottie," the director said. "If you can build a case for not returning them, I'll listen."

•　•　•　•　•

How would you proceed if you were Ms. Malden? What do you think of the way they handled the three recalls they received? What would happen if the librarian refused to return the document? Are there legal grounds upon which the librarian can refuse to give up a government publication?

20.
Over My Dead Body

· · · · · · · · · · · · · · · ·

A few years ago, Jordanville enjoyed a reputation as a quiet suburb. Now however, because of its proximity to one of the largest east coast cities, which is growing concentrically, it is being drawn into an ever-widening metropolitan area. As this has happened, its once almost exclusively Anglo-Saxon middle-class population has been becoming more heterogeneous in nature. Many of the older families, conservative and broadly cultivated, have died off or moved to remoter suburbs; they have been replaced by younger people of various races and nationalities who are seeking to escape deteriorating urban centers.

The present population of Jordanville is 49,000. The Jordanville Public Library, until recently, was housed in one of the oldest library buildings in the state, a building which, as the director put it, had long since "burst it seams." However, a successful bond issue several years ago provided funds for replacing the antiquated structure, and now the new Jordanville Public Library, which has just opened, is one of the most attractive and commodious in the state. The building is on two levels. The ground floor contains the children's library, a large meeting room, which can double as a small auditorium, with a seating capacity of 100, the audiovisual department, and space for future expansion. The second floor houses the main adult collection, a large browsing area, the administrative offices, and work areas.

Melvin Cohen has been director of the library for seven years. He realized the need for a new library from the moment he first saw the old building, and he worked very hard to convince the board and the community of that need. The library board consists of five members elected for five-year terms; there is no limit to the number of terms a member can serve. All its members are college graduates, working in either professional or managerial capacities. The chairman, Edgar W. Hudson, is the only "native" on the board; he is a retired lawyer from an old family in town. The other members are: Lionel D. Garrison, a vice president of a local bank; Rosemary Enright, a reporter with the local newspaper; Laura Cirillo, the owner of a clothing store; and Austin Legrand, the superintendent of schools in Jordanville.

The library board is having its first meeting in the new building, and the members and the librarian are in the process of formulating a set of policies.

HUDSON: What are we going to do about the meeting room? Since we didn't have one in the old library, we've never had the problem before. But are we going to open it up for use by various groups in town?

COHEN: I certainly think so, Ed. That was one of the reasons we decided to include a meeting room in the new building.

CIRILLO: When you suggested having a meeting room, Mel, did you intend it to be used by every group that wants to use it?

COHEN: Certainly. That was the idea.

LEGRAND: What about radical or extremist groups? Are we going to let them use it?

COHEN: I certainly think so. The *Library Bill of Rights* makes it clear that the library should welcome the use of its meeting rooms for discussion of current public questions and socially useful and cultural activities. The meeting rooms are to be available to all groups regardless of the beliefs and affiliations of their members. The meetings must be open to the public, however. To me, there's just no question about it.

HUDSON: Let's think for a moment about what this would mean. If the American Nazi party wanted to use it, we'd have to let them, right? If we had a Ku Klux Klan in town, they'd be able to use it? If the Black Panthers wanted it, they could?

COHEN: If their meetings were open to the public, yes.

ENRIGHT: You said something, Mel, when you were referring to the *Library Bill of Rights* about meeting rooms being used for socially useful and cultural activities. If the National Rifle Association wanted to meet in the library, would we say yes even though there is nothing socially useful or cultural about their activities?

COHEN: The other part of that statement, Rosemary, is that the meeting places should be available to all groups regardless of the beliefs and affiliations of their members, as long as the meetings are open to the public.

GARRISON: Isn't there a contradiction somewhere in that statement? On the one hand, it says we should welcome the use of the meeting rooms for socially useful and cultural activities and discussion of current public questions, and on the other it says the meeting places should be available to all groups. *Is* it all groups? Or is it socially useful and cultural groups who discuss current public questions? Maybe it's just me, but I'm confused by that statement.

HUDSON: So am I. How do you interpret it, Mel?

COHEN: I'm not sure there's a contradiction there. Take the NRA for a minute. They may or may not be socially useful or cultural, but they probably do discuss current public questions. Therefore, to my way of thinking, we should let them in, if they open their meetings to the public.

HUDSON: Then you're saying there isn't a group on earth that we could exclude.

COHEN: I can't think of any.

GARRISON: Well, who says we have to follow the *Library Bill of Rights* anyway?

COHEN: You endorsed the spirit and principle of the statement even before I came to the library.

GARRISON: I didn't. I wasn't on the board.

COHEN: I meant the board at the time did.

GARRISON: That doesn't mean we have to live with what they did at that time. I understood the board was to establish policy for the library on a continuing basis. What some other trustees did years ago isn't binding on me. I'm all for establishing our own policy in regard to the use of our meeting room. And I think we can do it without reference to the *Library Bill of Rights*. I don't want to see our library used by the Black Panthers or some other radical destructive group like the Young Socialist Alliance.

ENRIGHT: I'd far rather see *them* use it than the NRA, quite frankly.

HUDSON: The thought of the American Nazi party in here turns my stomach.

COHEN: It's precisely because people feel differently about different groups that the ALA has come up with its statement. I don't think we can let our personal preferences interfere with our policy. Look, next to each other on the shelves stand ideas that are poles apart. Why should we fear having them expressed orally rather than in written form?

CIRILLO: Books are not as dangerous as people. I mean you can throw a book away or close it. It can't become violent, while people can. Don't you think that if we have some controversial groups in here—the NRA, the American Nazi party, the Black Panthers—we're inviting trouble? There'll be others who won't want them here, and they might do something violent to keep them out and disrupt their meetings.

HUDSON: Do you still feel we should let all groups in, Mel?

COHEN: I do, and just as strongly as ever.

HUDSON: What about this question of balance, which you are always striving for? How do you balance the use of the meeting room?

COHEN: You let it balance itself. By that I mean you let the people in the community know that the meeting room is open to all, and then those who want to use it check to see if it's available when they want it.

GARRISON: Let me put this to you, Mel. Suppose the local Republican party wants to have a meeting in the library, would you go out and try to get the Democrats to come in and use the library?

COHEN: No, I wouldn't, but I'd let it be known that the Democrats could use it if they wanted to.

GARRISON: Aren't you being inconsistent, Mel? On the one hand, you balance your collection. You've told us that you try to have literature on the right and the left of an issue, as well as the center. If you have some leftist periodicals, you also have some rightist periodicals. You make an effort to have something of both when it comes to the collection—and we agree you should—but you're saying you don't when it comes to the meeting room.

COHEN: Lionel. Suppose we agree to let the TOPS group in. . . .

GARRISON: The what?

COHEN: The Take Off Pounds Successfully group. People who are overweight. Suppose we let fat people in, would we try to get a group of thin people in to balance the use of the meeting room? I say no. I say we let it be known that the room is available, and if thin people want to come in to discuss ways of gaining weight they can.

ENRIGHT: Well now, Mel, should the TOPS groups have access to the room at all? Are they socially useful and cultural and is what they discuss a current public question?

HUDSON: You begin to wonder who you're left with! What kind of group fills the bill in terms of the *Library Bill of Rights* requirement? There's the League of Women Voters, as long as their meetings are open to the public, because they are socially useful. Let me see—who else?

COHEN: I still maintain that any group has the right to meet here. If they can't be defined as socially useful and cultural, then they all could say they discuss current public questions. And as long as they open their meetings to the public, they're okay.

GARRISON: But that's if you use the *Library Bill of Rights* as your guide. I maintain that we can—and should—draw up our own statement of who can and cannot use the room.

COHEN: Are you proposing that we go through a list of groups in town and put a check mark beside those who can meet here and those who can't?

GARRISON: No. I think we can draw up a statement in general terms, and then when the various groups apply for use of the room we can see if they meet our requirements.

HUDSON: That makes sense to me, Mel. How about taking a stab at drawing up such a statement for our next meeting?

COHEN: I'm not opposed to having a statement, but before I work on it I want to clarify a few things. You disagreed earlier about the nature of some of the groups who might be able to use the meeting room. You, Ed, didn't want to see the American Nazi party use it. If I remember correctly, Rosemary didn't want the NRA, and Lionel didn't want the Black Panthers. Rosemary wasn't sure about the TOPS people. It's not going to be easy trying to please all of you. You, Lionel, were suggesting that we make an effort to balance the use of the room by actively canvassing for groups with different points of view. Would you want that reflected in the statement?

HUDSON: I would certainly think so. I think the statement should anticipate every contingency.

COHEN: Don't you think the statement in the *Library Bill of Rights* is adequate?

HUDSON: I would say definitely not. It doesn't answer many of the questions we've raised here. For instance, should the library go out and solicit people with other points of view to balance the presentation being made by one group? If we agree that political parties can use the meeting room and the American Conservative party asks for it, would we go out and ask the American Communist party to use it?

GARRISON: God forbid! That'll be the day, when I ask the Communists to come into our library. Over my dead body!

HUDSON: Could such socially useful groups as the Boy Scouts or Girl Scouts use it, since their meetings are not open to the public?

COHEN: It seems we're only left with the Great Book discussion group, the way you're talking.

CIRILLO: I'm afraid if we don't ask other groups to come in, for the purpose of balance, that we could be accused of taking sides. I mean if the Democrats want to use the library for a discussion, and Republicans don't, could we be accused of being pro-Democrat and anti-Republican?

ENRIGHT: That raises another question. Supposing a local candidate asks to use the room to plan his campaign. Would we allow that? If we did it for one, we'd have to do it for all. Would we invite the other candidates to use our facilities, when it didn't occur to them to ask?

COHEN: I still feel the *Library Bill of Rights* is an adequate statement, but I'll try to come up with a meeting room policy statement.

HUDSON: That sounds fine to me. The rest of you are nodding so I'll assume everyone is in agreement.

• • • • •

In Mr. Cohen's place, how would you draw up a statement governing the use of meeting rooms, considering all the points of view that were expressed? What should such a document say? In what respects, if any, is the *Library Bill of Rights* statement not adequate as a meeting room policy statement? Are there contradictions in the *Library Bill of Rights*, as one person in the case claims? Should the staff of the library actively try to solicit groups with other points of view to "balance" the points of view being expressed by those who might use the meeting room? How would you publicize the fact that a meeting room is open to the public?

21.
The Secretary and the Showgirl

· ·

"Oh, my word!" Violet Nolde exclaimed as she took the wrapper off the current issue of *Vacation Magazine.* "We can't put this in the library."

Ms. Nolde, a woman in her late fifties, is the secretary to Marjorie Bonsall, the principal of the Lillian B. Symonds High School in Torrens, a quiet, residential and conservative community of large estates and comfortable modern homes, with a population of 24,000.

Vacation Magazine is a monthly magazine for travel-minded, vacation-minded people. Each issue focuses attention on a particular place—either a country, a region, a state, or even a city. The articles are authoritative and written in a style calculated to appeal to the well-educated, general reader. The magazine lists and evaluates places of interest, current shows, exhibits, shopping areas, restaurants, night clubs, handicrafts, and hotel accommodations for the location. It also presents thoughtful essays on travel, hobbies, sports, and personalities, among other things, and it includes as regular features reviews of books, films, and recordings. As a rule, the articles are tastefully illustrated by eminent photographers and artists. All in all, it is a high-quality magazine, along the lines of *Holiday* and *Town and Country.*

The issue of *Vacation Magazine* that caused the secretary such concern featured Las Vegas as its vacation spot of the month. Right on the cover was a bright color photograph of a glamorous, extremely scantily clad chorus girl. Ms. Nolde, who checks in periodicals and prepares them for the display cases, decided to take the magazine to the principal. When she got to Ms. Bonsall's office, she announced she had something shocking to show her and slapped the magazine down on her desk. Ms. Bonsall looked at the cover, but before she could speak Ms. Nolde said she didn't think the magazine should be put out for public view in the library. Ms. Bonsall agreed that it would cause quite a commotion, particularly among the male students, but suggested that they might put it out, only without the cover.

"Do you mean we should remove the cover and put the magazine out in its regular place?" asked Ms. Nolde.

"Precisely," replied Ms. Bonsall, confidently.

"I don't know about that, Ms. Bonsall," Ms. Nolde said. "If we did that we'd be guilty of damaging library material, something we punish students for doing. I'm for leaving the old issue there, and just putting this one aside. I'm sure no one would pay much attention to the fact that the new one isn't there."

"Well, maybe you're right," Ms. Bonsall said. "Why don't you work it out with Lew Topping?"

Lewis Topping, a man of twenty-six, has been the school media specialist at Symonds for three years. He has two assistants, both library school graduates, but no clerical workers to serve the student body of 1,500. Ms. Bonsall has always been anxious to have Mr. Topping and his assistants devote themselves as much as possible to professional tasks in the media center, and, consequently, has been most cooperative in assigning routine clerical library jobs to her secretary and other clerical staff in her own office.

After she left the principal's office, Ms. Nolde went to the media center. She showed Mr. Topping the magazine and told him of her reaction and Ms. Bonsall's. Mr. Topping was taken aback. He said he felt it would be wrong to do what either the principal or her secretary were suggesting. It was his firm opinion that the magazine should go onto the shelves exactly as it was. "But it's an indecent photograph," the secretary exclaimed. "It'll cause quite a stir."

Mr. Topping had always had a reasonably good relationship with Ms. Nolde. She was not the easiest person to get along with, but he had learned during the three years he had been there how best to deal with her. He usually found that if he sympathized with the amount of work she had to do, or lent an ear when she sounded off about rude students, he could then get her to do the work he needed done. It was not the ideal way to work, he knew, but sometimes there is no other way. Now he was in a situation where he couldn't humor her, and he realized that she was dead in earnest about not wanting this issue of *Vacation* on the shelves.

"Look, Ms. Nolde," he said. "Let me have the magazine. I promise I won't put it out right away. I'd like to think the whole thing over for a couple of days. Maybe I'll decide your way. Who knows?"

"There isn't anything to think over," Ms. Nolde replied. "Ms. Bonsall doesn't want this issue out in the open. If you do put it out she wants the cover torn off."

Mr. Topping smiled and told her not to worry. "Don't forget now," she repeated confidently, "Ms. Bonsall doesn't want you to put it out."

Ms. Nolde went back to her office. "Damn it," Mr. Topping muttered to himself, "what a stupid mess to be in."

Mr. Topping took the magazine over to his two assistants, who had stood by wondering what their boss and the secretary had been talking about. He showed them the cover and told them the story, and they had a good laugh. "Imagine making a big deal out of that," Irene Marshall said, chortling heartily.

"What are you going to do, Lew?" Edgar Olorisa asked.

"For a start, I think I'll go down and see Bonsall," Mr. Topping replied. "But I'm in a spot. If I lose Ms. Nolde's respect, I'll have to work damned hard to build up a good relationship again—if that's possible. The old gal's been pretty helpful, but she's not one to cross. She holds grudges. She's still not talking to the head of the English department because he crossed her once. And not only that, I'm coming up for tenure this year. What a situation to be in—having to defend something I believe in at the risk of putting my job in jeopardy. This damn magazine may make the difference between my making it here or not."

"What's that old adage about he who fights and runs away lives to fight another day?" Edgar Olorisa interjected waggishly. "Why not try to fight this one, but if you see you're losing—give up. Is it worth your future here? There'll be plenty of other opportunities to take a stand and strike a blow for freedom. Think, too, of what effect bad references would mean for possible future jobs. From my experience, an employee never wins against a boss. Bonsall could screw you when you apply somewhere else."

"Anyway, we'd hate to see you go, Lew," Irene Marshall added. "You've been doing some great things here and everyone would miss you."

"You sound like Job's companions," Mr. Topping said. "But thanks for your opinions. I'm going down to see Bonsall now."

Anyone wanting to see Ms. Bonsall had to check with Ms. Nolde to see if she was available. Not to check with the secretary before entering the principal's office was to risk incurring Ms. Nolde's wrath. For the sake of harmony, Mr. Topping had long since decided to obey all the written and unwritten rules and laws of good faculty behavior. He announced to the secretary that he would like to see Ms. Bonsall and asked whether the principal had a few minutes. After checking, Ms. Nolde announced that Ms. Bonsall was very busy, but that she would give him a minute or two. Mr. Topping said thanks and went in.

"Hi, Lew," Ms. Bonsall said. "What can I help you with?"

The media specialist had the distinct impression that the nature of his visit was well known. "It's about the current issue of *Vacation*. Ms. Nolde informs me that you feel it should not go out on the shelves, at least with its cover on, that is."

"Yes. I think it would be better not to put it out. It's only going to draw a lot of attention. And it'll probably be stolen anyway."

"Somehow I don't feel right about not putting it out, or tearing off the cover. It sounds a bit like censorship."

"Come on now. You're a reasonable fellow. Why should we invite trouble?

This cover will stand out like a sore thumb. Anyway, with all the mothers who serve as aides in the library and in the classroom, we're bound to get complaints. You know that, Lew, so be reasonable."

"I still don't feel right about it," Mr. Topping replied.

"Well, look at it this way. You're not doing it, I am. And I don't feel the slightest bit guilty," the principal replied. "That should make you feel better. You can just say the boss made the decision. Put the blame on me if you like. Frankly, Lew, I think we're spending altogether too much time on something that isn't worth it. Look, give me the magazine and I'll tear the cover off right now."

●　●　●　●　●

If you were Mr. Topping what would you say or do at this point? What arguments might Mr. Topping have used with Ms. Nolde and Ms. Bonsall? Is the matter worth fighting over, considering that the question of Mr. Topping's tenure might be affected?

22.
The Business of Barbarians

* * * * * * * * * * * * * * * * * * *

The city of Hillstown lies in a western state, approximately eighty miles north of one of the state's largest cities. Its craggy soil has been devoted chiefly to timber, which, along with fishing, has been the chief source of income for the people of the area. It is predominantly a rural, low-to-middle-income district, and has a population of approximately 46,000. The people of Hillstown are markedly homogeneous politically, with the bulk of them always voting a straight conservative ticket. Hillstown, lying well outside a large metropolitan area, offers its inhabitants a wide range of group activities—patriotic, women's, hobby, special interest, religious, and such.

The Hillstown Public Library, currently under the direction of head librarian Albert Tolliver, was established largely by local effort and is financed primarily with local funds; it receives only a nominal grant-in-aid from the state and participates in regional operation for interlibrary loan. Its eight-member board is self-perpetuating, with the mayor, who serves as chairman ex-officio, usually suggesting any needed replacements as members' seven-year terms expire. Trustees may serve as many terms as they wish—the most recent addition to the current board has been a member for nine years. Members vary in age from fifty to eighty, with the average age being sixty-five. Never in the history of the Hillstown Public Library has a woman served as a trustee.

With the exception of Mr. Tolliver, who has been the head librarian for seven years, the staff has changed very little in recent years. He is the sixth librarian in the seventy-four year history of the library. A native of the state and a library school graduate, he came to Hillstown from a smaller library in the same state, where he had served as head librarian for two years.

Under the direction of Mr. Tolliver and his immediate predecessor, the library has tried to keep in tune with the times. As a result, the library provides many visual aids—films, projectors, filmstrips, recordings—as well as materials such as books, periodicals, and newspapers. The library also sponsors discussion groups, film programs, and story hours, and cooperates with community agenices by setting up special exhibits which these agencies request. It has been the policy of the board—never stated explicitly, however—that the library is to remain completely neutral as far as the issues of the day are concerned; as a consequence, the library has not been involved in any major controversies in the community. Mr. Tolliver, who does most of the selecting for the collection, has purchased some material slightly to the political right and left, but he has never strayed very far from center—although he has confided to friends that he would like to, as he put it, "spice up the collection considerably."

Recently, the local daily newspaper, *The Banner–Ledger*, hired a new editor. One of the first things he did upon arriving in Hillstown was assign a reporter to interview various officials in town, "so that they will be better known, and so that the people of Hillstown will have a better idea of what they do and what they think." The regular feature was announced, and a list of people to be interviewed was drawn up. The first person interviewed was the mayor, followed by the superintendent of schools, the police chief, the fire chief, and then the head librarian. The interviews, which appeared at the rate of one a week, gave the officials an opportunity to express their plans for their departments, their thoughts on various problems which they and the city faced, and some of their personal philosophies. The interviews included a picture and a brief biographical sketch. The interview with Mr. Tolliver follows.

BANNER-LEDGER: Mr. Tolliver, you've been with the library seven years now. Has the library changed much in that period of time?

TOLLIVER: I like to think so, but of course I'm prejudiced! Actually, I think we have made some important strides forward. For instance, we've seen our registration grow from 28 percent of the total population to 34 percent, an increase of 6 percent. We've seen our collection of books increase from 49,000 seven years ago to 74,000 at present; we're now subscribing to 156 periodicals and newspapers, whereas seven years ago we were receiving only 132. On the financial side, we've seen our allotment per capita increase from $3.57 to $4.78. Mind you, I would have liked to have seen it go higher, but I guess people in Hillstown feel the library is not as important in the great scheme of things as the fire department, the police department, and the schools.

BANNER-LEDGER: Do you resent that?

TOLLIVER: Well, naturally. I think we're just as important. I feel that ideas move the world, and we supply people with ideas.

BANNER-LEDGER: But do the people who make the decisions in the community get their ideas from the library?

TOLLIVER: To be honest, they don't seem to. They seem to be able to operate quite well without us, but we're working on that!

BANNER-LEDGER: Say some more about that!

TOLLIVER: Well, we've begun to send copies of articles which we think will be of interest to various boards and groups in town as we discover them in periodicals and newspapers. For instance, if we come across a table listing the comparative tax rates in the communities in the state or in the country, we send copies of it to the mayor and the finance committee. Or if the school officials are talking about the open classroom concept, as they are these days, we'll send them articles and references that might be of help. Things of that sort.

BANNER-LEDGER: Very interesting. What else do you have going that you would like people to hear about?

TOLLIVER: We've built up the library's stock of audiovisual equipment considerably. We have three stereo sets and an extensive collection of recordings. We also have two film projectors, one of which is available for use by groups in the city. We stipulate, however, that one of our trained projectionists must accompany the projector when it's loaned out, even if people say they have experienced projectionists of their own. This is a new policy which has become necessary because the projector was constantly being returned to us broken. We also have a good collection of framed prints for circulation. They go out for a three-month loan period. It is interesting to see the number of people who have borrowed our prints and who have then requested ordering information so that they can have a copy permanently. Of course, we try to do a good job of answering reference questions, but there are times when we have to give people short shrift because we're a bit understaffed in the reference department. We have three professional librarians—I hate the term—who handle reference questions, but one of them also catalogs and another handles our exhibits. After school and in the evenings we're quite busy and can't always do the in-depth research we would like.

BANNER-LEDGER: How many additional people would you like to have on the staff, if you had your way?

TOLLIVER: I think we could easily find work for two more professional librarians and three more nonprofessional people—that is, circulation clerks and library assistants in the cataloging department. I had requested two additional people for this year, but as you know the city has been on an economy kick and we didn't get them.

BANNER-LEDGER: So far, we've been talking about the services and the staff and the collection. Let's shift our focus to the role of the library in Hillstown. What do you see the purpose of the library to be?

TOLLIVER: That's a pretty broad question, but I think I can answer it. I see our role as threefold: educational, recreational, and informational. I think, too, that the library should represent the democratic ideal of tolerance. We have in the library field what is known as the *Library Bill of Rights*. It states in effect that libraries should present the widest spectrum of views, however unpopular the people are who are presenting them, and that censorship should be avoided. Of course, that's often easier said than done.

BANNER-LEDGER: Do you present all points of view in this library?

TOLLIVER: Not as many as I would like, really. We tend to be prudent, for the most part.

BANNER-LEDGER: What could you be doing that you're not doing now?

TOLLIVER: I've been at a few library conferences recently where the question of whether libraries should remain impartial was discussed. I have to admit that I'm wondering whether the library should merely act as an impartial mirror to society or whether it shouldn't be attempting to influence public opinion. I haven't resolved this question in my mind, but I'm beginning to think that libraries have remained aloof for too long. I sometimes get the feeling that they're fiddling while the country burns.

BANNER-LEDGER: Could you be more specific?

TOLLIVER: Well, all over the country we have people out demonstrating against injustice, corruption, high prices, and so on, and in the meantime we're back in our libraries setting up exhibits on flower arranging and cooking and boating. It's not that these things don't have their place, but I question whether they should have all the place. I'm wondering if we have an obligation to represent all sides of a controversial issue equally, or whether we shouldn't be getting into the fray now and then and taking sides. I mean, I'm wondering if there isn't something so right that we can fight for it—lend our weight as libraries to one side over the other. Perhaps we should be attempting to influence people. I'm beginning to think that where there is no issue in a community a librarian should create one. For instance, where civil rights is not an issue in a community, perhaps the librarian should attempt to make it one. We in libraries should come down hard against discrimination, and we should set up exhibits and purchase materials that are antidiscrimination. Can discrimination be justified by rational, civilized human beings? Civilized people don't discriminate against people of other races, religions, and sex. Shouldn't we in the library therefore be attempting to help create a race of civilized people? Is this not one of our educational functions?

BANNER-LEDGER: You've asked quite a few questions. How about answering some of them!

TOLLIVER: Take war, for instance. Surely no one can be for war and its horrors. Napoleon said that war is the business of barbarians. Surely no one can be for brutality. Take Hitler's annihilation of the Jews at Auschwitz and Treblinka. Surely no one in his right mind can sanction the incredible barbarism of Hitler's attempts to exterminate the Jews. I mean, if we were to set up an exhibit in the library on man's inhumanity to man, would we have to balance our presentation by putting in material that would express and justify a Hitler point of view? I don't think we would.

BANNER-LEDGER: Are these exhibits that you speak of—which I presume consist of posters, photographs, and books—going to influence many people anyway? You set them up in the library and only those people who come into the library see them, and maybe even some of them don't look at them.

TOLLIVER: That's true, but I've been toying with the idea of asking the local banks and stores if they would permit us to put up some of our exhibits in their windows.

Before we go on, I'd like to correct an impression I may have left you with earlier in regard to exhibits. I do feel they have a place in a library, and we have a very artistic and imaginative person in the library who sets them up. This person has a flair for arrangement and the use of color, and she comes up with some ingenious displays. We've tended, however, to avoid controversial topics in our displays and exhibits. We've had displays on planning a party, world cookery, arm-chair travel, collecting antiques, books that have stood the test of time, animal ways—things of that sort. The closest we've come to getting involved was when we put up an exhibit on voting, stressing that people should get out and vote. But who can quarrel with that? I'd like to see us set up an exhibit on the horrors of war, for example. I think we could show pictures of the bombings of Hiroshima and Nagasaki and pictures of the mangled and scarred survivors who were exposed to radiation. We could show pictures of the concentration camps at Auschwitz and Treblinka and the naked, emaciated human bodies being swept along by bulldozers. And the massacre at My Lai, and the pictures of the children running down the road trying desperately to escape the effects of napalm. I would present the goriest pictures of man's inhumanity to man—we've all seen them in magazines and newspapers—in the hope that people would realize how horrible war is. Perhaps if more people could see the ravaging effects of war more of them would refuse to fight. I would also gather a collection of antiwar writings, books by Bertrand Russell, Jean-Paul Sartre, and others.

BANNER-LEDGER: Are you suggesting that a country should never defend itself? Are you suggesting that all wars are bad?

TOLLIVER: I think we in America would have to fight if we were attacked, but only then. I would hope that if more people could be brought to see what war does to people, mostly innocent victims, they might feel differently about fighting. If the terrible effects of war could be personalized so that every person could feel the effects on himself, if he could see himself as one of the scarred, brutalized victims, he might feel differently. That's what I'm suggesting.

BANNER-LEDGER: You said something earlier about representing the democratic ideal of tolerance and the library's obligation, which seems to be understood in this community, of representing all points of view. This would be an antiwar exhibit, wouldn't it? You would then be taking a side, wouldn't you?

TOLLIVER: Well, perhaps war is one of those issues about which there can't be any debate. It is to be avoided at all costs, in my opinion. And if we can help people see how atrocious war is, then we'll be doing something good.

BANNER-LEDGER: Have you discussed this with the trustees of your library?

TOLLIVER: No. But just because the exhibit, which would probably be in the library rather than in a store or bank window, might bother some people, and they might contact the trustees, I will.

BANNER-LEDGER: We shall watch with interest to see how you make out with this exhibit. Thank you for the interview.

Mr. Tolliver did not tell any of the trustees about the specific nature of his interview with the newspaper. He had mentioned at one of their meetings that he would be included in the series, and they seemed pleased to hear it. A day after the write-up appeared in the paper, Mr. Tolliver got a call from the chairman of the board, who was also the mayor. The mayor indicated he thought the interview was interesting, adding that he felt the board had better discuss the idea of an antiwar exhibit to see whether the members considered it a breach of the library's commitment to remain completely neutral on all issues. He said he was surprised to read that Mr. Tolliver might have been influenced by things he heard at library conventions, adding that he was also amazed to hear that librarians would be talking of such things. "For what it's worth," he said, "my initial reaction is negative to the exhibit you're contemplating. I feel it definitely goes against our policy of noninvolvement."

Mr. Tolliver replied, "Willy-nilly, the library does take sides. It chooses to select safe and acceptable material. And that definitely is taking sides."

The mayor asked the librarian what had come over him, stating that Tolliver had always accepted the position of the trustees before. "We've got a good library, Al. You don't want to do anything to ruin it."

The conversation closed with the mayor saying he was sure the trustees would want to discuss the opinions expressed in the interview at the next board meeting. In the meantime, several members of the staff indicated to Mr. Tolliver that they thought the library should not put up an antiwar exhibit; and when Mr. Tolliver encountered residents of Hillstown—in the library, in the stores, or on the street—many of them offered their opinions, which were mostly negative. By the time the trustees met, Mr. Tolliver's unofficial survey of reactions was four to one against the exhibit. Many people were concerned that the pictures would be ugly and disturbing, and felt, as one person expressed it, that "unpleasant reminders of things of that sort should not be kept in front of people's eyes." Very few people in the community discussed the pros and cons of the library's taking sides, but when they did they were unanimously against it.

At the trustees' meeting, the mayor, as chairman, opened the discussion with a reference to the interview and the possibility of an antiwar exhibit, stating that he thought such an exhibit went against the board's policy of impartiality. He further reported that he had discussed the matter with several people in town and that they felt as he did. He then invited other members of the board, all eight of whom were at the meeting, to offer their comments. One said that "for the library to take a stand against war, repugnant as war is, would be to open the way to turning the library into a center for propaganda." Another said that "such a display would violate the principle to which a library is dedicated, that is, to provide a sanctuary for the free exchange of ideas, without becoming a symbol of a particular point of view."

Many other members spoke along the same lines, the essence of their comments being that it would be dangerous precedent for the library to take sides even on an issue as apparently safe as this one, and that they did not want to see the library move from a passive role to an active one.

● ● ● ● ●

Does a library have a right to push a particular point of view, as Mr. Tolliver suggests? What do you think of his view? Pay particular attention to his assertion that "willy-nilly, the library takes sides. It chooses to select safe and acceptable materials." Consider, too, his statement, "I'm wondering if we have an obligation to represent all sides of a controversial issue equally, or whether we shouldn't be getting into the fray now and then and taking sides."

23.
Rated "X"

• • • • • • • • •

Associate Professor Myron B. Schwartz offers a freshman course in the Department of Speech and Dramatic Art at Dexter State University; it is required of all students who plan to major in broadcasting and film. Entitled Cinematography Techniques, the course carries three semester hours of credit toward the baccalaureate degree and deals with the expressive possibilities of film and the techniques by which these are carried out. Students screen many different types of film during the semester, including samples from the realist and romantic traditions, from the cinéma vérité directors, and from the independent film-makers of today.

Dexter State was one of the first universities in the country to accept a program of courses in film-making for academic credit. The program, which has achieved national recognition, is offered within the context of a liberal education, and is designed to help students understand the nature of the broadcasting and film industries and their relationship to the broader field of the communication arts.

The university was established in 1897 by an act of the state legislature. As a land-grant institution, Dexter State derives its support from state legislature appropriations, from student fees, and from private gifts and other grants. The coeducational campus, which occupies over 800 acres of rural property in the midwestern part of the country and comprises thirty major buildings has a student body of approximately 10,000, three-fourths of whom are enrolled in undergraduate degree programs.

The university's main library is a modern, air-conditioned building with a total of more than 1,200,000 items, including bound volumes, periodicals, manuscripts, maps, sheet music, films, and recordings. The facilities of the library include microfilm and microcard reading rooms, seminar and conference rooms, listening rooms for recordings, film viewing rooms, and carrels for graduate students.

The audiovisual librarian at Dexter is Joseph Campanella. One of his jobs involves coordinating the use of the library's audiovisual materials, including the use of the film viewing room, and arranging for men and women students to run the projectors.

One day at the end of the spring semester, as Professor Schwartz was booking the film viewing room for the coming fall with Mr. Campanella, he mentioned that he had bought some "hard-core" pornographic films and planned to show them to his Cinematography Techniques class as examples of that genre of film-making. Mr. Campanella's reaction was one of surprise and interest. "Where did you get them?" he asked.

"At an adult bookstore in New York when I was there recently. They're examples of what used to be known as 'stag' films. They have no sound track, the lighting is poor—you know the kind of thing. I want my students to see the really bad so they can have some appreciation of the good, like *Scorpio Rising* or *I am Curious (Yellow)*."

"I think I'd better see them beforehand," the librarian said, "to determine whether I should show them myself or whether I should let the student aides do it as usual. If they're anything like some I've seen, some of the projectionists might be upset by them."

Professor Schwartz assured the librarian that he would bring them in a few days before they were to be shown. The two men then concluded their business with talk of where each would be spending his summer vacation.

Summer passed, and it wasn't long before Dexter State was in the middle of its fall term. Two days before the scheduled showing of the pornographic films, Professor Schwartz appeared in Mr. Campanella's office.

"Hi, Joey," he said. "I just remembered that you asked me to let you preview the pornographic films I bought last spring."

"I completely forgot about them, Myron. Thanks for bringing them over. When are they to be shown?"

"The day after tomorrow," was Professor Schwartz's reply. "But, look, I've got a slight problem. My department head and I are leaving right away for a film convention out of town and we won't be back until Thursday. As a matter of fact, our plane doesn't get in until about half an hour before my class. So I'll probably be a trifle late. I told the students last time about the films—some are quite anxious to see them!—so they'll be in the screening room at 2:30. Would you be a good guy and start without me, since I'll probably not make it on time?"

Mr. Campanella told the professor not to worry, that he would be glad to get things started. Professor Schwartz left four films with the librarian, who said again that either he or one of his aides would show them on Thursday. Later, Mr. Campanella went into the film viewing room. After watching a total of sixty minutes of uninhibited nudity and sexual convolutions, including a great deal of fellatio and cunnilingus, he concluded that he would run the projector himself.

That day at the lunch table, he told Ruth Gibson, the associate director of the library and his immediate boss, and other librarians about the films, mentioning that the cinematography professor intended to show them to his class on Thursday. Several people said they wished Mr. Campanella had apprised them of the screening so they could have attended. But Ms. Gibson was more serious. "Did you check the state obscenity laws, Joey, to see if we're on safe ground legally to show them?" she inquired.

Mr. Campanella said he hadn't, admitting it had not occurred to him to do so. Ms. Gibson suggested that it might be a good idea. She went on to say that she remembered reading in the *New York Times* some time ago about police breaking into a classroom at Notre Dame where students were preparing to show a pornographic film, and how they seized the film and sprayed the audience with Mace. During the discussion which followed, several people offered their opinions, pro and con, on whether the films should be shown at Dexter State. One thought universities might be exempt from any laws since they are educational institutions; another said that the chances of anyone outside the university hearing about the showing were exceedingly slight; and another thought that the educational value of the experience outweighed all other considerations, including what he called "repressive" laws.

As he left the lunch table, Mr. Campanella told his boss that he would check the state obscenity statutes and give her a report on his findings. He spent the early part of the afternoon reading the pertinent sections of the General Laws of the State.

As he sat and pondered the statements, he began to wonder whether Professor Schwartz's films should be shown.

• • • • •

After examining the laws appended to this case, what would you do at this point if you were Mr. Campanella? In reporting to Ms. Gibson, what recommendations would you offer?

APPENDIX

Law 272.28. *Obscene things; possession; distribution to persons under 18; introduction into family or place of education.*

Whoever sells or distributes, or imports, prints or publishes for the purpose of selling or distributing, to a person under the age of eighteen years a book, pamphlet, ballad, printed paper, phonographic record or other thing which is obscene, indecent or impure, harmful to minors, or manifestly tends to corrupt the morals of youth, or an obscene, indecent or impure print, picture, figure, image or description, which is harmful to minors or manifestly tends to corrupt the morals of youth, or introduces into a family, school or place of education, or buys, procures, receives or has in his possession any such book, pamphlet, ballad, printed paper, phonographic record, obscene, indecent or impure print, picture, figure, image or other thing, either for the purpose of sale, exhibition, loan or circulation to a person under the age of eighteen years or with intent to introduce the same into a family, school or place of education, shall be punished by imprisonment in the state prison for not more than five years or in jail or house of correction for not more than two and one half years, or by a fine of not less than one hundred dollars nor more than five thousand dollars, or by both such fine and imprisonment in jail or the house of correction. In order to obtain a conviction under this section, it shall not be necessary to prove that the book, pamphlet, ballad, printed paper, phonographic record, print, picture, image, description or other thing which the accused is alleged to have dealt with in a manner prohibited by this section has been adjudged to be obscene, indecent or impure under the provisions of sections twenty-eight C to twenty-eight H, inclusive.

As used herein, the words "harmful to minors" mean that quality of description or representation of nudity, sexual conduct or sexual excitement which appeals predominantly to the prurient, shameful or morbid interest of minors under eighteen years of age, is patently contrary to prevailing standards of adults in the community as to suitable material for such minors, and is utterly without redeeming social importance for such minors.

Law 272.28A. *Importing, printing, distributing or possessing obscene things.*

Whoever imports, prints, publishes, sells or distributes a pamphlet, ballad, printed paper, phonographic record, or other thing which is obscene, indecent or impure, or an obscene, indecent or impure print, picture, figure, image or description, or buys, procures, receives or has in his possession any such pamphlet, ballad, printed paper, phonographic record, obscene, indecent or impure print, picture, figure, image or other thing, for the purpose of sale, exhibition, loan or circulation, shall be punished by imprisonment in the state prison for not more than five years or in a jail or house of correction for not more than two and one half years, or by a fine or not less than one hundred dollars nor more than five thousand dollars, or by both such fine and imprisonment in jail or the house of correction.

Law 272.28B. *Importing, printing, distributing or possessing obscene books.*

Whoever imports, prints, publishes, sells, loans or distributes, or buys, procures, receives, or has in his possession for the purpose of sale, loan or distribution, a book, knowing it to be obscene, indecent or impure, or whoever, being a wholesale distributor, a jobber, or publisher sends or delivers to a re-

tail storekeeper a book, pamphlet, magazine or other form of printed or written material, knowing it to be obscene, indecent or impure, which said storekeeper had not previously ordered in writing, specifying the title and quantity
of such publication he desired, shall be punished by imprisonment in the state
prison for not more than five years or in a jail or house of correction for not
more than two and one half years, or by a fine of not less than one hundred
dollars nor more than five thousand dollars, or by both such fine and imprisonment in jail or the house of correction.

Law 272.28C. *Information or petition against obscene books; order of notice to show cause; notice of order; interlocutory adjudication.*

Whenever there is reasonable cause to believe that a book which is being
imported, sold, loaned or distributed, or is in the possession of any person
who intends to import, sell, loan or distribute the same, is obscene, indecent
or impure, the attorney general, or any district attorney within his district,
shall bring an information or petition in equity in the superior court directed
against said book by name. Upon the filing of such information or petition in
equity, a justice of the superior court shall, if, upon a summary examination
of the book, he is of opinion that there is reasonable cause to believe that such
book is obscene, indecent or impure, issue an order of notice, returnable in or
within thirty days, directed against such book by name and addressed to all
persons interested in the publication, sale, loan or distribution thereof, to
show cause why said book should not be judicially determined to be obscene,
indecent or impure. Notice of such order shall be given by publication once
each week for two successive weeks in a daily newspaper published in the city
of Boston and, if such information or petition be filed in any county other
than Suffolk county, then by publication also in a daily newspaper published
in such other county. A copy of such order of notice shall be sent by registered
mail to the publisher of said book, to the person holding the copyrights, and
to the author, in case the names of any such persons appear upon said book,
fourteen days at least before the return day of such order of notice. After the
issuance of an order of notice under the provisions of this section, the court
shall, on motion of the attorney general or district attorney, make an interlocutory finding and adjudication shall be of the same force and effect as the
final finding and adjudication provided in section twenty-eight E or section
twenty-eight F, but only until such final finding and adjudication is made or
until further order of the court.

Law 272.28D. *Answer to notice; right to jury trial.*

Any person interested in the sale, loan or distribution of said book may appear and file an answer on or before the return day named in said notice or
within such further time as the court may allow, and may claim a right to trial
by jury on the issue whether said book is obscene, indecent or impure.

Law 272.28E. *Order of default; adjudication.*

If no person appears and answers within the time allowed, the court may at once upon motion of the petitioner, or of its own motion, no reason to the contrary appearing, order a general default and if the court finds that the book is obscene, indecent or impure, may make an adjudication against the book that the same is obscene, indecent and impure.

Law 272.28F. *Hearing; evidence; adjudication.*

If an appearance is entered and answer filed, the case shall be set down for speedy hearing, but a default and order shall first be entered against all persons who have not appeared and answered, in the manner provided in section twenty-eight E. Such hearing shall be conducted in accordance with the usual course of proceedings in equity including all rights of exception and appeal. At such hearing the court may receive the testimony of experts and may receive evidence as to the literary, cultural or educational character of said book and as to the manner and form of its publication, advertisement, and distribution. Upon such hearing, the court may make an adjudication in the manner provided in said section twenty-eight E.

Law 272.28G. *Objection that mere judgment sought and no relief claimed on issue of knowledge.*

An information or petition in equity under the provisions of section twenty-eight C shall not be open to objection on the ground that a mere judgment, order or decree is sought thereby and that no relief is or could be claimed thereunder on the issue of the defendant's knowledge as to the obscenity, indecency or impurity of the book.

Law 272.28H. *Proceedings under section 28C as evidence in trial under section 28B; presumptions as to knowledge.*

In any trial under section twenty-eight B on an indictment found or a complaint made for any offence committed after the filing of a proceeding under section twenty-eight C, the fact of such filing and the action of the court or jury thereon, if any, shall be admissible in evidence. If prior to the said offence a final decree had been entered against the book, the defendant, if the book be obscene, indecent or impure, shall be conclusively presumed to have known said book to be obscene, indecent or impure, or if said decree had been in favor of the book he shall be conclusively presumed not to have known said book to be obscene, indecent or impure, or if no final decree had been entered but a proceeding had been filed prior to said offence, the defendant shall be conclusively presumed to have had knowledge of the contents of said book.

24.
The Interview

· · · · · · · · · · ·

"The big boss wants to see you," the head of the reference department at the Morley Public Library announced as she approached Frank Keller, who was sitting at the reference desk.

"She wants to see me?" Mr. Keller asked, somewhat apprehensively. "Why?"

"Don't be alarmed. She does this with all new employees. She likes to get to know the staff better and find out what they think. Things of that sort. I'll cover the desk so you can go in."

Frank Keller is a young man who has just graduated from library school; this is his first professional job, which he has held for two months. The job in Morley was not his first choice, but, as he expressed it to a friend, jobs were scarce and he had to settle for this one. He felt that the community and the library were quite conservative, but he rationalized having accepted the job by saying he "had to start somewhere."

Morley is the largest city in May County, a low-income, rural area in the Midwest, whose principal products are cattle, dairy products, grain, and vegetables. The county itself is thinly settled, but Morley has a population of 38,000; it serves as the county's principal shopping area. The people of May County earn incomes slightly lower than the national average and the educational level is also somewhat lower; the people of Morley tend to be more middle-class and middle-income, but basically they share the same conservative and culturally complacent attitudes of the people in the surrounding county.

The "big boss," as the head of reference called her, is Diane Fullerton, a woman in her late fifties, who has been the director of the Morley Public Library for twelve years. She joined the library as a young woman after completing a bachelor's degree in English at a university in the state, making her way up through various staff positions until she ultimately became director. Having served the library with unselfish devotion for close to thirty years, she is regarded as "the very heart and soul of the library," as she was once described in the local newspaper. She is considered to be keenly in tune with the expressed desires of the community as far as library service is concerned, and many people, particularly the library trustees, have complete confidence in her.

After Frank Keller had been on the staff for a month or so, Ms. Fullerton decided to let him help with the selection of fiction, his undergraduate work having been in English. Accordingly, he has been going through various reviewing journals and initialling reviews of books he thinks the library should purchase. A book will be purchased, however, only if Ms. Fullerton also has put her initials beside those of the selector. This tells the order clerk to send for the book; otherwise the selection is to be ignored. A few days ago, at coffee, the order clerk mentioned casually to the new librarian that several of his selections were not being initialed by the director. He appeared to be somewhat irritated, but managed to mutter something about "needing more experience."

Mr. Keller knocked on Ms. Fullerton's door. She motioned him to come in and sit down.

FULLERTON: Hi, Frank, how are you?

KELLER: Fine, thanks, Ms. Fullerton.

FULLERTON: You've been with us two months now, and I thought it was time we should have an uninterrupted chat, away from the lounge and the reference desk and other people. Your supervisor tells me that you are doing a fine job on reference, and I've heard a couple of good things about you from some of the patrons. They've said you're helpful and considerate. It looks as if we made the right choice in hiring you. I wanted to take this opportunity to get to know you better and find out how things are going.

KELLER: Quite well. I'm enjoying the job so far. I like the staff, and the working conditions are fine.

FULLERTON: Good! I'm glad to hear it. I don't know whether you know, but I haven't always approved some of the books you've thought we should purchase. We're operating on a tight budget and can't buy everything we'd like to. I feel, too, that in many cases the community isn't ready for much of the fiction being published today, and perhaps you've been selecting a few items that aren't suitable for our clientele. I don't mean this to sound like a criticism, but I wanted you to know why I was turning down some of your suggestions. After you've been here a while, you'll realize what the community likes and wants, and will gear your selections accordingly.

KELLER: I'm glad you mentioned this to me. I *had* heard you weren't initialing some of my suggestions, and now I know why. But if the community isn't ready for what is being published, isn't it part of our job to make them ready?

FULLERTON: What do you mean exactly?

KELLER: I realize we have an obligation to consider the community's wishes, but that doesn't mean capitulating to them completely, does it?

FULLERTON: No, certainly not. It's our job to guide them in their reading, but not to take them from good to bad. I mean, does education and guidance mean we prepare people to read dirty and violent books? Is that our ultimate goal?

KELLER: I'm not sure I know what you mean.

FULLERTON: Let me try to be clearer. Is the dirty book at the pinnacle of all literature, and is our purpose to bring people to that pinnacle? You know how educators take people from the simple to the complex. Well, are we to take patrons from good books to that kind of book? Do you see what I'm getting at?

KELLER: I think so. I don't think I'm suggesting that so-called dirty books are the best, or that we should be trying to get people to the point where they can handle them. I'm merely saying that they should be side by side on the shelves with other, "safer" books. It's our duty to defend the right of all books to be there. We can't impose our values on people. What's the expression about he who pays the piper calls the tune? I think if some of our taxpayers who support this library want to read dirty books, then they should.

FULLERTON: They can get their dirty books in other places. They don't have to get them here.

KELLER: Can you tell me why we have certain books in a locked case behind the circulation desk?

FULLERTON: They're too controversial to be left out in the open. I'd feel very uncomfortable with them out. Not only that, many of them are sex education books, and they would be stolen or mutilated. As a matter of fact, I once put a few on the open shelves as an experiment, and they disappeared.

KELLER: Ms. Fullerton, you said when I came in today that you wanted to get to know me better and find out how things are going. Again, I like the job. People have been fair and good to work with. But that locked case disturbs me. I can't accept the idea, particularly when I see what's in there.

FULLERTON: As I said, we have the locked case to protect the books from damage, from being stolen, and because some parents would not want them accessible to the young. I, myself, am not sure that young people should get their hands on them. They need reading guidance and have to be brought to the point where they can handle the material there.

KELLER: I think it's a nuisance and embarrassing to have to ask permission to see those books. That's treating people like children, and even children shouldn't be treated that way.

FULLERTON: The alternative is to restrict access to certain parts of the library. To have an "adults only" section. As you know, we now have a completely open library. Everyone—children, young adults, adults—is free to wander anywhere. Some libraries have no locked case, but they have an "adults only" room, or something like that. To have a completely open library, you must have a locked case. But even that doesn't deal with the problem of theft and mutilation. It's not an easy problem to solve.

KELLER: I know it isn't, but the ALA has a very clear policy statement against restricted access, and I feel we should try to abide by it.

FULLERTON: I've read the statement, and I don't think we're violating it. We're keeping the books away from people because they might be stolen or mutilated. You know, it's very easy for people in Chicago at the ALA headquarters to come up with these policies. They don't have to deal with the problems. They can make us feel terribly guilty for not doing this or for doing that. I'd like to see them deal with some of our problems. They tell us what to do, but they never face the problems themselves.

KELLER: But we need people to produce guidelines, wouldn't you agree?

FULLERTON: Maybe my comments were a little unfair, but I still believe it's a lot easier to tell people what should be done than it is to do it.

KELLER: It's a pity we restrict some of the books we do. We have some excellent things in that locked case. I was surprised we actually have some of the books we do own.

FULLERTON: Many were bought because they were requested. I purchased others because I feel they should be available somewhere in the community. They're books you hear about all the time. But I still feel they should be locked up. I don't know whether you've looked in the case to see how many times the books have been charged out, but you'd find they almost never go out; some have been charged out once, maybe twice, and some never.

KELLER: Perhaps people don't want to ask for them.

FULLERTON: Oh, go on! Our staff is very friendly and helpful.

KELLER: That may be, but people are embarrassed by having to ask for books that are stashed away. They wonder what the circulation clerks might be thinking about them.

FULLERTON: I'm sorry, but I'd feel too uncomfortable having them out in the open. As you know, we have books on sex education and drugs there, and many parents are violently opposed to such subjects being taught in the schools.

KELLER: It seems to me that the parents' sensibilities cannot be the criterion for what we do in the library. The *Restricted Access* statement warns about the library acting *in loco parentis*. It's up to the parents to supervise what their children read.

FULLERTON: We have an obligation to see to it that young people don't get what their parents don't want them to get.

Just then, the telephone rang, and Ms. Fullerton asked Mr. Keller if they might resume their talk later.

• • • • •

What do you think of the arguments raised by both people? After examining the contents of the locked case in the appended lists, would you agree with the junior librarian that they should be put on the open shelves? How would you deal with problems of theft and mutilation? How would you deal with parents who object to having material of this sort on the open shelves? What do you think of the director's statement, "To have a completely open library, you must have a locked case?"

APPENDIX A: SOME BOOKS FOUND ON THE OPEN SHELVES AT THE MORLEY PUBLIC LIBRARY

Allen, *Anthony Adverse*
Blanchard, *American Freedom and Catholic Power*
Buck, *The Good Earth*
Capote, *Breakfast at Tiffany's*
Cobb, *The Swimming Pool*
Connelly, *The Green Pastures*
Cronin, *The Judas Tree*
Drury, *Advise and Consent*
Fast, *Citizen Tom Paine*
Frank, *The Diary of Anne Frank*
Griffin, *The Devil Rides Outside*
Heggen, *Mr. Roberts*
Heller, *Catch 22*
Hemingway, *The Sun also Rises; A Farewell to Arms*
Huie, *The Revolt of Mamie Stover*
Joyce, *Ulysses*

Kerouac, *On the Road*
King, *Stride Towards Freedom*
Lederer, *The Ugly American*
Lee, *To Kill a Mockingbird*
Lewis, *Elmer Gantry*
Mailer, *The Naked and The Dead*
McCarthy, *The Group*
Metalious, *Peyton Place*
Miller, *The Crucible*
O'Hara, *From the Terrace*
Rand, *Atlas Shrugged*
Smith, *Strange Fruit*
Steinbeck, *Of Mice and Men; The Grapes of Wrath*
Vidal, *The Best Man*
Wilson, *Memoires of Hecate County*
Wolfe, *Look Homeward, Angel*

APPENDIX B: BOOKS IN THE LOCKED CASE AT THE MORLEY PUBLIC LIBRARY

Andrews, *The Parents' Guide to Drugs*
Baldwin, *Another Country*
Birdwood, *The Willing Victim: A Parent's Guide to Drug Abuse*
Bohannan, *Love, Sex and Being Human: A Book About the Human Condition for Young People*
Brenner, *Drugs and Youth: Medical, Psychiatric, and Legal Facts*
Brown, *Sex and the Single Girl*
Browne, *Manchild in the Promised Land*
Burn, *Better than the Birds, Smarter than the Bees; No-Nonsense Answers to Honest Questions About Sex and Growing Up.*
Cain, *Young People and Drugs*
Caldwell, *God's Little Acre*

Cleaver, *Soul on Ice*
Densen-Gerber, *Drugs, Sex, Parents, and You*
Duval, *Facts on Life and Love for Teenagers*
Fraswe, *Sex, Schools, and Society; International Perspectives*
Ginsberg, *Howl and Other Poems*
Girdano, *Drug Education: Content and Methods*
Goldhill, *A Parent's Guide to the Prevention and Control of Drug Abuse*
Greenberg, *The Wonderful Story of How You Were Born*
Gregory, *Nigger*
Griffin, *Black Like Me*
Guttmacher, *Planning Your Family*

Harris, *My Life and Loves*
Hitler, *Mein Kampf*
Huxley, *Brave New World*
Johnson, *Sex: Telling It Straight*
Jones, *From Here to Eternity*
Kazantzakis, *Last Temptation of Christ*
Kinsey, *Sexual Behavior of the American Male; Sexual Behavior of the American Female*
Lawrence, *Lady Chatterly's Lover*
Lingeman, *Drugs from A to Z, a Dictionary*
Mao, *Quotations from Chairman Mao Tse-Tung*

Masters and Johnson, *Human Sexual Response*
Marx, *Das Capital*
Miller, *Tropic of Cancer*
Nabokov, *Lolita*
Orwell, *1984*
Robbins, *The Carpetbaggers*
Salinger, *Catcher in the Rye*
Rubin, *Do it*
Spock, *A Teenager's Guide to Life and Love*
Thomas, *Down These Mean Streets*
Vidal, *Myra Breckenridge*
Wright, *Black Boy*

25.
Probable Cause

· · · · · · · · · · · ·

Originally, the town of Tayler was situated in an amphitheater of low, timber-covered hills, dotted with vast quantities of rock debris. Gradually, the sturdy farming stock who first settled in the area cleared away many of the trees and rocks, converting much of the rolling countryside into arable soil and pasture land. Now, two hundred and fifty years after its incorporation, Tayler is a lively commercial city, the seat and center of a productive agricultural and manufacturing county. The county has a total population of 56,000 and a land area of 120 square miles. Modern-day farmers, of whom there are still many, continue to fell trees and clear rocks as their ancestors did, to prepare the land for grass for sheep and cattle, and for cultivation.

As with the majority of towns in the state, the community was built around a public square, which continues to be the center of community life and business activity. Main Street is a broad thoroughfare with many large buildings, the most impressive of which is the new county library, a handsome contemporary structure of brick, glass, aluminum, and poured concrete. Wesley Drummond, the director of the Tayler County Library, has the well-founded reputation of trying to meet the different library needs of all the people of the county. Very early in his nineteen-year career at the library, Mr. Drummond recognized that the library needs of the typical city dwellers were quite different from those of the farmers in the rural sections of the county. He found, for one thing, that the farmers were very much interested in practical, how-to-do-it material; consequently, he built up a good collection of manuals on repairing equipment and machinery, seed selection, better farming methods, crop rotation, and so forth. He has also attended to the needs of the other audiences of Tayler—the business and professional men and women, retired people, and school children—and has acquired a diversified assortment of print and nonprint materials. So pleased were people with Mr. Drummond's efforts on behalf of the community that the trustees encountered little opposition when they asked for a new library building.

A new phenomenon has occurred lately which has the inhabitants very disturbed. Although, to the casual observer, the city gives the impression of moderate calm despite its industrial hum, it has been bothered by a series of bombings and bomb threats. Two bombs actually have gone off—the first in the Veteran's Hall when it was empty, and the second in the east-end high school, where a custodian was killed—and three other bombs were discovered and dismantled. Two or three times a week, the police have been receiving anonymous warnings by telephone of bombs that are supposed to be planted in various buildings around town, but which, when they check them out, turn out to be hoaxes. Twice the library has had to be vacated while the police searched for bombs which were said to be there, but which, it turned out, were not.

Before the second bomb went off, the police were happy to report one day that they had found one of the culprits in the act of placing a bomb in City Hall. The malefactor, a young man in his senior year at one of the city's high schools, refused to name any accomplices, stating that he was not part of any organized group. Upon questioning him, the police found he had learned how to make explosives from books he had obtained from the county library. His friends and acquaintances were all questioned, but to no avail. Not long after he was convicted and jailed, the second bomb went off—in the high school where the custodian was killed. The community was outraged at this senseless act, and the police were "ordered to step up their investigations and not overlook any possible leads," as the local newspaper described it.

Shortly after the second bombing, a detective dropped in to see Mr. Drummond. He reminded the library director that the young man who had been arrested had said he learned how to make explosives from library books. He then asked the library director if he knew which books they might be, adding that the young man said he couldn't remember any specific titles. Mr. Drummond pointed out that the information was available in a number of sources, including several reference books. The detective suggested the staff determine which books they might be and then remove them from the shelves. The director balked at the idea. "With a collection of 160,000 volumes it would be nearly impossible to do this. I'll check and see what we have under 'explosives' and 'bombs' in the card catalog, though." The two men went over to the catalog and found the following books listed:

Cook, Melvin A. *Science of High Explosives.* Van Nostrand Reinhold, 1958.

Langefors, U., and Kihlstrom, Bjorn. *Modern Techniques of Rock Blasting.* Wiley, 1967.

Lenz, Robert R. *Explosives and Bomb Disposal Guide.* C. C. Thomas, 1971.

Stoffel, Joseph F. *Explosives and Home-made Bombs.* C. C. Thomas, 1972.

Ye Yaremenko, N., et al. *Properties and Preparation of Explosives.* CCM Information Corp., 1971.

The detective asked Mr. Drummond to tell him who had taken any of these books out recently. The library director said it was impossible to do this with their transaction card charging system; they did not keep any record of who had borrowed specific books.

"Why would you have books like this in the collection?" the detective inquired.

"Because the farmers use them all the time. They are always blasting out roots of trees and large rocks. In a way, I'm glad you asked that question. With most controversial material, people often ask why the library has to have it when it's readily available elsewhere—in bookstores, drug stores, etcetera. Well, these books are not available anywhere else in town. I try to have things that people need, and the farmers need this information."

"Do you keep the books where people can get at them easily?"

"They're on the open shelves."

"Don't you think that's dangerous? Anybody can get them. Presumably, the boy in jail took one out, and look what's happened. One man's dead, and the town's worried. And we're still getting bomb threats. You've even had them here."

"I know the situation is serious," admitted the director. "And we have to find out who the guilty people are, but I'm not sure the answer is to gather up all our books on explosives and restrict their use."

"I think what I'd like you to do is take them out of circulation and then tell us who asks for them. This is a criminal investigation. I needn't tell you that we're trying to track down killers."

Mr. Drummond paused for so long, the detective spoke up again. "Since you can't tell us who took the books out, you can at least tell us who wants to take them out."

"What would you do with the information?"

"Well, of course, we'd question the people who wanted them. If their reasons seem legitimate, then they have nothing to fear."

"If word got out that we're keeping tabs on who takes the books out, don't you think people will stop asking for them?"

"How can you be arguing with me?" said the detective sharply. "This is a serious matter."

"I know it is. But I'm the type of person who likes to think about what he's being asked to do."

"Well, why would word have to get out?" snapped back the detective.

"People would be suspicious, and if we didn't tell them, you would when you'd investigate them."

"Your point is a valid one. I think we could merely keep an eye on the borrowers."

"I'd like to review what you're asking, if I could," Mr. Drummond stated. "First of all, we can't tell you who took the books on explosives out, because our charging system doesn't permit us to. Let's go back even before that. You think the people who are planting bombs are learning how to make them from our library books."

"Right," said the detective. "And we're pursuing every possible lead."

"I understand that. But let me continue. Now, you would like us to identify which books in our collection have information on how to prepare bombs and explosives. Then you would like us to take these books off the shelves, and if anyone asks for them to give you their names. Well, here's my reaction. I see this as a breach of professional ethics. We're dealing with a professional–client relationship. Doctors don't go around broadcasting what's wrong with their patients, and priests don't go around telling everyone what they hear in the confessional."

"I would remind you that people's lives are at stake, including your own, because a bomb could go off here. But let me see if I have you right. As I understand it, you're reluctant to go along with our request—and I definitely feel some reluctance on your part—because you don't want to be guilty of a breach of some kind of library ethics; and the ethics are that you don't give out information on who took out what because you consider it private."

"That's true," the library director said. "But since you have said that lives are in danger, including my own, which is your way of personalizing this whole thing so that I see it your way, let me ask you this. Supposing you had a case of ulcers and didn't want people to know about it, and you came down to the library and took out several books on ulcers. Would you want me to broadcast that around? Or suppose you were considering a divorce and you didn't want people to know, and you took out books on divorce. Would you want me to tell people? I think this is the same thing."

"I see your point, but I disagree," responded the detective. "In the one case, only one person, or a few, are affected. In the case of bombings, several people are affected—indeed a whole community. Look at it this way. If you saw some people in danger, wouldn't you rush to help them? If you saw someone walking perilously close to the edge of a dangerous cliff, and he didn't realize the danger, wouldn't you warn him? If you saw a blind man about to walk into a trench, wouldn't you rush up to stop him? Well, we're like blind men looking for help. In fact, I look upon this as similar to national security. The government often has to protect itself, so—under certain circumstances—it wiretaps. Now wiretapping is a dirty business, but so too are criminal acts. We have to weigh society's need for protection against an individual's need for privacy. I think the circumstances here justify this kind of surveillance, and I think we could get a 'probable cause' warrant to do it."

"Well, when you put it that way, I guess I have no choice but to go along.

Okay, I'll have the books kept behind the circulation desk and when people ask for them, we'll take note of their names and pass them on to you. I don't know what we can do about the reference books."

"I think it might be enough to start with books that circulate. I sure appreciate the fact that you're doing this. You had me worried for a while that you weren't going to go along!"

•   •   •   •   •

Evaluate the arguments raised by the discussion between the library director and the detective. Would you have assented to the detective's requests?

26.
Knowing the Community

· ·

"You know, Bill, I've been thinking," Elaine Osgood said, as she sat at the reference desk. "I've been at the library three years and you've been here two, and I think we've accomplished quite a bit, But I don't really feel we know what the community thinks of our library."

"What do you mean?" William DeBekker inquired.

"Well," Ms. Osgood continued, "we've never undertaken a survey to find out what the community likes and dislikes about the library, or found out what services they would like to see us provide, or anything of that sort."

"I think we could say that they're reasonably happy with what we're doing," Mr. DeBekker offered. "They've never given our budget a tough time at town meetings the way they have with some of the other departments."

"True, but we've never made exorbitant demands for money, either," Ms. Osgood stated. "In fact, we've been entirely too reasonable, I sometimes think."

"Are you suggesting we should undertake a community survey?" Mr. De-Bekker asked.

"Yes," was Ms. Osgood's reply.

Elaine Osgood is the head librarian of the Abernathy Memorial Library in Vanderlin, a town of some 12,000 inhabitants about thirty-five miles northwest of one of the largest cities on the east coast. She and William DeBekker, who is the reference and cataloging librarian, are the only library school graduates on the staff—in fact, before Ms. Osgood came to Vanderlin there had never been a library school graduate at the town's public library. Together, Ms. Osgood and Mr. DeBekker have been able to build up what they consider to be a fairly good reference collection, and they have undertaken to strengthen the general collection in several areas.

One of the first moves the new head librarian made upon arriving at the Abernathy Memorial Library was to request another professional librarian in her first budget. She tried to convince the board of trustees and the town manager that she could use an assistant librarian, but they felt the library was too small to warrant the position at the time; they did agree, however, to her counter-proposal, that a professional librarian be hired to look after reference and cataloging. William DeBekker was hired to fill the new position shortly after the townsfolk approved the library's budget at the town meeting that year.

The team of Ms. Osgood and Mr. DeBekker appeared to be a good one. While Ms. Osgood was known officially as head librarian, she did spend a considerable portion of her time at the reference desk, spelling Mr. DeBekker while he did the cataloging. There were two others on the staff who manned the reference desk when Ms. Osgood and Mr. DeBekker were not there, usually during the evening hours, but most of the time these two worked at the circulation desk; although neither had been to library school, both were certified as professional librarians by virtue of having met the state certification requirements.

The Abernathy Memorial Library came into existence in 1910 when Cyrus Abernathy, a bachelor and life-long resident of Vanderlin, died. In his will, he had stated that his colonial mansion was to be given to the town and used as a library. A few rearrangements were made internally in the house—walls were knocked down and floors underpinned to accomodate the weight of stacks and books—but the facade remained the same as it had always been. Wedged in between a grocery store and the post office, there was virtually no place for patrons to park, unless they were fortunate enough to find vacant places in the small parking area behind the library or a spot on the street in front.

Vanderlin could be characterized as an upper-middle-class community, most of whose inhabitants are staunchly Republican. They believe in education, assigning most of their tax dollars to the public schools; and close to 4,000 people, including children and young people, are registered borrowers at the Abernathy Library. The town is administered by a full-time town manager, who appoints the five members of the board of library trustees, each of whom serves a seven-year term. At the present time, the board is made up of three men and two women—all fairly senior members of the community, with the exception of the chairman, James Anthelme, who is a young professor of government at a nearby university and a native of Vanderlin. The board meets regularly on the first Monday of every month. At these meetings the members merely approve of what Ms. Osgood and her staff are doing, offering a few suggestions from time to time.

As a result of their discussion at the reference desk, the head librarian and her assistant decided they would undertake a survey which would get the opinions of the users and nonusers of library service in Vanderlin. They decided that Mr. DeBekker would do a search through library literature to see what kinds of printed questionnaires were already in existence, and then put one together, selecting pertinent questions from the ones he liked. Ms. Osgood would then take the questionnaire to the board and the town manager for their reactions.

In about a month, Mr. DeBekker came up with a questionnaire, which he showed to Ms. Osgood. She went over it carefully, making minor changes here and there. They agreed that it would be very helpful to know how the community felt about certain articles in the *Library Bill of Rights*, so they designed questions which would deal specifically with the question of the library's role vis-a-vis intellectual freedom. Ms. Osgood then had copies of the proposed questionnaire typed up, and she sent them to the board members and the town manager before the next regularly scheduled board meeting. She mentioned in the covering letter to the town manager, who did not attend the trustees' meetings unless there was a reason for him to do so, that she would give him a report after the trustees had had a chance to react to the idea of the survey.

After a good deal of discussion at the trustees' meeting as to what would be done with the results of the questionnaire—it was agreed that they would wait until the results were in before they made any decisions—the board members gave Ms. Osgood their consent to proceed with it. It was decided that three copies of the questionnaire would be mailed to every household in Vanderlin, in the hope that more than one person at every home would respond, and that a self-addressed, postage-free envelope would be included to encourage people to return them. The trustees agreed to pay the cost of mailing and returning the questionnaires. Ms. Osgood informed the town manager the next day of the trustees' decision, and he gave the project his blessing. He said he would like to attend the meeting at which they planned to discuss the results.

The questionnaires were mailed out to every household, of which there were 4,500, and it wasn't long before the results started coming in. Ms. Osgood and Mr. DeBekker read the first few questionnaires with considerable interest, but then decided merely to collect them and summarize them later. After a month had elapsed, they concluded that the people who were going to respond had done so, and they began to tabulate the results.

They were delighted to discover that some 3,000 people, many of whom were not registered library borrowers, had taken the trouble to give their views. The filled-in questionnaires, which had included questions (with space to amplify on the answers) about the library building itself, parking, frequency of use, hours, types of materials, friendliness and helpfulness of staff, and ease of access of materials, were most edifying. For instance, the overwhelming majority of respondents found parking a problem; they complained about having to wait too long for popular books; they wanted a new building; and they wished the library would be open on Sundays. On the plus side, they were generally content with the staff and the materials being purchased.

Most interesting of all were the responses to the two questions dealing with intellectual freedom and censorship. To the question, "Do you think the library should present all points of view concerning the problems and issues of our times, international, national, and local?" 65 percent said, "no;" 20 percent said "yes;" and 15 percent left the question blank. Those who chose to expand upon their negative answers indicated that they were strongly opposed to representation of the radical left; the periodical they most often objected to was *Ramparts*, which the library did receive. To the question, "Do you think the adult collection should be open to everyone, including young people and children?" 68 percent said "no;" 25 percent said "yes;" and 7 percent did not answer. The answers revealed that most people thought the library should institute "limited-access shelves," where material considered harmful to minors (defined as people under eighteen) should be kept. Several respondents offered the names of certain well-known authors whose books should not be made available to young people; included were Henry Miller, Philip Roth, William Burroughs, Hubert Selby, Jr., with many of the titles for which these authors are well known. The library had many of them.

After the staff had compiled a summary, Ms. Osgood sent a copy to each of the trustees and the town manager, so they could study it before the next board meeting. The board met as usual, and the entire meeting was devoted to the results of the questionnaire. The town manager was particularly gratified to see that people were dissatisfied with the present library building, and he spoke of presenting a proposal for a new one, which pleased the board members and the librarian. He said, too, that he would try to alleviate the parking problem by designating certain spaces on the street for library use only.

The chairman of the board said he thought the results should be published in the local newspaper so the townsfolk would be able to see how the community felt about its library. Another member suggested that the trustees and the staff should try to implement as many of the suggestions, and alleviate as many of the problems, as possible, letting the townsfolk know in the same newspaper release what they were going to do. Ms. Osgood stated that she and other members of the staff, including Mr. DeBekker, would be willing to work from 2:00 to 5:00 P.M. on Sundays, if a bit more money could be scraped up to handle the additional cost. The town manager said he didn't think that could be done this year, but suggested that they provide for Sunday hours in next year's budget. Ms. Osgood suggested that the library might consider the MacNaughton Plan, which she described, to alleviate the problem of demand books. The response was positive.

Then, Mr. Anthelme suggested they discuss the two controversial questions. "It would seem to me," he said, "in regard to the questions of access to adult material and representation of all points of view, that it is very clear how the majority of the community feels. Since we're going along with most of the respondents' suggestions, we had better go along with these as well. I think we had better have restricted shelves and cancel our subscription to *Ramparts*. What do you think, Elaine?"

"I've been thinking about these two questions, Jim," Ms. Osgood replied, "and I'm not sure what to say."

"I can understand your hesitation," the chairman said. "But we have a clear mandate from the majority of the community as to what they want. They want restricted shelves and don't want all points of view represented. In a democracy, the majority rules, and we have a majority here."

"But it may not be a majority," the librarian said. "Only 3,000 people replied to the questionnaire."

"Well, 3,000 is enough for us to say we should be open on Sundays, and try for a new building, and subscribe to this MacNaughton Plan," Mr. Anthelme said. "Why isn't it enough for restricted shelves?"

Ms. Osgood asked the other trustees to express their opinions on these two questions. The others agreed that they had to go along with the wishes of the community. The town manager sided with the trustees, citing the contemporary community standards test as one way of determining whether a thing is obscene or not. He reminded Ms. Osgood that the Supreme Court used this element to help them determine whether to declare something obscene. "Contemporary community standards in Vanderlin should be taken into consideration in determining what the library should do in regard to offensive material," he added.

"I think we have to apply the 'Ad Hoc Balancing' test of the First Amendment here," the chairman said. "That test weighs and balances the interest of freedom of expression against the social interest involved in restricting freedom. You have our thoughts on the matter, Elaine. Why don't you mull them over and let us know what you think at the next meeting. We'll wait until then before we publish the results of the survey."

• • • • •

How would you respond to the trustees and the town manager if you were Ms. Osgood? What should she do at this point? In light of the ALA's statement on *Restricted Access to Library Materials*, how would you resolve the dilemma of the community's apparent wishes? What are the implications of the "contemporary community standards" test of obscentity? Are librarians always in a position of "Ad Hoc Balancing?" Should majority rule determine what the library should purchase or subscribe to?

27.
The Other Side—I

• • • • • • • • • • • • •

"You take it with cream and sugar, don't you, Beth?" Priscilla Wirt asked.

"Yes, thanks," Beth Keyes replied.

"How are things going in the library today?" Ms. Wirt inquired, returning to the table.

"You mean, the media center?" Ms. Keyes answered with a smile.

"Right! I always forget. One of these days I'll get it right!"

Ms. Keyes chuckled. "We're very busy. Ever since we've gone to the open classroom concept we've had people wandering in and out all day long. Sometimes I pine for the days when we had a few minutes away from the kids between periods. But not really!" she added quickly.

Beth Keyes is the assistant media specialist at the Waldo A. Fitch Elementary School in Bowesville, a city of 600,000 located in one of the central states. She joined the staff three years ago, working under the direction of Ms. Nancy Aiken, the media specialist, who has been at Fitch for twelve years. Both women are library school graduates.

Ms. Keyes found Ms. Aiken a bit more conservative in her selection policies than she would have liked, but aside from that fault (which she considered quite minor) she thought her boss a very good person to work for. They enjoyed an excellent relationship, finding always that when they disagreed with each other they could discuss matters amicably and reach mutually satisfactory solutions.

Priscilla Wirt has been a fifth grade mathematics teacher at Fitch for four years. She is very popular with both students and her fellow teachers. When she was at college, just prior to coming to Fitch, she was active in student affairs, championing many of the popular causes of the day.

"Say, Beth," Ms. Wirt went on. "I've been meaning to speak to you about something. I was glad to see today that my free period and your coffee break coincided. A few teachers in the city are forming a group called Teachers against Discrimination. Have you heard anything about it?"

"Yes, I've been asked to join—probably because I'm black. I don't know very much about it though, but I can figure out from the name what it deals with."

"Well, we're just getting underway. In fact, we've only had one meeting. We elected a president and a few other officers the other night. But we still have to decide what our approach is going to be. One of the first things we agreed to do was examine the material we use in the classroom and check our libraries—er, rather, media centers—to see if there's anything that treats minority groups in an unfavorable light or that discriminates openly or covertly against them. We haven't decided, as I said, what we will do once we've collected this information, but this is the first step."

"Have you checked our media center and found anything you don't think should be there?" the assistant media specialist inquired.

"Yes, I went through the card catalog the other day looking specifically for *Little Black Sambo*, and guess what? You have it. That's one title we were asked to look for."

"Anything else?"

"I didn't really look. I'm not that familiar with the titles of children's books. Everyone knows *Little Black Sambo*, though. It's one of the worst."

"I have to admit that I've been wondering if we should have it in our collection. It's been the subject of quite a bit of controversy for some time now."

"Well, as I said, we're not sure what we'll do, but I wanted to mention our group to you and say that *Little Black Sambo* will probably come in for some fire."

"Maybe next time you come around it won't be there," Ms. Keyes ventured with a confident smile.

"Say, great! Let me know what you do."

When Ms. Keyes got back to the media center, she went directly to the shelves to look for *Little Black Sambo*. Finding it there, she took it over to her desk and began to thumb through it. It was dated 1951 and published by Lippincott. She put it down and began to stare idly into space. Just then, Ms. Aiken came over and asked her how her day was going. The media specialist could see that her assistant was in some sort of reverie, so she waved her hand in front of her eyes and said jokingly; "Hey, where are you?"

Ms. Keyes snapped out of her daze and smiled. "I was just thinking about *Little Black Sambo*," she said. "You know, I don't think we should keep it anymore. It's outdated, the kind of book we no longer need in our collection. I think it's a dangerous and cruel book," she went on, becoming quite excited. "It depicts us in a very unfavorable light. It makes us appear to be inferior human beings who white people are expected to laugh at. I think if we're going to continue to make strides towards equality, then books such as *Little Black Sambo* have to go."

Ms. Aiken realized that her assistant was very serious and that she was deeply disturbed by the book. She said nothing but pulled up a chair. A child came over to ask if someone would help her select a film loop. In a very nice way, Ms. Aiken suggested to the child that she ask one of the aides behind the desk to help her.

The assistant media specialist continued, "I think this book distorts children's views of black people and I know it causes blacks great mental anguish. We constantly weed out old materials, and it would seem to me that we could easily weed out this book. Wasn't it written back around the turn of the century?"

"It was written in the late 1890s by Helen Bannerman," Ms. Aiken said. "You know, of course, that the setting is India and not Africa, and that the book doesn't concern blacks but Indians."

"I think I did hear something to that effect, but now Black Sambo is looked upon as being black. Even if you tell people that the characters are Indians, isn't it still demeaning to the people of India? But Sambo is thought to be black, and that's what's important."

"You know, Beth, if you used the date when a book was written as a criterion for whether it it should stay or go," Ms. Aiken explained, "you'd have to get rid of the works of some of the best writers of children's books—Robert Louis Stevenson, Mark Twain, Louisa May Alcott, and others."

"But that assumes that *Little Black Sambo* is a classic," Ms. Keyes observed. "It's not a classic, it's just an offensive and insulting work of an insensitive person who wanted to amuse people."

"That may be a little harsh, Beth."

"In an age when intelligent, thinking people have an obligation to be socially responsible, it seems to me that it's being socially responsible to get rid of *Little Black Sambo*."

"I'm not at all sure that you're being consistent, Beth, if I may say so. You've accused me of practicing censorship when I've hesitated to purchase certain books dealing with sex. Or even better than that, when I wanted to put *In the Night Kitchen* behind the desk you said we couldn't because that would be censorship. What's the difference between what you're suggesting and what I wanted to do?"

"I think the issue is different. All our lives we blacks have lived with a banjo-strumming, foot-shuffling, slow-witted image, and *Little Black Sambo* perpetuates that negative stereotype. It's dehumanizing and doesn't help the black man in his search for identity. We blacks have been persecuted all our lives. We don't like *Little Black Sambo*. Can't people today try to compensate for how we've been treated in the past and grant us the humble request that we no longer keep *Little Black Sambo* around? Is that asking much? It's an unpleasant reminder of the way things were. It impedes progress."

"You know, Beth, I don't want you to think because I'm resisting the suggestion that *Little Black Sambo* be removed from the shelves that I'm against the black man or that I'm a racist. I find it so very hard to know what to do when it comes to black literature—and blacks, for that matter. If I don't buy lots of black literature I'm prejudiced, and if I do I'm a white do-gooder. Is someone who wants *Little Black Sambo* off the shelves a better person than someone who doesn't? Is that the implication? I thought we were committed to something higher than that—to a principle, to a freedom of speech, to the *School Library Bill of Rights.* You've certainly helped me to see that; and while I personally would have preferred not to purchase some of the books we have purchased, I've realized that we can't let our own preferences interfere with selection. Now, you're doing the same thing, but because *you* believe in the cause, it's all right. I don't get the logic, Beth. Really, I don't."

Ms. Keyes began to rub her forehead. "I know it doesn't look as if I'm being consistent," she said wearily, "but this isn't book censorship, it's book weeding. The book has been given longer life than it deserves. A stupid story about a boy outsmarting tigers. We don't hesitate to weed out other books which we think have outlived their usefulness; in fact, we're always chiding ourselves that we don't do more of it. Now I suggest weeding *Little Black Sambo* and we hesitate."

"If I'm not mistaken, *Little Black Sambo* appears in a collection or two which we have. I think it's Hutchinson's *Chimney Corner Stories.* Let me check." Ms. Aiken got up and went over to get the book, stopping on the way back to pick up their copy of *The Elementary School Library Collection: A Guide to Books and Other Media.* "Here, you look and see if it's recommended in *The Elementary School Library Collection* and I'll look in Hutchinson."

"I don't see it listed in this book," Ms. Keyes said.

"It's in Hutchinson," Ms. Aiken said. "Do you think we should take Hutchinson's book off the shelves because it has *Little Black Sambo* when there are fifteen other folk tales in it? Or, should we cut out the pages it appears on the way some librarians did with *Sylvester and the Magic Pebble?*"

"That's a little mean," Ms. Keyes said indignantly.

"I don't want to be mean, Beth. But I can see no justification for taking the book off the shelves. As far as I'm concerned it should stay. You've often told me that you couldn't understand anyone suppressing *Catcher in the Rye* or *To Kill a Mockingbird.* I hate to hammer away at you like this, but I'm trying to show how hard it is to resist wanting to suppress what *we* don't want to hear. Goodness knows, I've learned that, and you've helped me to see it. If something touches a sore spot with us, we want to get rid of it. Maybe it's good we have some materials that we as librarians would like to see suppressed, for then we can better understand the censor."

"Well, if you use that argument, how would you like it if you were depicted as a stupid, inferior savage? Think of that for a moment. I've noticed that it's been the white Anglo-Saxon Protestants who think that Jews and blacks and other minorities shouldn't be upset when their races are slurred. I wish they'd be more sensitive."

"I'm sure I wouldn't like being the object of slurring, but I'd live with it," the older woman observed.

"Oh, that's easy to say because you're white. I bet you'd want to see it stop. How do you think I feel charging out *Little Black Sambo* to some white kid?"

"But how can we possibly know whether the kids who read it feel hostile toward blacks?"

"There's always the chance that one or two might be affected by it, and that's enough. It has to go, Nancy. For the sake of all that's decent, it has to go. The Teachers against Discrimination group will be after us to get rid of it anyway."

Just then, one of the media aides came over to say that the principal wanted Ms. Aiken on the phone.

•   •   •   •   •

What do you think of the arguments of both Ms. Aiken and Ms. Keyes? Are there times when some form of censorship is justified and necessary in the best interests of groups of people and progress? Would your reaction to the arguments presented be the same, if the school was in a predominantly black neighborhood? Can a controversial book ever be weeded from a collection the way an outdated noncontroversial book is without suspicion of censorship? What approach should Ms. Aiken take with Ms. Keyes at this point? Is *Little Black Sambo* a harmful book, in your opinion? Would you buy the book if the library didn't own it?

28.
The Other Side—II

• • • • • • • • • • • • • • • •

"You take it with cream and sugar, don't you, Beth?" Priscilla Wirt asked.

"Yes, thanks," Beth Keyes replied.

"How are things going in the library today?" Ms. Wirt inquired, returning to the table.

"You mean, the media center?" Ms. Keyes answered with a smile.

"Right! I always forget. One of these days I'll get it right!"

Ms. Keyes chuckled. "We're very busy. Ever since we've gone to the open classroom concept we've had people wandering in and out all day long. Sometimes I pine for the days when we had a few minutes away from the kids between periods. But not really!" she added quickly.

Beth Keyes is the assistant media specialist at the Waldo A. Fitch Elementary School in Bowesville, a city of 600,000 located in one of the central states. She joined the staff three years ago, working under the direction of Ms. Nancy Aiken, the media specialist, who has been at Fitch for twelve years. Both women are library school graduates.

Ms. Keyes found Ms. Aiken a bit more conservative in her selection policies than she would have liked, but aside from that fault (which she considered quite minor) she thought her boss a very good person to work for. They enjoyed an excellent relationship, finding always that when they disagreed with each other they could discuss matters amicably and reach mutually satisfactory solutions.

Priscilla Wirt has been a fifth grade mathematics teacher at Fitch for four years. She is very popular with both students and her fellow teachers. When she was at college, just prior to coming to Fitch, she had been active in student affairs, championing many of the popular causes of the day.

"Say, Beth," Ms. Wirt went on. "I've been meaning to speak to you about something. I was glad to see today that my free period and your coffee break coincided. A few teachers in the city are forming a group called Teachers against Discrimination. Have you heard anything about it?"

"Yes, I've been asked to join. I don't know very much about it though, but I can figure out from the name what it deals with."

"Well, we're just getting underway. In fact, we've only had one meeting. We elected a president and a few other officers the other night. But we still have to decide what our approach is going to be. One of the first things we agreed to do was examine the material we use in the classroom and check our libraries—er, rather, media centers—to see if there's anything that treats minority groups in an unfavorable light or that discriminates openly or covertly against them. We haven't decided, as I said, what we will do once we've collected this information, but this is the first step."

"Have you checked our media center and found anything you don't think should be there?" the assistant media specialist inquired.

"Yes, I went through the card catalog the other day looking specifically for *Little Black Sambo*, and guess what? You have it. That's one title we were asked to look for."

"Anything else?"

"I didn't really look. I'm not that familiar with the titles of children's books. Everyone knows *Little Black Sambo*, though. It's one of the worst."

"I have to admit that I've been wondering if we should have it in our collection. It's been the subject of quite a bit of controversy for some time now."

"Well, as I said, we're not sure what we'll do, but I wanted to mention our group to you and say that *Little Black Sambo* will probably come in for some fire."

"Maybe next time you come around it won't be there," Ms. Keyes ventured with a confident smile.

"Say, great! Let me know what you do."

When Ms. Keyes got back to the media center, she went directly to the shelves to look for *Little Black Sambo*. Finding it there, she took it over to her desk and began to thumb through it. It was dated 1951 and published by Lippincott. She put it down and began to stare idly into space. Just then, Ms. Aiken came over and asked her how her day was going. The media specialist could see that her assistant was in some sort of reverie, so she waved her hand in front of her eyes and said jokingly; "Hey, where are you?"

Ms. Keyes snapped out of her daze and smiled. "I was just thinking about *Little Black Sambo*," she said. "You know, I don't think we should keep it anymore. It's outdated, the kind of book we no longer need in our collection. I think it's a dangerous and cruel book," she went on, becoming quite excited. "It depicts blacks in a very unfavorable light. It makes them appear to be inferior human beings who white people are expected to laugh at. I think if blacks are going to continue to make strides towards equality, then books such as *Little Black Sambo* have to go."

Ms. Aiken realized that her assistant was very serious and that she was deeply disturbed by the book. She said nothing but pulled up a chair. A child came over to ask if someone would help her select a film loop. In a very nice way, Ms. Aiken suggested to the child that she ask one of the aides behind the desk to help her.

The assistant media specialist continued, "I think this book distorts children's views of black people and I know it causes blacks great mental anguish. We constantly weed out old materials, and it would seem to me that we could easily weed out this book. Wasn't it written back around the turn of the century?"

"It was written in the late 1890s by Helen Bannerman," Ms. Aiken said. "You know, of course, that the setting is India and not Africa, and that the book doesn't concern blacks but Indians."

"I think I did hear something to that effect, but now Black Sambo is looked upon as being black. Even if you tell people that the characters are Indians, isn't it still demeaning to the people of India? But Sambo is thought to be black, and that's what's important."

"You know, Beth, if you used the date when a book was written as a criterion for whether it should stay or go," Ms. Aiken explained, "you'd have to get rid of the works of some of the best writers of children's books—Robert Louis Stevenson, Mark Twain, Louisa May Alcott, and others."

"But that assumes that *Little Black Sambo* is a classic," Ms. Keyes observed. "It's not a classic, it's just an offensive and insulting work of an insensitive person who wanted to amuse people."

"That may be a little harsh, Beth."

"In an age when intelligent, thinking people have an obligation to be socially responsible, it seems to me that it's being socially responsible to get rid of *Little Black Sambo*."

"I'm not at all sure that you're being consistent, Beth, if I may say so. You've accused me of practicing censorship when I've hesitated to purchase certain books dealing with sex. Or even better than that, when I wanted to put *In the Night Kitchen* behind the desk you said we couldn't because that would be censorship. What's the difference between what you're suggesting and what I wanted to do?"

"I think the issue is different. All their lives, blacks have lived with a banjo-strumming, foot-shuffling, slow-witted image, and *Little Black Sambo* perpetuates that negative stereotype. It's dehumanizing and doesn't help the black man in his search for identity. Blacks have been persecuted all their lives. They don't like *Little Black Sambo*. Can't people today try to compensate for how they've been treated in the past and grant them the humble request that we no longer keep *Little Black Sambo* around? Is that asking much? It's an unpleasant reminder of the way things were. It impedes progress."

"You know, Beth, I don't want you to think because I'm resisting the suggestion that *Little Black Sambo* be removed from the shelves that I'm against the black man or that I'm a racist. I find it so very hard to know what to do when it comes to black literature—and blacks, for that matter. If I don't buy lots of black literature I'm prejudiced, and if I do I'm a white do-gooder. Is someone who wants *Little Black Sambo* off the shelves a better person than someone who doesn't? Is that the implication? I thought we were committed to something higher than that—to a principle, to a freedom of speech, to the *School Library Bill of Rights.* You've certainly helped me to see that; and while I personally would have preferred not to purchase some of the books we have purchased, I've realized that we can't let our own preferences interfere with selection. Now, you're doing the same thing, but because *you* believe in the cause, it's all right. I don't get the logic, Beth. Really, I don't."

Ms. Keyes began to rub her forehead. "I know it doesn't look as if I'm being consistent," she said wearily, "but this isn't book censorship, it's book weeding. The book has been given longer life than it deserves. A stupid story about a boy outsmarting tigers. We don't hesitate to weed out other books which we think have outlived their usefulness; in fact, we're always chiding ourselves that we don't do more of it. Now I suggest weeding *Little Black Sambo* and we hesitate."

"If I'm not mistaken, *Little Black Sambo* appears in a collection or two which we have. I think it's Hutchinson's *Chimney Corner Stories.* Let me check." Ms. Aiken got up and went over to get the book, stopping on the way back to pick up their copy of *The Elementary School Library Collection: A Guide to Books and Other Media.* "Here, you look and see if it's recommended in *The Elementary School Library Collection* and I'll look in Hutchinson."

"I don't see it listed in this book," Ms. Keyes said.

"It's in Hutchinson," Ms. Aiken said. "Do you think we should take Hutchinson's book off the shelves because it has *Little Black Sambo* when there are fifteen other folk tales in it? Or, should we cut out the pages it appears on the way some librarians did with *Sylvester and the Magic Pebble?*"

"That's a little mean," Ms. Keyes said indignantly.

"I don't want to be mean, Beth. But I can see no justification for taking the book off the shelves. As far as I'm concerned it should stay. You've often told me that you couldn't understand anyone suppressing *Catcher in the Rye* or *To Kill a Mockingbird.* I hate to hammer away at you like this, but I'm trying to show how hard it is to resist wanting to suppress what *we* don't want to hear. Goodness knows, I've learned that, and you've helped me to see it. If something touches a sore spot with us, we want to get rid of it. Maybe it's good we have some materials that we as librarians would like to see suppressed, for then we can better understand the censor."

"Well, if you use that argument, how would you like it if you were depicted as a stupid, inferior savage? Think of that for a moment. I've noticed that it's been the white Anglo-Saxon Protestants who think that Jews and blacks and other minorities shouldn't be upset when their races are slurred. I wish we'd be more sensitive."

"I'm sure I wouldn't like being the object of slurring, but I'd live with it," the older woman observed.

"Oh, that's easy to say because you're white. I bet you'd want to see it stop if you were black. Every time I let some white kid have *Little Black Sambo*, I feel terrible."

"But how can we possibly know whether the kids who read it feel hostile toward blacks?"

"There's always the chance the one or two might be affected by it, and that's enough. It has to go, Nancy. For the sake of all that's decent, it has to go. The Teachers against Discrimination group will be after us to get rid of it anyway."

Just then, one of the media aides came over to say that the principal wanted Ms. Aiken on the phone.

• • • • •

What do you think of the arguments of both Ms. Aiken and Ms. Keyes? Are there times when some form of censorship is justified and necessary in the best interests of groups of people and progress? Would your reaction to the arguments presented be the same, if the school was in a predominantly black neighborhood? Can a controversial book ever be weeded from a collection the way an outdated noncontroversial book is without suspicion of censorship? What approach should Ms. Aiken take with Ms. Keyes at this point? Is *Little Black Sambo* a harmful book, in your opinion? Would you buy the book if the library didn't own it?

29.
The Confrontation—I

Earl Skinner hadn't known quite what to expect on his job as the new director of the Hamersley Public Library. He had been born not far from Hamersley twenty-eight years ago and was glad to be back in the area.

Hamersley is a rather fashionable "bedroom" community of 35,000 just outside one of the larger cities in the East. The community enjoys the reputation of being a prestige location, having all these prerequisites: it is in sound shape financially, it is reported to have excellent schools, and it affords many opportunities for cultural and recreational activities.

As his wife drove him to work that first Monday morning, Earl Skinner reflected on how pleased he was that his predecessor had departed the previous Friday. He had not wanted any overlap time with Giles Chisholm, the former director, who had retired, for he had not been impressed with him when he came to be interviewed by the board of trustees for the directorship. Mr. Skinner also knew his predecessor by reputation to be representative of the "old school" librarian, and so felt there was little that the older man could pass on to him of much worth. He wanted to start his first director's job with a clean slate—no preconceptions, no biases, no opinions.

The Hamersley Public Library has a total book collection of 110,000 volumes and a staff of twenty-four people, including four other professionally trained librarians, three of whom worked at the adult reference desk and one who was the children's librarian. The collection was housed in an old structure whose capacity had long since been exhausted. Being an old building with many varied but minor additions, it had several hidden nooks and crannies— the bane of the staff, for these areas were difficult to supervise. The building was ideally situated in one regard, in that it was in the center of town, but poorly situated in that there were now no parking facilities. Directly across the street from the library was the one undeveloped area in the entire downtown complex—a small park block with playground facilities in the middle and benches fronting the surrounding sidewalks. Here the old-timers in the town sat and talked; and here, too, many of the young people in the town congregated, often driving the old-timers away.

After having served in various positions in two larger public libraries in the Midwest, working up to assistant director in one of them before he took over the directorship of the Hamersley Public Library, Mr. Skinner felt he knew his way around libraries quite well. His mind was full of new and creative ideas which he was anxious to try in Hamersley. One of the first things he did was arrange his schedule so that he would spend a few hours a week at the reference desk, "just to keep his hand in the operation and to meet some of the patrons and get a feel for their requests"—something, he learned later, Mr. Chisholm had never done. Indeed, one day a staff member, Emily Foster, told him that the former director spent most of his time in his office and had very little contact with the public. "He didn't really understand our problems," the woman said, "and when we would mention them to him he would listen and say he would do something about them, but he always treated them lightly and indicated that perhaps we were dramatizing them. Sometimes we just threw up our hands in despair."

Things seemed to go along quite well in Mr. Skinner's first few days at the Hamersley Public Library. The staff warmed to him and he was pleased with them. In his discussions, however, he found that many staff members had some excellent ideas which they apparently had never suggested to Mr. Chisholm. One day, he broached the subject with Olive Keegan, one of the reference librarians.

"Well," Ms. Keegan started, hesitantly, "it's not easy to talk about. I don't really know if I should say anything; I wouldn't want you to misunderstand me. I liked Mr. Chisholm very much—we all did—although we found him somewhat reserved and almost stand-offish. We used to make suggestions, but then we stopped when we realized he wasn't doing anything with them." She offered no explanation as to why this was.

Although there were numerous procedures to become acquainted with, budget matters to look into, and files to go through, the director decided he would spend a considerable amount of his time in the library, observing the scene and talking to the staff. About 4:30 one afternoon, as he was standing at the circulation desk, he observed a group of five or six boys in their late teens enter the library, making what he thought was a great deal of noise by deliberately dragging their feet, and join a group of boys already seated around one of the tables in the main reading room. The recent arrivals went to other tables, grabbed up unoccupied chairs, and carried them to where their friends were sitting. Mr. Skinner noticed that not one of them had a magazine or a newspaper in front of him, and that they were all engaged in a merry conversation, which sometimes got exceedingly loud.

"I hate it when they come in," Ms. Leland, a desk clerk, said, noticing that Mr. Skinner was taking it all in. "My pulse starts beating faster when I see them."

"Do they come in often?"

"Several times a week."

"Well, what do we do when they're here? Do we just let them sit around and gab like this?"

"Sometimes the reference people speak to them and ask them to leave. We can't leave the desk, so the reference people talk to them."

Mr. Skinner glanced over and noticed that Ms. Foster, who was covering the reference desk at the time, was busy searching through the card catalog with two young girls. He decided to approach the group. One or two of the boys looked up as he got closer, and one of them nudged another with his elbow. Most of them looked up at him as he stood by the table, but a few kept right on with their conversation, appearing to ignore him.

"How about keeping the noise down, fellows, and getting something to look at while you're here," the director said firmly. The boys who were talking stopped, but no one really looked at him. They either looked at each other and smiled, or looked nowhere in particular. No one moved. Mr. Skinner appeared uneasy.

"Did you hear me?" he said in a stern tone.

Two of them slowly and deliberately shuffled out of their chairs, and then stood looking at the others. Again, no one said anything.

"Okay. Now how about getting something to read?" the director said to the two who were standing.

Slowly, they went over to the newspaper and magazine area; the others continued to sit motionless.

"What about you others?" Mr. Skinner demanded.

By this time, the attention of everyone in the room was riveted on what was going on. Mr. Skinner felt even more uncomfortable. Finally, he decided the boys had better leave. "Okay. It looks as if you're not here to do much of anything but talk, so you all better go." But by now, the two who had gone for magazines had returned and reoccupied their seats. "You'd better all leave," he repeated.

One of the boys with a magazine said, "I've got something to read, why should I go?"

"You can stay," Mr. Skinner said, after a second's thought. "But you others must go."

"If we get magazines, can we stay?" one of them asked.

The director hesitated before he spoke. "All right. But spread yourselves around the room."

The others ambled over to the magazine racks, grabbed anything that came to hand, and returned to the table. Mr. Skinner continued to stand there. Not one of them took a chair back to another table, so the annoyed director reminded them that he wanted them to break up and sit at different tables. With deliberate motions, and as noisily as possible, they began to move the chairs back to the tables. Mr. Skinner started back to the desk, glancing back at what was going on as he went. He noticed that they smiled at each other as they glanced around from their new locations.

"Is it like this often?" he asked Ms. Leland, as he returned to the desk.

"Oh, yes," she replied, quickly. "Sometimes they come in and we don't know where they've gone, but we're sure they're up to no good wherever they are. We're all uneasy when they're here. We could tell you some stories of some of the things they've done over the years."

"Has this been going on for some time?" Mr. Skinner asked, almost incredulously.

"Ever since I've been here, and that's six years. Some of our older troublemakers have disappeared, but we always get a new batch to replace them."

Ms. Foster was free at the reference desk now, so he went over to see her. "What has our policy been toward kids who come in merely to lounge around and pass the time of day, Ms. Foster?" he asked. "I don't know whether you noticed, but I had to go over and speak to that gang of boys and ask them to keep down the noise."

"Oh, those. They're always in here and they always have to be spoken to about noise. Actually they're quite tame today. Wait till you see some of our really bad days."

"What sorts of things have they done?" Mr. Skinner asked, his interest keenly piqued.

"Oh, they've come in and taken books from one section of the shelves and moved them to another part of the library; they've marched all through the library in a single file and in step, in and out of the stacks, up and down the stairs; they've spread themselves all over the main reading room and let out weird cackles when we weren't looking, and we couldn't tell where the noises were coming from; they've smoked in the stacks. Things like that. And they're so bold and deceitful. You talk to them and they deny everything. And the way they stare you down! When I was a girl and someone in authority spoke to me, once was enough! With these kids you have to tell them the same thing every day; they never seem to remember. Sometimes I go home a wreck after chasing them around. After speaking to them, I often come back to the reference desk so upset I can't concentrate on my work; sometimes I'm actually shaking."

Mr. Skinner stood listening and watching the group of boys. They were talking again, so he went over and told them to get out. They stared at him and gave him a look that signified they would like to "take care" of him outside. He repeated his command. Finally they left, but as they got to the door they let out hoots and hollers, loud enough for everyone in the library to hear. Other young people in the library, who had not been causing any disturbance, began to laugh. The boys lingered for a moment on the front steps, then crossed the street and sat on the park benches.

The director looked bewildered and irritated. He returned to the reference desk. "I'm glad you've seen some of this," Ms. Foster said to him. "Perhaps you'll be able to do something about it. One time some of them stayed in here after the library was closed—hid somewhere when we locked up at night—and the next morning we came in to find the front lobby piled up with books; there were matches and cigarette butts all over the place, too. Really, we don't know what to do. If we're too hard on them they might get tough with us or our children, and we have to live here. I even feel uncomfortable walking down the street when I see them because often they will point me out to each other. Maybe if we make them mad or antagonize them they'll do even worse things than they're doing."

"Who are these boys anyway?" Mr. Skinner asked angrily. "Doesn't the staff know who they are?"

"Well, we know some of them."

"I don't intend to let them run this place."

The reference librarian went on to say that several staff members, whom she declined to identify, had discussed the possibility of leaving the library because of lack of support in dealing with the problem.

Over the next few days, Mr. Skinner found that the boys who caused the trouble spent most of their time across the street on the park benches. In discussing the situation with other staff members, he discovered that a fairly small group of some forty or so were the cause of most of the trouble, and that many of them were school drop-outs, both voluntary and forced. He also found that, on occasion, the situation had become so unmanageable the police had to be called in; but calling the police was frequently of little use because they took so long to get there—if they came at all—that the boys had often left on their own before the police arrived. The staff felt that even the less troublesome young people had a tendency to be quite boisterous in the library because the others got away with so much. He was most startled to hear that many adults were staying away altogether because they looked upon the public library as an extension of the high school, and they were disturbed by the unruliness that so often prevailed.

Toward the end of Mr. Skinner's first week at Hamersley, a reporter appeared from the local paper to interview him. The new director devoted almost the entire interview to a discussion of the disciplinary problem, severely criticizing the former director for not having taken action with "the unsavory teenagers who look upon the library as some sort of country club." He stated that as the new director he was going to "clean up the library and get rid of the thugs that cause such a disruption." He said he had a good staff and that he didn't want to see them wasting their time "on a bunch of reprobates."

The interview appeared in print two days later, the day before Mr. Skinner's first board meeting. Several members of the staff said they were glad to hear the new director was planning to take steps to correct the disciplinary problem, but one or two others thought he had been hard on his predecessor.

Mr. Skinner answered by saying that he believed "in calling a spade a spade, and if Chisholm was negligent why should I cover for him?"

At the trustees' meeting that night, he was welcomed officially. The chairman opened the meeting with the comment that he was quite surprised to hear that Mr. Skinner thought there was a disciplinary problem in the library. Another board member said she hadn't noticed any problem when she was there; and a third said that if there really were a problem, "Mr. Chisholm would have taken care of it in the proper manner," adding that she thought the new director had been "extremely unkind" to his predecessor in his comments. Another trustee offered the opinion that there were no "unsavory" teenagers in Hamersley, and that, unlike some of the surrounding towns and cities, Hamersley was a very respectable community "that doesn't have trouble with its young people the way some towns do." Mr. Skinner attempted to explore the problem with the board, but the members were disinclined to talk about it. The chairman said he hoped the new director would refrain from making any more comments of the type he made in the paper and that he would "stop worrying so much about a few boys when there are 35,000 other people to take care of." The meeting terminated at this point; but it was obvious the members were dissatisfied with Mr. Skinner's behavior. The library director tried to assure the board that he was not magnifying the problem, but they refused to discuss it further.

The next day, about 3:30 in the afternoon, as he was glancing out one of the windows, Mr. Skinner noticed what he had come to refer to as the "troublemakers" lolling around the park benches. As he stood watching them, someone notified him he was wanted on the telephone.

Shortly afterwards, he returned to the main reading room. He was astonished to see the entire group he had been watching a few minutes earlier now occupying seats all over the room. Not one of them had any library materials in front of him, and each had a look of defiance as he sat there.

Mr. Skinner went to his office and called the police chief. He asked him to send over some officers right away—stressing that it was important they come immediately. When the policemen arrived, he told them he wanted to get the names of all the boys in the library, explaining that they were causing trouble. As soon as the boys saw the uniformed men, they scattered all over the library—into the stack areas, the newspaper room, and the music room. One of the policemen went after the scampering boys, while the other stood by the front door to corral them. Mr. Skinner helped track them down. As the boys were lined up by the front door, one of the officers jotted down their names and addresses. Most said they were not causing trouble, and some maintained they were there for serious purposes when they were found in the stacks. The police officer took down all the names, however, regardless of the protests. After their names and addresses were written down, the angry director told them he didn't want to see them back in the library again. There were twenty-six names on the list.

That day, Mr. Skinner composed the following letter to the boys' parents:

Dear (name of parents):

Your child, (name of child), has been coming to the library with the sole purpose of causing trouble. When he is in the library, he is disruptive and disrespectful. The library is a place for serious work; it is not a place to act the fool, which is what your child has been doing when he is here. We are anxious that people in Hamersley use the public library, but we want them to observe a few simple rules—such as keeping quiet, behaving in an orderly way, and making use of library materials constructively. Your boy is one of the reasons several people in the community are avoiding using the library. It is my unpleasant task, therefore, to inform you that your child is not to enter the library until you come with him to give me assurances that he will not misbehave again.

I will be happy to see you at any time, and look forward to welcoming your son back into the library.

A personalized copy of the letter was sent to the parents of every boy on the list. At the same time, Mr. Skinner called the local paper and told the reporter who had interviewed him what had happened and what he had done. The reporter asked for details, which the director gave willingly. "Would you write something up?" he asked the reporter. "And indicate that we have a 'get-tough' policy here and will not stand for any fooling around?" The next day, the following article appeared in the evening paper:

LIBRARY GETS TOUGH WITH KIDS

Earl Skinner, newly appointed director of the Hamersley Public Library, has issued an ultimatum ·o the parents of twenty-six boys in town that unless their boys behave in the library they will not be welcome there. With the aid of two policemen, the new director rounded up the youngsters yesterday afternoon. According to Skinner, the boys had been in the library with the express purpose of causing a disturbance. He says he and the staff have had to deal with these boys on numerous occasions in the past, and the library is not going "to tolerate this kind of behavior any longer." He pointed out that his predecessor, Giles Chisholm, let the boys do whatever they wanted to in the library, and as a result many adults were staying away because of "the unruliness that prevailed there." He said further that his staff spends most of its time after school is out acting as policemen, "which is not what the city is paying us to be."

Skinner has sent a personal letter to the parents or guardians of the boys, informing them of his action and telling them that their boys will be welcome in the library only after the parents come down and give the library director assurances there will be no further problems of this sort.

Skinner has been on the job for just over two weeks.

Late that same afternoon, Mr. Skinner received a call from the father of one of the boys who had been in the library.

"This is Phillip Ruthven," the father said. "I received a letter today stating that my son has been causing a disturbance in the library, and I saw this evening's paper, which says that twenty-five other parents have received similar letters. I can't speak for them, but I want to tell you that my son told me he was doing nothing wrong at all in the library. He says—and I believe him—that he was merely looking up a book in the stacks when a policeman told him to leave. I think you have done a foolish thing, and I have no intention of coming to see you about my son getting back into the library. I am going to see if there isn't some way I can sue you for defamation of character. I'm sure there must be libel laws to protect people from this kind of irresponsible slander. I'm going to look into this, but in the meantime I want you to know that you haven't heard the last from me."

Before Mr. Skinner could respond, the man hung up. A moment later, the telephone rang again. It was the chairman of the board. "What on earth are you doing at the library, Earl?" he asked indignantly. "I saw the evening paper and couldn't believe my eyes. How could you have done that? What were you thinking of? I'm going to call an emergency meeting of the board for tonight to discuss what action we should take. It'll be an executive session, which means you can't attend. I'll get back to you tomorrow to tell you what we decide."

The beleaguered librarian repeated his claim that he was merely trying to make the library a place people would want to visit by getting rid of those who were disruptive. He reminded the chairman of the trouble the staff was having with the boys, stating that they could not tolerate the situation any longer. In the discussion that followed, Mr. Skinner told of the threatening telephone call from the father. The chairman expressed further annoyance with the way the librarian was handling the situation.

Early next morning, Mr. Skinner received a call from the chairman. "We spent a great deal of time discussing the situation, and you specifically, last night," he said. "We talked about asking for your resignation, but decided to give you another chance. In order for you to stay, however, you must promise us that you will not concern yourself with this problem any more; and you must also promise us that you will not say a single word about the problem to anyone—the staff, the newspapers, or anyone else. We also want you to know that we think you have acted very unprofessionally in regard to Mr. Chisholm. We think it's disgraceful how you have criticized him. Don't you have a code of ethics? And doesn't it say anything about speaking disparagingly about fellow librarians? We're going to seek counsel on the question of libel and slander which Mr. Ruthven has raised. We would appreciate knowing what you can find out in this regard. Now remember, Earl, not a word to anyone about the boys or Mr. Chisholm. We want you to clear everything with us before you speak. Do you understand—everything?"

The director said he understood what was being said. He told the chairman that he would look into the question of libel; but he maintained that the library had the legal right to keep people who did not observe library rules out of the building. It was in the state laws, he said. The chairman told him to try to devote himself to more important matters.

That afternoon, Mr. Skinner telephoned the librarian who was chairman of the Intellectual Freedom Committee of the state library association. He explained the situation to her and asked if he could meet with the committee to discuss how he should proceed in light of the directive not to speak. A meeting was set for the following Tuesday. In the meantime, two sets of parents came to the library to apologize for their sons' behavior and to say it would not be repeated. Mr. Skinner heard nothing further from Mr. Ruthven, nor from the board.

He met with the Intellectual Freedom Committee as planned, outlining all the details of what had happened. He requested the members to intercede on his behalf and inform the board that they could not take away his right to speak as he wished.

•   •   •   •   •

If you were a member of the Intellectual Freedom Committee, how would you respond to Mr. Skinner's request? Would you intercede on his behalf? On what basis? What do you think of the way Mr. Skinner had handled the situation thus far? Is it unethical to speak disparagingly of fellow librarians? Does Mr. Ruthven have grounds for legal action against the library and/or Mr. Skinner? How could he have handled the situation differently, to avoid such a confrontation?

30.
The Confrontation—II

Ellie Skinner hadn't known quite what to expect on her job as the new director of the Hamersley Public Library. She had been born not far from Hamersley twenty-eight years ago and was glad to be back in the area.

Hamersley is a rather fashionable "bedroom" community of 35,000 just outisde one of the larger cities in the East. The community enjoys the reputation of being a prestige location, having all these prerequisites: it is in sound shape financially, it is reported to have excellent schools, and it affords many opportunities for cultural and recreational activities.

As her husband drove her to work that first Monday morning, Ellie Skinner reflected on how pleased she was that her predecessor had departed the previous Friday. She had not wanted any overlap time with Giles Chisholm, the former director, who had retired, for she had not been impressed with him when she came to be interviewed by the board of trustees for the directorship. Ms. Skinner also knew her predecessor by reputation to be representative of the "old school" librarian, and so felt there was little that he could pass on to her of much worth. She wanted to start her first director's job with a clean slate—no preconceptions, no biases, no opinions.

The Hamersley Public Library has a total book collection of 110,000 volumes and a staff of twenty-four people, including four other professionally trained librarians, three of whom worked at the adult reference desk and one who was the children's librarian. The collection was housed in an old structure whose capacity had long since been exhausted. Being an old building with many varied but minor additions, it had several hidden nooks and crannies—the bane of the staff, for these areas were difficult to supervise. The building was ideally situated in one regard, in that it was in the center of town, but poorly situated in that there were now no parking facilities. Directly across

the street from the library was the one undeveloped area in the entire downtown complex—a small park block with playground facilities in the middle
and benches fronting the surrounding sidewalks. Here the old-timers in the
town sat and talked; and here, too, many of the young people in the town congregated, often driving the old-timers away.

After having served in various positions in two larger public libraries in the
Midwest, working up to assistant director in one of them before she took over
the directorship of the Hamersley Public Library, Ms. Skinner felt she knew
her way around libraries quite well. Her mind was full of new and creative
ideas which she was anxious to try in Hamersley. One of the first things she
did was arrange her schedule so that she would spend a few hours a week at
the reference desk, "just to keep her hand in operation and to meet some of
the patrons and get a feel for their requests"—something, she learned later,
Mr. Chisholm had never done. Indeed, one day a staff member, Emily Foster,
told her that the former director spent most of his time in his office and had
very little contact with the public. "He didn't really understand our problems," the woman said, "and when we would mention them to him he would
listen and say he would do something about them, but he always treated them
lightly and indicated that perhaps we were dramatizing them. Sometimes we
just threw up our hands in despair."

Things seemed to go along quite well in Ms. Skinner's first few days at the
Hamersley Public Library. The staff warmed to her and she was pleased with
them. In her discussions, however, she found that many staff members had
some excellent ideas which they apparently had never suggested to Mr. Chisholm. One day, she broached the subject with Olive Keegan, one of the reference librarians.

"Well," Ms. Keegan started, hesitantly, "it's not easy to talk about. I don't
really know if I should say anything; I wouldn't want you to misunderstand
me. I liked Mr. Chisholm very much—we all did—although we found him
somewhat reserved and almost stand-offish. We used to make suggestions,
but then we stopped when we realized he wasn't doing anything with them."
She offered no explanation as to why this was.

Although there were numerous procedures to become acquainted with,
budget matters to look into, and files to go through, the director decided she
would spend a considerable amount of her time in the library, observing the
scene and talking to the staff. About 4:30 one afternoon, as she was standing
at the circulation desk, she observed a group of five or six boys in their late
teens enter the library, making what she thought was a great deal of noise by
deliberately dragging their feet, and join a group of boys already seated
around one of the tables in the main reading room. The recent arrivals went
to other tables, grabbed up unoccupied chairs, and carried them to where
their friends were sitting. Ms. Skinner noticed that not one of them had a
magazine or a newspaper in front of him, and that they were all engaged in a
merry conversation, which sometimes got exceedingly loud.

"I hate it when they come in," Ms. Leland, a desk clerk, said, noticing that Ms. Skinner was taking it all in. "My pulse starts beating faster when I see them."

"Do they come in often?"

"Several times a week."

"Well, what do we do when they're here? Do we just let them sit around and gab like this?"

"Sometimes the reference people speak to them and ask them to leave. We can't leave the desk, so the reference people talk to them."

Ms. Skinner glanced over and noticed that Ms. Foster, who was covering the reference desk at the time, was busy searching through the card catalog with two young girls. She decided to approach the group. One or two of the boys looked up as she got closer, and one of them nudged another with his elbow. Most of them looked up at her as she stood by the table, but a few kept right on with their conversation, appearing to ignore her.

"How about keeping the noise down, boys, and getting something to look at while you're here," the director said firmly. The boys who were talking stopped, but no one really looked at her. They either looked at each other and smiled, or looked nowhere in particular. No one moved. Ms. Skinner appeared uneasy.

"Did you hear me?" she said in a stern tone.

Two of them slowly and deliberately shuffled out of their chairs, and then stood looking at the others. Again, no one said anything.

"Okay. Now how about getting something to read?" the director said to the two who were standing.

Slowly, they went over to the newspaper and magazine area; the others continued to sit motionless.

"What about you others?" Ms. Skinner demanded.

By this time, the attention of everyone in the room was riveted on what was going on. Ms. Skinner felt even more uncomfortable. Finally, she decided the boys had better leave. "Okay. It looks as if you're not here to do much of anything but talk, so you all better go." But by now, the two who had gone for magazines had returned and reoccupied their seats. "You'd better all leave," she repeated.

One of the boys with a magazine said, "I've got something to read, why should I go?"

"You can stay," Ms. Skinner said, after a second's thought. "But you others must go."

"If we get magazines, can we stay?" one of them asked.

The director hesitated before she spoke. "All right. But spread yourselves around the room."

The others ambled over to the magazine racks, grabbed anything that came to hand, and returned to the table. Ms. Skinner continued to stand there. Not one of them took a chair back to another table, so the annoyed director reminded them that she wanted them to break up and sit at different tables. With deliberate motions, and as noisily as possible, they began to move the chairs back to the tables. Ms. Skinner started back to the desk, glancing back at what was going on as she went. She noticed that they smiled at each other as they glanced around from their new locations.

"Is it like this often?" she asked Ms. Leland, as she returned to the desk.

"Oh, yes," the woman replied, quickly. "Sometimes they come in and we don't know where they've gone, but we're sure they're up to no good wherever they are. We're all uneasy when they're here. We could tell you some stories of some of the things they've done over the years."

"Has this been going on for some time?" Ms. Skinner asked, almost incredulously.

"Ever since I've been here, and that's six years. Some of our older troublemakers have disappeared, but we always get a new batch to replace them."

Ms. Foster was free at the reference desk now, so the director went over to see her. "What has our policy been toward kids who come in merely to lounge around and pass the time of day, Ms. Foster?" she asked. "I don't know whether you noticed, but I had to go over and speak to that gang of boys and ask them to keep down the noise."

"Oh, those. They're always in here and they always have to be spoken to about noise. Actually they're quite tame today. Wait till you see some of our really bad days."

"What sorts of things have they done?" Ms. Skinner asked, her interest keenly piqued.

"Oh, they've come in and taken books from one section of the shelves and moved them to another part of the library; they've marched all through the library in a single file and in step, in and out of the stacks, up and down the stairs; they've spread themselves all over the main reading room and let out weird cackles when we weren't looking, and we couldn't tell where the noises were coming from; they've smoked in the stacks. Things like that. And they're so bold and deceitful. You talk to them and they deny everything. And the way they stare you down! When I was a girl and someone in authority spoke to me, once was enough! With these kids you have to tell them the same thing every day; they never seem to remember. Sometimes I go home a wreck after chasing them around. After speaking to them, I often come back to the reference desk so upset I can't concentrate on my work; sometimes I'm actually shaking."

Ms. Skinner stood listening and watching the group of boys. They were talking again, so she went over and told them to get out. They stared at her but did nothing. She repeated her command. Finally they left, but as they got to the door they let out hoots and hollers, loud enough for everyone in the library to hear. Other young people in the library, who had not been causing any disturbance, began to laugh. The boys lingered for a moment on the front steps, then crossed the street and sat on the park benches.

The director looked bewildered and irritated. She returned to the reference desk. "I'm glad you've seen some of this," Ms. Foster said to her. "Perhaps you'll be able to do something about it. One time some of them stayed in here after the library was closed—hid somewhere when we locked up at night—and the next morning we came in to find the front lobby piled up with books; there were matches and cigarette butts all over the place, too. Really, we don't know what to do. If we're too hard on them they might get tough with us or our children, and we have to live here. I even feel uncomfortable walking down the street when I see them because often they will point me out to each other. Maybe if we make them mad or antagonize them they'll do even worse things than they're doing."

"Who are these boys anyway?" Ms. Skinner asked angrily. "Doesn't the staff know who they are?"

"Well, we know some of them."

"I don't intend to let them run this place."

The reference librarian went on to say that several staff members, whom she declined to identify, had discussed the possibility of leaving the library because of lack of support in dealing with the problem.

Over the next few days, Ms. Skinner found that the boys who had caused the trouble spent most of their time across the street on the park benches. In discussing the situation with other staff members, she discovered that a fairly small group of some forty or so were the cause of most of the trouble, and that many of them were school drop-outs, both voluntary and forced. She also found that, on occasion, the situation had become so unmanageable the police had to be called in; but calling the police was frequently of little use because they took so long to get there—if they came at all—that the boys had often left on their own before the police arrived. The staff felt that even the less troublesome young people had a tendency to be quite boisterous in the library because the others got away with so much. She was most startled to hear that many adults were staying away altogether because they looked upon the public library as an extension of the high school, and they were disturbed by the unruliness that so often prevailed.

Toward the end of Ms. Skinner's first week at Hamersley, a reporter appeared from the local paper to interview her. The new director devoted almost the entire interview to a discussion of the disciplinary problem, severely criticizing the former director for not having taken action with "the unsavory teenagers who look upon the library as some sort of country club." She stated that as the new director she was going to "clean up the library and get rid of the thugs that cause such a disruption." She said she had a good staff and that she didn't want to see them wasting their time "on a bunch of reprobates."

The interview appeared in print two days later, the day before Ms. Skinner's first board meeting. Several members of the staff said they were glad to hear the new director was planning to take steps to correct the disciplinary problem, but one or two others thought she had been harsh on her predecessor. Ms. Skinner answered by saying that she believed "in calling a spade a spade, and if Chisholm was negligent why should I cover for him?"

At the trustees' meeting that night, she was welcomed officially. The chairman opened the meeting with the comment that he was quite surprised to hear that Ms. Skinner thought there was a disciplinary problem in the library. Another board member said she hadn't noticed any problem when she was there; and a third said that if there really were a problem, "Mr. Chisholm would have taken care of it in the proper manner," adding that she thought the new director had been "extremely unkind" to her predecessor in her comments. Another trustee offered the opinion that there were no "unsavory" teenagers in Hamersley, and that, unlike some of the surrounding towns and cities, Hamersley was a very respectable community "that doesn't have trouble with its young people the way some towns do." Ms. Skinner attempted to explore the problem with the board, but the members were disinclined to talk about it. The chairman said he hoped the new director would refrain from making any more comments of the type she made in the paper and that she would "stop worrying so much about a few boys when there are 35,000 other people to take care of." The meeting terminated at this point; but it was obvious the members were dissatisfied with Ms. Skinner's behavior. The library director tried to assure the board that she was not magnifying the problem, but they refused to discuss it further.

The next day, about 3:30 in the afternoon, as she was glancing out one of the windows, Ms. Skinner noticed what she had come to refer to as the "troublemakers" lolling around the park benches. As she stood watching them, someone notified her she was wanted on the telephone.

Shortly afterwards, she returned to the main reading room. She was astonished to see the entire group she had been watching a few minutes earlier now occupying seats all over the room. Not one of them had any library materials in front of him, and each had a look of defiance as he sat there.

Ms. Skinner went to her office and called the police chief. She asked him to send over some officers right away—stressing that it was important they come immediately. When the policemen arrived, she told them she wanted to get the names of all the boys in the library, explaining that they were causing trouble. As soon as the boys saw the uniformed men, they scattered all over the library—into the stack areas, the newspaper room, and the music room. One of the policemen went after the scampering boys, while the other stood by the front door to corral them. Ms. Skinner helped track them down. As the boys were lined up by the front door, one of the officers jotted down their names and addresses. Most said they were not causing trouble, and some maintained they were there for serious purposes when they were found in the stacks. The police officer took down all the names, however, regardless of the protests. After the names and addresses were written down, the angry director told them she didn't want to see them back in the library again. There were twenty-six names on the list.

That day Ms. Skinner composed the following letter to the boys' parents:

Dear (name of parents)

Your child, (name of child), has been coming to the library with the sole purpose of causing trouble. When he is in the library, he is disruptive and disrespectful. The library is a place for serious work; it is not a place to act the fool, which is what your child has been doing when he is here. We are anxious that people in Hamersley use the public library, but we want them to observe a few simple rules—such as keeping quiet, behaving in an orderly way, and making use of library materials constructively. Your boy is one of the reasons several people in the community are avoiding using the library. It is my unpleasant task, therefore, to inform you that your child is not to enter the library until you come with him to give me assurances that he will not misbehave again.

I will be happy to see you at any time, and look forward to welcoming your son back into the library.

A personalized copy of the letter was sent to the parents of every boy on the list. At the same time, Ms. Skinner called the local paper and told the reporter who had interviewed her what had happened and what she had done. The reporter asked for details, which the director gave willingly. "Would you write something up?" she asked the reporter. "And indicate that we have a 'get-tough' policy here and will not stand for any fooling around? The next day, the following article appeared in the evening paper:

Library Gets Tough With Kids

Ellie Skinner, newly appointed director of the Hamersley Public Library, has issued an ultimatum to the parents of twenty-six boys in town that unless their boys behave in the library they will not be welcome there. With the aid of two policemen, the new director rounded up the youngsters yesterday afternoon. According to Skinner, the boys had been in the library with the express purpose of causing a disturbance. She says she and the staff have had to deal with these boys on numerous occasions in the past, and the library is not going "to tolerate this kind of behavior any longer." She pointed out that her predecessor, Giles Chisholm, let the boys do whatever they wanted to in the library, and as a result many adults were staying away because of "the unruliness that prevailed there." She said further that her staff spends most of its time after school is out acting as policemen, "which is not what the city is paying us to be."

Skinner has sent a personal letter to the parents or guardians of the boys, informing them of her action and telling them that their boys will be welcome in the library only after the parents come down and give the library director assurances there will be no further problems of this sort.

Skinner has been on the job for just over two weeks.

Late that same afternoon, Ms. Skinner received a call from the father of one of the boys who had been in the library.

"This is Phillip Ruthven," the father said. "I received a letter today stating that my son has been causing a disturbance in the library; and I saw this evening's paper, which states that twenty-five other parents have received similar letters. I can't speak for them, but I want to tell you that my son told me he was doing nothing wrong at all in the library. He says—and I believe him—that he was merely looking up a book in the stacks when a policeman told him to leave. I think you have done a foolish thing, and I have no intention of coming to see you about my son getting back into the library. I am going to see if there isn't some way I can sue you for defamation of character. I'm sure there must be libel laws to protect people from this kind of irresponsible slander. I'm going to look into this, but in the meantime I want you to know that you haven't heard the last from me."

Before Ms. Skinner could respond, the man hung up. A moment later, the telephone rang again. It was the chairman of the board. "What on earth are you doing at the library, Ellie?" he asked indignantly. "I saw the evening paper and couldn't believe my eyes. How could you have done that? What were you thinking of? I'm going to call an emergency meeting of the board for tonight to discuss what action we should take. It'll be an executive session, which means you can't attend. I'll get back to you tomorrow to tell you what we decide."

The beleaguered librarian repeated her claim that she was merely trying to make the library a place people would want to visit by getting rid of those who were disruptive. She reminded the chairman of the trouble the staff was having with the boys, stating that they could not tolerate the situation any longer. In the discussion that followed, Ms. Skinner told of the threatening telephone call from the father. The chairman expressed further annoyance with the way the librarian was handling the situation.

Early next morning, Ms. Skinner received a call from the chairman. "We spent a great deal of time discussing the situation, and you specifically, last night," he said. "We talked about asking for your resignation, but decided to give you another chance. In order for you to stay, however, you must promise us that you will not say a single word about the problem to anyone—the staff, the newspapers, or anyone else. We also want you to know that we think you have acted very unprofessionally in regard to Mr. Chisholm. We think it's disgraceful how you have criticized him. Don't you have a code of ethics? And doesn't it say anything about speaking disparagingly about fellow librarians? We're going to seek counsel on the question of libel and slander which Mr. Ruthven has raised. We would appreciate knowing what you can find out in this regard. Now remember, Ellie, not a word to anyone about the boys or Mr. Chisholm. We want you to clear everything with us before you speak. Do you understand—everything?"

The director said she understood what was being said. She told the chairman that she would look into the question of libel; but she maintained that the library had the legal right to keep people who did not observe library rules out of the building. It was in the state laws, she said. The chairman told her to try to devote herself to more important matters.

That afternoon, Ms. Skinner telephoned the librarian who was chairman of the Intellectual Freedom Committee of the state library association. She explained the situation to her and asked if she could meet with the committee to discuss how she should proceed in light of the directive not to speak. A meeting was set for the following Tuesday. In the meantime, two sets of parents came to the library to apologize for their son's behavior and to say it would not be repeated. Ms. Skinner heard nothing further from Mr. Ruthven, nor from the board.

She met with the Intellectual Freedom Committee as planned, outlining all the details of what had happened. She requested the members to intercede on her behalf and inform the board that they could not take away her right to speak as she wished.

●　●　●　●　●

If you were a member of the Intellectual Freedom Committee, how would you respond to Ms. Skinner's request? Would you intercede on her behalf? On what basis? What do you think of the way Ms. Skinner has handled the situation thus far? Is it unethical to speak disparagingly of fellow librarians? Does Mr. Ruthven have grounds for legal action against the library and/or Ms. Skinner? How could she have handled the situation differently, to avoid such a confrontation?

Sample Analysis of Case 26
by JAMES HOGAN

The case under examination here is extremely important as it deals with a problem fundamental to the very existence of librarianship as a profession. It is a problem that, in one form or another, will probably confront all librarians at some point in their careers. The solution to this problem, then, must be carefully chosen and even more carefully implemented. It is unfortunate that all too often in our professional and personal lives solutions to problems are worked out emotionally on the basis of too little relevant information. Would-be problem solvers attack their troubles with an enviable gusto but little intelligence. The results are often disappointing. Anticipated solutions turn out to be no solutions at all but rather stop-gap measures that later breed new problems of their own.

The problem solver in such a situation wonders where he went wrong. He appears to be constantly on the defensive, constantly reacting. He never seems to have control over the forces operating against him. It is suggested here that one of the major causes for this happening is the simple fact that such a person has no previously worked out problem-solving methodology. He merely throws himself against each problem, aiming at the most visible annoyances and never seeing the true cause of his troubles.

There are several problem-solving models that one might choose and it is not necessarily important which particular one is chosen. What is important is that the solver choose the one that works for him. The solution to this case will be built around one model that has worked for many people. It is a flexible model that lends itself very well to the very human type of problem that frequently confronts the librarian.

This model has been successfully used for many years at some of the nation's leading business and professional schools. In his book, *Case Analysis and Business Problem Solving,* Kenneth E. Schnelle proposes a six-step problem-solving model that is admirably suited to the case method of library education. Thus, before moving into the specifics of the "Knowing the Community" case it might prove helpful to briefly discuss the Schnelle model.

The six steps suggested by Schnelle are as follows:

1. Statement of the problem.
2. Statement of the pertinent facts.
3. Statement of alternative courses of action.
4. Advantages and disadvantages of the alternative courses of action.
5. Evaluation of the advantages and disadvantages.
6. Selection of the best alternative.[1]

The statement of the problem is undoubtedly the single most important step in the process. It is crucial to isolate, identify, and articulate the correct problem. For it goes without saying, if the wrong problem is initially stated, the wrong problem is going to be solved. The problem solver will discover that, having acted, he is still confronted with his original trouble. Extreme care and much thought must be given to insure that the correct root problem is clearly stated at the outset.

Once this has been accomplished the problem solver can proceed to gather all the pertinent information. He clearly knows the nature and scope of his problem and should not be led astray by interesting but irrelevant facts. This search for information must be as full and as thorough as time will allow. Adequate factual data is crucial to a successful solution.

The statement of alternative courses of action is the step in which the problem solver can throw to the wind the cold calculation that categorizes the rest of the process. Here he is free to give full rein to his imagination. It is suggested that in listing alternative courses of action he not discount even the wildest possibility. Often it turns out that the most outlandish ideas can contribute to a solution either in whole or in part.

With a batch of possible alternatives at hand the solver returns to the use of logic and carefully scrutinizes *all* the advantages and disadvantages of *each* alternative. None should be neglected, for even the most seemingly minute adverse effect can have a way of telescoping into a major problem if left unattended.

Some weight or sense of priority must now be given to each of the above-listed advantages and disadvantages. A sense of balance must be achieved. Frequently a single disadvantage may be enough to outweigh several advantages. In such a case the alternative, however appealing, must be abandoned.

Once this sense of order has been achieved the problem solver can proceed to select the best *possible* alternative. It is important to remember that even this solution may not be ideal. It may even be one that the solver personally does not like very much. However, if the problem-solving model has been faithfully followed, if all the pertinent facts have been collected, then the chosen alternative should at least have a viable chance of solving the problem. It is better to learn to live with a true solution that one does not especially care for than to opt for a pleasant course of action that is bound to lead to failure.

With these thoughts in mind it is now time to proceed with the case of Ms. Osgood and her troublesome questionnaire.

It might be suggested by some that had Ms. Osgood never dreamed up the questionnaire in the first place she would not now be confronted with her problem. The questionnaire has all the appearance of Pandora's box. It has opened to Ms. Osgood problems and dissatisfactions that she did not know existed in the town. This line of speculation is not especially useful. The attitudes that Ms. Osgood has uncovered apparently have existed for some time. They were bound to come out at some point. It is better that they surfaced as a result of a library-instigated survey than in some other perhaps unexpected manner.

The problem faced by Ms. Osgood is not simply whether *Ramparts* should be discontinued or whether shelves should be restricted or purified of offensive materials. The real problem is whether the town of Vanderlin is going to continue to enjoy free and unrestricted communication. Is a small but vociferous group going to be able to impose its own moral and political beliefs on the town as a whole? As guardians of man's recorded communications librarians are deeply involved in problems of this nature. They are fundamental to the profession and to our continuance as a free society.

Explicitly stated, the problem is whether or not Ms. Osgood is going to proceed to knowingly censor material that she or someone else considers to be offensive. Is she going to allow someone or some group to interfere with her role as the guardian of man's recorded communication?

With the true problem clearly in mind Ms. Osgood can now begin the process of gathering all the facts pertinent to that problem. Her questionnaire has been returned to the library by some three thousand inhabitants of Vanderlin, a town of twelve thousand. Sixty-five percent of the respondents indicated that they were opposed to the library's presenting all points of view concerning the problems and issues of our times. Many of these people expressed a desire to eliminate those points of view which especially upset them. They seemed to find the magazine *Ramparts* especially offensive.

Sixty-eight percent (2,040) of the respondents thought that the library should institute a policy of limited access for certain materials. Some of them even suggested a few titles that young people (under eighteen years of age) should not be allowed to see.

It should be noted that an overwhelming majority of the respondents also favored longer library hours, better parking facilities, and a new library building. Both the board of trustees and the town manager thought that at least the first of these two desires could be accommodated since clearly a "majority" of the citizens were in favor of them. However, by logical extension, they also felt that if a "majority" should be accommodated on these issues then the same should apply to the question of *Ramparts* and the offensive titles.

Statistics have a way of adding an aura of authenticity and strength to a weak argument. Conversely, they can also bolster a valid contention, and it would appear that at least part of Ms. Osgood's solution is going to have to rely on a clever use of statistics. Just what are the real results of the survey? As will be clear from Tables 1, 2, and 3, the figures can really be interpreted three different ways. It is readily clear that in reality nowhere near a majority of the townspeople have advocated the censoring action that Mr. Anthelme is so anxious to enforce. Purely on the basis of figures his argument that Ms. Osgood should follow the wishes of the majority falls apart. The majority has not spoken.

Table 1

INTERPRETATION OF DATA BASED ON TOTAL RESPONDENTS

	Response	No response	Yes	No
All points of view question	2,550(85%)	450(15%)	600(20%)	1,950(65%)
Open collection question	2,790(93%)	210(7%)	750(25%)	2,040(68%)

Table 2

INTERPRETATION OF DATA BASED ON TOTAL NUMBER OF QUES-TIONNAIRES

	Response	No response	Yes	No
All points of view question	2,550(66%)	450(11%)	600(15%)	1,950(49%)
Open collection question	2,790(69%)	210(5%)	750(14%)	2,040(51%)

Table 3

INTERPRETATION OF DATA BASED ON THE TOTAL POPULATION OF VANDERLIN

	Response	Yes	No
All points of view question	2,550(21%)	600(5%)	1,950(16%)
Open collection question	2,790(23%)	750(8%)	2,040(17%)

Using their initial interpretation of data, the four members of the board agreed with Mr. Anthelme, as did the town manager. The latter further confused the issue by "citing" the contemporary community standards doctrine as a method of determining obscenity. Evidently, he viewed the data as an indication of the standards of Vanderlin.

The facts in this case then are plain and clear. Ms. Osgood has the full board of trustees, her town manager and a couple of thousand of her fellow townsfolk urging her to morally and politically censor material in her library collection. One of her major (some might say her principal) duties, that of wisely and fairly selecting library materials, has been challenged. And, more importantly, a small group of citizens is urging that their own and their fellow citizens' rights of free communication and expression as guaranteed by the First Amendment be suspended.

There are approximately five courses of action open to Ms. Osgood at this point. First, she could agree to all the demands being made upon her. Second, she could completely resist all the demands being made upon her. Third, she could partly accede and partly resist, hoping for a compromise. Fourth, she could simply declare that her own convictions are at odds with those of the town and resign. Fifth, she could use the time allotted to her (one month) to conduct an intensive campaign attempting to persuade the committee to her point of view.

With her alternatives clearly listed, Ms. Osgood, in the quiet of her office or home, must mull over all the advantages and disadvantages of each.

Alternative number one has a major advantage. By simply giving in to the suggestions of the respondents, Ms. Osgood will have apparently solved one problem. She will have avoided a conflict with her board, her town manager, and a sizeable portion of the citizenry. However, this "solution" bears no relationship to the real problem facing Ms. Osgood. Having given in once, she would be forced to do the same again and again. She would find herself continually faced with the very problem she thought she had solved.

It should further be pointed out that if Ms. Osgood accedes to the demands of the censors she will have abdicated her responsibility as a librarian. She will, furthermore, be flying in the face of guidelines established by her professional organization. Concerning the infamous Proposition 18 that the voters of California were faced with in 1972, the ALA said:

> The library is the only traditional or contemporary institution which functions primarily to provide free and untrammeled access to books and materials presenting all points of view concerning problems and issues of the past, present and future. Free availability of these materials and equal access to them for all library patrons are the purpose for and objective of the librarian and are crucial to the free exchange of ideas in a free society. . . . In a democracy, each individual is free to determine for himself what he wishes to read and each group is free to determine

what it will recommend to its freely associated members. But no group has the right to impose its own concept of politics or morality upon other members of a democratic society. Freedom is no freedom if it is accorded only to the accepted and inoffensive.[2]

This statement appears to be almost tailor-made to the troubles facing Ms. Osgood. While it is true that the ALA has no legal authority, its pronouncements carry a certain weight for professional librarians.

In addition it is suggested that Ms. Osgood remember the *Library Bill of Rights*. Each of the six articles of the bill are applicable to this case and should guide Ms. Osgood's thinking.

It would seem that if Ms. Osgood were to opt for the first alternative she would be doing so contrary to the established guidelines of her profession. In addition, Ms. Osgood might remember that while it is true that in America the majority rules, that majority cannot operate in such a way as to deprive any person or group of persons of their basic constitutional rights. The First Amendment guarantees free speech to all Americans; no legislative or judicial body can abridge that right. Some would agree with the town manager that the "contemporary community standards" doctrine enunciated by the Supreme Court would seem to hedge on that First Amendment guarantee. However in a 1964 case, Justice William Brennan of the United States Supreme Court commented, ". . . contemporary community standards . . . refer to the community in the sense of society at large . . . the public or people in general . . . thus . . . the concept of obscenity would have a varying meaning from time to time—not from county to county, or town to town."[3]

The Brennan opinion indicates that the whim of a particular town, even if that whim is embraced by a majority of the citizens, cannot operate in a manner contradictory to the first amendment.

It also bears stating at this point that even a majority must operate within certain defined parameters. There are some things that even the majority cannot dictate. Elected and appointed officials are not compelled to accede to the demands of the majority if they honestly feel that those demands are immoral or illegal.

The second alternative is exactly the reverse of the first. One can envision Ms. Osgood meeting with the board of trustees one month hence and saying that *Ramparts* stays and none of the "offensive" books will go on a restricted shelf. It is possible that an extremely strong individual who had been head librarian for several years and who thoroughly dominated her board of trustees might get away with this tactic. Such a person could cite the Brennan opinion, the First Amendment, the *Library Bill of Rights*, etc., and flatly state that the case was closed. Ms. Osgood would never get away with this. She has not dominated her board of trustees or the town manager. There is, however, one major advantage to this alternative. Ms. Osgood would leave the conflict with a clear conscience. She would know that she had not compromised on a basic

American principle. She would have done the "right thing" and none of her professional colleagues could fault her for her action. However, one must ask what she would leave behind her, as she would surely be fired. A new librarian, possibly Mr. DeBekker, would be appointed. And that new librarian would be under the strict control of the board. The censorship policies would be implemented. Ms. Osgood would become a martyr to a few people, but most would say good riddance to her. Once again, the real problem would not have been solved. It would remain and perhaps grow with time. Ms. Osgood's conscience would be saved but little else would be accomplished. Here, as with alternative number one, the disadvantages clearly outweigh the advantages and alternative number two should be discarded.

Alternative number three is very appealing. It is a sort of compromise that may assuage egos and allow each party to halt short of total commitment. It would allow Ms. Osgood to go the "democratic" route and heed the wishes of the "majority." At the same time it would not force elected officials to appear to be going against the populace and would prevent an unpleasant split between the board and the town manager on the one hand and the librarian on the other hand.

Just what sort of compromise could be envisioned here? For one thing, Ms. Osgood might not cancel any subscriptions or remove any books. However, offensive magazines like *Ramparts* could be held behind the desk, placed in a locked case, or simply kept on a high shelf in a dark corner with no identifying sign. Undesirable books could be placed on reserve, held behind the desk or locked up. They could be made available to adults upon request but would not be given to minors. This sort of compromise would probably please all but extremists on both sides.

Arrayed against all these advantages is one single disadvantage. It is a policy fraught with peril. The First Amendment freedoms are like virginity. One either has them or one does not. There is no such thing as an almost virgin and there is no such thing as being almost free. If one is restricted, then one is not free.

An attempt at striking a position between freedom and restriction is an exercise in self-delusion. Ms. Osgood's first compromise will later be met with other requests for compromises. Ultimately, because she will have failed to solve her true problem, she will lose her authority and the "solution" will simply lead to more problems.

In addition, Ms. Osgood should recall that the ALA has come out strongly against restricted-access shelves. Furthermore, article five of the *Library Bill of Rights* advises against discrimination on the basis of age. Article one advises that materials should not be "proscribed or removed from the shelves because of partisan or doctrinal disapproval." The ALA has also issued a statement advising against the labeling of certain books as "dirty," "un-American," or "politically offensive."

The attempt to restrict the reading of the young rests on the belief that what one reads can influence one's actions. It is felt that if the young read "dirty" books, they will commit immoral acts; and if they read "un-American" books, they will act in such a way as to subvert American society. Until recently, there has been precious little information to either support or refute this belief. However, *The Report of the Commission on Obscenity and Pornography*, published in 1970, while not definitive and conclusive, states that there is little evidence to support the contention that exposure to pornography leads to immoral or anti-social actions. It really shakes the foundations of the argument in support of restricting the reading of the young. The whole question is still open to debate, and it would appear that the best course for the librarian is to restrict what his child reads, that is his prerogative. The librarian cannot and should not do it for him.

The question of politically sensitive materials can be dealt with much more easily. The *Library Bill of Rights* is quite specific in condemning such censorship. Furthermore, such censorship actually flies in the face of our constitutional guarantees. Long ago Justice Marshall pointed out that included under the First Amendment's guarantee of free speech is "the right to receive information and ideas, regardless of their social worth."

While alternative number three might cool the fires for a short period of time it would do nothing toward solving the basic problem facing Ms. Osgood. She would in effect be censoring, although in a more subtle way. She would have abdicated her responsibility just as completely as if she had adopted alternative number one. She would have done nothing to preserve her role as selector of library materials not to preserve the First Amendment guarantees of free speech. In fact she would probably be striking an unwitting blow against free speech.

Once again the disadvantages appear to far outweigh the advantages, and Ms. Osgood should reject alternative number three.

The fourth alternative is really an offshoot of the second. It has one advantage for Ms. Osgood. She could simply state that she objects to censoring and hand in her resignation. She and the board could part as friends, and there would be no black marks in Ms. Osgood's dossier. She would not have to explain a dismissal to future employers. At the same time she would not have hanging on her conscience the fact that she had censored library materials.

However, most of the disadvantages that applied to the second alternative also apply to this one. It is the easy way out for Ms. Osgood. The problem has not been solved. It will undoubtedly face her again in future library situations. Equally important, the problem in terms of the town of Vanderlin will not have been solved. The basic rights of the citizens of the town will have been trampled, and they will be the poorer for it. A bad precedent will have been set, and future librarians will have an even more difficult time opposing censorship proposals.

As with the previous three alternatives, this one should be rejected as a course of action.

Alternative number five also has several disadvantages. It immediately places Ms. Osgood in opposition to the board, the town manager, and a large group of citizens. It prophecies an indefinite period of strife and antagonism, not a pleasant prospect. Ms. Osgood faces the prospect of public criticism, especially if someone publicizes the results of the questionnaire before the end of the month. And it must be remembered that if Ms. Osgood does not succeed with her program of education she could still be faced with her problem—in fact she could still lose her job. In other words, it is a gamble.

On the other hand, if Ms. Osgood succeeds with her program, even partially, she will have made major progress toward solving her real problem. This alternative has the very distinct advantage of being the only one with even the slightest possibility of solving the real problem. All things considered, Ms. Osgood would appear to have at least a fifty–fifty chance of succeeding. And, unlike each of the previously considered alternatives, succeeding with alternative number five means solving the real problem.

It is thus strongly suggested that Ms. Osgood opt for the fifth alternative. Having selected a viable alternative, Ms. Osgood should now proceed to outline her course of action.

The old adage that honesty is the best policy applies in this case. Ms. Osgood should ask for a special meeting of the board, or she should speak with each member individually and inform them that she probably will not act to restrict the suggested titles or cancel the subscription. She should point out that she will be spending the allotted month attempting to prove her case with each of the board members. However she must be careful at this point not to offend or insult the members. Her aim is to educate them to her point of view. A simple victory over the board on this one point will not solve the problem.

At this point Ms. Osgood will probably realize that all along she has actually been failing in one of her major responsibilities as a librarian. She should have been conducting a program to educate the board from her first day as director. She should have convinced the board that one of their major duties is to defend the librarian's freedom to act. As Alex P. Allain points out in his discussion of libraries and intellectual freedom, "A librarian does not have to yield to that kind of pressure (to censor library materials), and library governing bodies are there to protect him and back him."[4]

Ms. Osgood should long ago have exposed the board to the *Library Bill of Rights* and the *Freedom to Read Statement*. They as well as she should be committed to the principles stated in these two documents. Since she has not yet done this, she must now undertake a sort of crash program to make up for lost time. After asking the board members to read the two statements, she should flood them with articles from the professional literature. She should see that they get to see issues of the *Intellectual Freedom Newsletter*. Perhaps a neighboring librarian who has been through a similar situation should be invited to speak to the board.

The question of ad hoc balancing can be turned to Ms. Osgood's favor. She should point out that librarians are constantly involved in ad hoc balancing.

Librarians are restricted in what they can purchase by lack of money as well as by considerations of the content of materials. The decision of what should be purchased must be left up to the librarian. She should point out that in balancing one consideration against another her good judgment must be trusted.

Based on what has been said so far, Ms. Osgood should probably suggest to the board that what is needed in Vanderlin is a solid professional policy of book selection. Library literature is full of good policies. One such policy that might be adopted is quoted below.

> The board of this library recognizing the pluralistic nature of this community and the varied backgrounds and needs of all citizens, regardless of race, creed or political persuasion, declares as a matter of book selection policy that:
>
> 1. Book and/or library material selection is and shall be vested in the librarian and under his direction such members of the professional staff who are qualified by reason of education and training. Any book and/or library material so selected shall be held to be selected by the board.
>
> 2. Selection of books and/or other library material shall be made on the basis of their value of interest, information and enlightenment of all people of the community. No book and/or library material shall be excluded because of the race, nationality or the political or social views of the author.
>
> 3. This board believes that censorship is a purely individual matter and declares that while anyone is free to reject for himself books which he does not approve of, he cannot exercise this right of censorship to restrict the freedom to read of others.
>
> 4. This board defends the principles of the freedom to read and declares that whenever censorship is involved no book and/or library material shall be removed from the library save under the orders of a court of competent jurisdiction.
>
> 5. This board adopts and declares that it will adhere to and support: (a) The *Library Bill of Rights,* and (b) the *Freedom to Read Statement* adopted by the American Library Association, both of which are made a part hereof.[5]

An obvious ally of Ms. Osgood will be Mr. Anthelme. He is a political scientist and an educator. As such he must be constantly exposed to the ideas and sentiments that Ms. Osgood will be presenting to the board; he could perhaps even add to her arguments. Once he is won over to her point of view, his weight as chairman of the board will certainly be helpful in converting the town manager and the rest of the board. It must be assumed that he will be susceptible to a barrage of arguments soundly grounded in American constitutional theory and practice. As a professional himself, he can be expected to understand the *Librarian's Code of Ethics* under which Ms. Osgood must function.

At the end of the one month of concentrated proselytizing, Ms. Osgood will

be ready to face the board for her final argument. She can present her interpretation of the results of the questionnaire, pointing out that if the board and
the librarian act to censor, they will be doing so on the advice of a very small
percentage of the populace of Vanderlin. While it is true that 65 percent of the
respondents indicated a desire not to have all points of view represented and
68 percent indicated opposition to an open collection, this is certainly not a
total majority. It is only a majority of the people who responded to the questionnaire. As can be seen from Table 2, of the four thousand people who received questionnaires, only 49 percent were opposed to having all points of
view represented and only 51 percent were opposed to an open collection.
This is hardly a mandate to censor. Furthermore, when the entire town of
twelve thousand is considered the percentage of people opposing the open
collection drops to 17, and those not wanting to see all points of view represented falls to 16 percent. Clearly, to censor on the strength of these numbers
would not be a case of majority rule but rather of the tyranny of the minority.

It should be pointed out to the board that they are not a legislative or judicial body. In fact they are not constituted to censor. Only the courts can determine that an item is obscene (and even they have great difficulty doing
this). As the distinguished lawyer Charles Rembar points out, ". . . officials
who seek to interfere with free expression on their own—that is prior to a judicial determination that the book should be suppressed—will be stopped by
the courts.[6] Clearly, then, even if there were a majority calling for censorship,
they could not ask the librarian to go beyond her jurisdiction and usurp the
rightful powers and responsibilities of the courts.

Assuming that the board and the town manager (who by the way has no jurisdiction over the library board of trustees and is included as a political cour-
tesy), can be won over, there is still a good job of public education to be undertaken. The results of the questionnaire are going to be published in the
local newspaper, and Ms. Osgood will have to interpret them and fully explain her policies and beliefs. Perhaps a good beginning would be a regular
column in the paper. Here Ms. Osgood could discuss the concept of intellectual freedom from time to time. She could point out that her purchase of
a book or magazine does not necessarily signify her approval of the point of
view contained therein. She could state that the library will have an open collection and that the responsibility for overseeing children's reading must rest
with the parents. Further, she might consider a series of public education programs aimed at promoting the concept of intellectual freedom. Speakers,
films, and discussions might prove a good beginning.

This then is the proposed course of action for Ms. Osgood. She must educate the board and then she must educate the public. Much will depend on the
manner she employs and the energy and dedication she can muster. It will not
be an easy task, and it will not be done quickly. The results, however, could be
stupendous.

The real problem defined at the outset of this case stands a good chance of being solved. The uncontested selector of library materials for the town of Vanderlin will be its librarian. She will not be hampered by restrictive rules of censorship. Her good judgment will prevail. The town of Vanderlin will have its constitutional guarantees of free speech protected. This is not to say that all will be rosy and bright forever. The censor will rear its ugly head again. But when it does the library will be ready. A sound and healthy precedent has been set. The librarian and the board of trustees will be unified and organized and prepared to meet the threat.

NOTES

1. Kenneth E. Schnelle, *Case Analysis and Business Problem Solving* (New York: McGraw-Hill, 1967), p. 38.
2. "ALA Position Statement Regarding Proposition 18," *California Librarian*, (October 1972), p. 237.
3. *California Librarian*, XXXIII (October 1972), p. 240.
4. Alex P. Allain, "Public Library Governing Bodies and Intellectual Freedom," *Library Trends*, XIX (July 1970), p. 57.
5. *Ibid.*, p. 48.
6. *Ibid.*

Sample Analysis of Case 27—I

by DOROTHY HIRSHFIELD

• •

"Maybe it's good we have some materials that we as librarians would like to see suppressed, for then we can better understand the censor."

INTRODUCTION

There are a multitude of problems involved in "The Other Side," predominantly educational, all overlapping. These areas of concern have been separated for clarity and development. What we are studying is not merely another side of a familiar childhood story, we are trying to understand another side of a familiar problem—censorship.

It is important to state at the outset that this paper is by no means the last word on *Little Black Sambo*. Excluded are studies on the effects of stereotypic literature on children. Such studies are often poorly controlled, contradictory, and inconclusive. For these reasons, the entire area of child psychology has been bypassed for the purpose of this case.

In the first part of this study, the educational concerns have been divided into "The Censorship Problem" and "The Distorted View of Blacks." This censorship, as we will view it initially, involves both the removal or banning of *Little Black Sambo* (by librarians/teachers/parents) and the contingent attitudinal problems (generally based on social responsibility as viewed by the censors). The distorted view of blacks initially involves black stereotyping; the editions problem (i.e., which edition of *Sambo* is actually being discussed); and the reviewing problem (i.e., whether certain children's books have ever been adequately reviewed).

Part II delineates areas of concern for all libraries, especially school libraries, regarding censorship. "Protective Censorship" is considered first. This term covers censorious practices brought about by a zealous desire to protect others from prejudice or from seemingly prejudicial materials. Considered next is "The Higher Commitment of Libraries," regarding *The School Library Bill of Rights*, the social function of libraries, and the educational function of libraries. Unless some conclusions can be reached regarding overriding commitment, the censorship problem cannot be fully understood.

If Part III appears much more subjective than the foregoing sections of the study, it is because herein we will find (for all they are worth) the analyst's own feelings about the book. Technically, this will amount to subjective delineation of some of the educational problems that will have been covered—the editions problem, black stereotyping, and the attitudinal problems involved.

The shortest section of this analysis, the conclusion, is something of an educational plea. Although of specific concern to school librarians and teachers, the conclusion hopefully has general application.

PART I

The Censorship Problem

Whether *The Story of Little Black Sambo* has been the victim of masked censorship (via selective weeding or locking) or the victim of blatant banning, the fact remains that this well-known children's story has been under fire for at least twenty years. A chronological study of some of the better-publicized instances of censorship might begin with an article which originally appeared in the *New York Times* on February 4, 1956. Reported later in the *Newsletter on Intellectual Freedom*, the article concerned Canadian librarians protesting the Toronto Board of Education's decision to remove *Little Black Sambo* from school shelves. This decision was made after the board had heard group complaints that "the popular book was a cause of mental suffering to Negroes in particular and children in general."

W. R. Castell, Calgary librarian in defense of *Sambo*, pointed out that the book was written in 1898 by Mrs. Helen Bannerman for her two children and that the setting is India, not Africa. "The book does not even concern Negroes," he had said. "Everything in it pertains to India, even the clothing and the house where Black Sambo lived." (Some of the points raised herein will be discussed further in the editions problem.) In the opinion of Jean Thomson, a Toronto children's librarian, "all the boys and girls who have read *Little Black Sambo* have done so without any suggestion of harboring derogatory feelings."[1]

Removed from a New York school library back in 1959 when a black resident charged that the book was racially derogatory, *Little Black Sambo* underwent a committee ruling. The charge was "unfounded" and the book was restored.[2] Removed in the fall of 1965 from public schools in Lincoln, Nebraska upon complaint from the Human Relations Council, Sambo warranted an Associated Press release entitled "Black Sambo Banished":

Little Black Sambo, the fairy tale type story about a dark-skinned boy pursued by a tiger through the jungle, has been banished from the Lincoln public school system. School Superintendent Steven N. Watkins confirmed he ordered the book removed from elementary school libraries after a letter from the Lincoln Human Relations Council. "It's not worth making an issue over," said Watkins. "There are plenty of good stories left."

But Watkins' future change of heart was picked up in an editorial in the Sioux City, Iowa *Journal* on October 27, 1965, q.v.: *Sambo* "will not be a part of the [Lincoln] instructional program, [but] it will be available to those who want to read it as optional material."[3]

The 1971 banning of *Sambo* by Montgomery, Alabama, county schools was well publicized. All copies of the book and of filmstrips and records telling the story were removed from the county school libraries following a parent's complaint. A committee of principals, librarians, teachers, and one county staff member voted six to one for removal, calling *Sambo* "inappropriate" and "not in keeping with good human relations." The lone vote of dissent came from a librarian who called the book fantasy and said "humor is good for everyone."[4] Montgomery's director of educational media and technology reported in a memo to principals and librarians that "the decision is not to be construed as book burning, but rather as book selection." The director found *Sambo* "derogatory" and "didn't think they still had things like that in libraries." She announced that the public libraries would be her "next target."[5]

Less than a year later an article entitled "Sambo Removal Sought By National Black Coalition" appeared in *Library Journal*. The Montreal-based Canadian coalition wanted the book off school and library shelves. It was reported that in Hamilton, Ontario, objections to the story in school readers "resulted only in teachers ordering pupils to tear out the pages from the readers." Successful also were efforts in New Brunswick to ban *Little Black Sambo*.[6]

The same issue of *Library Journal* included an article by Mavis Wormley Davis, "Black Images in Children's Literature: Revised Editions Needed," which discussed the controversial Lippincott editions of *Little Black Sambo* in light of their stereotypic illustrations. The article pointed out that although new, improved editions of *Sambo* have been published "with Sambo portrayed as a most attractive little black boy," local libraries were allegedly surprised at a directive by the superintendent of schools that all copies of *Sambo*, regardless of edition, were to be discarded from school library shelves. Unfortunately, Ms. Davis' article lost its impact in the end. Because of a "black incident" at her school, she ultimately agreed with the superintendent's censorious decision.[7]

In spring of 1972 a tri-ethnic committee in Dallas, Texas, also became upset about *Little Black Sambo*. Their formal complaint was that *Sambo* "distorts a child's view of black people and should be taken out of the city's school libraries." Apparently the book had been removed in 1965, prior to the formal ban, but later had been put back. An investigation ensued in the school district. Said the assistant school superintendent at the time, "The facts boil down to the question: are we going to deprive our children of literary freedom?"[8]

The summer of 1972 saw another attack on the use of *Sambo*, this time in London libraries and schools. *Little Black Sambo* symbolized "the kind of dangerous and obsolete books that must go," in the words of the teachers against racism who campaigned against *Sambo*. A Pakistani backer of that campaign said that the story "depicts the Negro as an almost unclothed, illiterate and inferior savage from whose antics great humor can be derived." In his words, when he had been a schoolboy in England and the book had been read to his class, "I suddenly became *Little Black Sambo* to my classmates."[9]

In spring of 1973, when the author was busy rounding up editions of *Little Black Sambo* for this study, assistance was sought at one point from a children's librarian at the Boston Public Library. It seems that the main branch of the BPL has a Lippincott edition (1951?), a Stokes edition (no date), and numerous copies of Hutchinson (1925). At the time of the initial research on *Sambo*, the Lippincott was kept under lock and key in the library office because it was considered "potentially damaging to a child's ego." The irony of this practice will be evident in our discussion of the editions problem. Perhaps more ironic is the fact that the librarian in question admitted to remembering fondly the colorful Tenggren edition which she had read in her childhood. The Tenggren illustrations had made quite an impression on her as a child, and that impression apparently was a positive one.[10]

Perhaps the school superintendents, citizen committees, concerned parents, teachers, and librarians who have committed or condoned these acts of censorship have one common bond—a strong sense of social responsibility, as they interpret it. And perhaps what is being overlooked is the concomitant educational responsibility, to be discussed in the second part of the case. An interesting book on just this attitudinal problem, *The Censors and the Schools*, succinctly asks of a controversial work, "How is the material intended to be used in the schools? Is the student taught to accept unthinkingly everything he reads, or is he taught to evaluate and discriminate?"[11]

The Distorted View of Blacks

"Negro children have generally been written of in the same terms as their mothers and fathers, as quaint, living jokes, designed to make white children laugh."[12] At the time when those words were first written, there was indeed a high degree of black stereotyping in children's literature. But thirty-four years later, the coordinator of children's services at the New York Public Library wrote an article on the portrayal of blacks in books for children—and there seems not to have been much progress in this area. She wrote about the importance of illustration sans caricature. But caricature takes on many forms. "Is the black character merely a clown or buffoon, the object of ridicule, and the butt of humor? . . . It is [also] important to be critical of books which describe blacks in derisive terms and which use derogatory names and epithets" [such as "Black Sambo," "Black Mumbo" and "Black Jumbo"?].[13]

Investigation specifically into the language problem turned up some interesting findings. Various dictionaries, including Webster's *New Collegiate* (1956 edition), the *New World* (1964), and the *New International* (second edition), have defined "sambo," a noun allegedly of Spanish derivation (Sp. *sambo*: Negro, mulatto, monkey), as "an Indian or mulatto and Negro half-breed." And an article written much more recently considered it quite a "problem when an author calls her principal character Sambo (a name in minstrel shows made almost synonymous with a character who was black and supposedly simple-minded)."[14]

If the citations above are enough to make the readers run out and burn all available copies of *Sambo*, perhaps this is the time for examination of a specific question raised in the case: "How can we possibly know whether the kids who read [*Little Black Sambo*] feel hostile toward blacks?" In this analyst's opinion, there has been no conclusive study to date on the effects of stereotypic literature on children; now is it within the realm of this case for the author to play child psychologist. Obviously, then, the most painful aspect of this case as here interpreted has been the need to remain (or become) unbiased in the study of literature which is not necessarily unbiased.

Banned Books, in its chapter on textbook censorship, cited well-meaning censors of recent years. The NAACP by constitution directed local branches to "study material used in the schools and seek to eliminate material therefrom which is racially derogatory." This directive resulted in attacks on Stephen Foster songs in music books, on sections of history books pertaining to the Civil War, and on literature anthologies containing *Huckleberry Finn*. Similarly, the Anti-Defamation League of the B'nai B'rith has opposed in the past the use in schools of *The Merchant of Venice* and *Oliver Twist*, in attempts to eliminate religious stereotypes in school materials.[15]

Regarding the problem of racially stereotypic materials, works such as *Image of the Black in Children's Fiction* [16] and the unpublished "Wanted: Black Writers for Black Children's Literature"[17] make readers uncomfortably aware of a long history of black stereotyping. Perhaps a book like *Jubilee*, poignantly told from the black point of view, will help lead the way back and help us to understand.[18]

The subjects of black stereotyping and the editions problem regarding *Little Black Sambo* are not unrelated. In fact, the analyst has found it very important to establish (where possible) just what edition of *Sambo* is being disputed and for what reasons. The *Chimney Corner Stories* collection referred to within the case is the first volume of a very popular four-volume children's set written in the mid-1920s by Veronica S. Hutchinson and illustrated by Lois Lenski. Not a classic but certainly a standard in children's collections, the Hutchinson *Sambo* seems to fare better on library shelves than the Lippincott editions.

Although the Lippincott editions (especially the 1946) are the most often reviled, this analyst found that *Sambo* suffers as retold by Hutchinson. First of all, omitted are all written or illustrated references to tiger "ghi" (ghee), "as it is called in India."[19] There are in fact six black-and-white illustrations in the Hutchinson as opposed to the twenty-seven colorful Lippincott drawings, which appear as copied from the originals by Helen Bannerman.

Furthermore, although Lois Lenski's illustrations in Hutchinson for all of the other stories in the collection seem not only cute but appropriate, those for *Sambo* are pure caricature. He and his family look funny; and a reader unaware that tigers are indigenous only to Asia might think the story African.[20]

But "the only authorized American edition" (quoth the Lippincott) indicated in its preface to *Little Black Sambo* that the story took place in India and was composed by Helen Bannerman on a train. More than likely the illustrations were not researched or intended to be representational. The Lippincott illustrations were "copied as exactly as possible" from Helen Bannerman's drawings in the original.[21] It is ironic that the Lippincott editions are most often in the line of fire and least often on library shelves. Although the Sambo story may not appear as recommended reading in such books as *The Elementary School Library Collection*, Hutchinson to date has been an undisputed standard in children's collections.

To add to the confusion, there are well over fifty distinct editions of Sambo, some of which are difficult if not impossible to obtain. For clarity—if such is possible—the early Lippincott edition, which identifies itself as the only authorized American edition, is cataloged 19—and may have appeared at the time of the Stokes edition in 1923—two years before the Hutchinson; the 1946 Lippincott is dated as such; and the third Lippincott, also identified as "the only authorized American edition," is marked 1951?. It is this edition which Ms. Keyes now holds in her hands.

If we can tear ourselves away from the editions problem, some time can be spent analyzing another critical aspect of this censorship study—the reviewing problem. Dorothy Broderick, in *Image of the Black* and in an article entitled "Lessons in Leadership," has long been pointing out the history of *black stereotyping in books recommended by the Children's Catalog*. Such books have consistently "met with the approval of the leaders of the library world, both individuals and periodicals."[22] Although Broderick does not mention explicitly the problem of *Little Black Sambo*, the Sambo story appears in many recommended forms.

The aim of Hutchinson's *Chimney Corner Stories*, according to the *Children's Catalog*, has been to include stories of unquestioned merit that have found favor with children and whose illustrations have been both interesting and amusing. Early editions of the catalog (first through third) list *Sambo* under Helen Bannerman, and later editions and supplements list Hutchinson, probably the most popular collection including *Little Black Sambo*. To date, Hutchinson's *Chimney Corner Stories* is still being recommended in the most recent edition of the *Children's Catalog*. Furthermore, the influential *Anthology of Children's Literature*—slightly dated but still a standard on reference shelves of children's collections—lists Bannerman's story (and makes reference to India, by the way). Very interesting, though, is the omission, in the graded reading list of the anthology, of Hutchinson's *Chimney Corner Stories*.[23]

PART II

Protective Censorship

The reviewing problem is no less touchy than any of the other problems encountered in this study. For instance, in a letter entitled "Selection and Racism," librarian David Cohen expressed the anguish of those who have been reviewing many of the old standards in children's literature. "If we agree that these books are racist in content, should we stand by and let matters take their course or should we exercise our professional prerogatives as book selectors by saying that books [like these] no longer meet the criteria for a 'recommended' book? Is this professional judgment or is it censorship?"[24]

There are many possible answers to such disconcerting questions, some of which will be discussed at greater length below. It is worth considering in the meantime that the criteria for recommending a book are rarely static—they often reflect the Zeitgeist, the spirit or trends of the times; and more often they reflect the spirit or trends of former times. When Mr. Cohen mentioned in the same breath our prerogatives as selectors and the books that no longer deserve formal recommendation, perhaps he was implying that a book which should no longer appear as recommended reading for children should no longer appear on the shelves either.

Then, in the title words of an article which concerns protective censorship, "Where Do You Draw the Line?" Mother Goose, like Sambo, has been on the firing line; and some librarians have been expressing concern over the removal under organized group pressure of old standards such as these. Succinctly stated by one of those librarians, "thoughts cannot be concealed by concealing evidence that they exist."[25] Likewise, it is important, though painful, for us to remember the historical, political, and social setting of England—especially as pertains to India—in the late nineteenth century when Bannerman penned her book. Like it or not, the British attitude toward blacks and Indians at that time was a matter of fact—not fiction; and "censorship does not repress the historical fact [of nationalism, racial slur, and suppression]. The suppression of ideas, the withdrawal of books, and the evasion of facts are negative responses. They serve no good educational purpose."[26]

The Higher Commitment of Libraries

It is the educational purpose just mentioned with which we should concern ourselves at this time. There is a growing realization that the author of *Banned Books* was right: benevolent censors are no less emotional or difficult to reason with than any other censors and certainly no less self-righteous. Protective censorship is still censorship, and it does not mix well with what perhaps should be the overriding commitment of libraries to the public. Nevertheless, all of the statements on freedom of the press—amendments to the Constitution, the *Library Bill of Rights*, the *Freedom to Read* statement, the *School Library Bill of Rights*, and so on forever—all of these and more will not automatically insure a library against censorship. There will always be patrons/librarians/teachers/school boards quite deliberately unaffected by any or all of these documents and very determined to act accordingly.

If a case cannot be built on supportive documents such as the *School Library Bill of Rights*—and this analyst thinks it cannot—then perhaps something of the social function of libraries should be considered next. The current function of libraries goes well beyond the original concept of patronizing the public with well-guarded offerings of culture—primarily as interpreted by the librarian. Although library function in society is still evolving, in an age when nonprint materials are having quite an impact we can still appreciate a librarian's analysis of the impact of reading on the mind: "The role of the library is an extremely important one because it is the only organized social institution which fosters the reading of books."[27]

This analyst in fact does not agree that libraries are the only organized social institutions fostering book-reading—or even that book-reading itself is the end-all. Most libraries also foster free access to information and the freedom of ideas. These freedoms of information and ideas deserve and need protection.

An editorial in the *Wilson Library Bulletin* over ten years ago painstakingly explained how to give "An Answer to the Censors." Writing in favor of free access to books in public (and school) libraries, the editorialist considered libraries a primary source of information and freedom: "Our free society is based on the right of each individual to form his own opinion, and I have faith in the ability of our people to think for themselves."[28]

This brings us to the educational function of libraries. Nothing particularly new or original will be said here; it has all been said by others before. George Bernard Shaw had made an attempt to explain the freedom to read in terms of open and closed minds: "You must be careful what books you give adults, for they may be corrupted; but children may read anything. . . ." There are, of course, great numbers of doubters regarding this ability of children to think and to choose for themselves—and the concomitant educational responsibility of librarians/teachers/parents should not be overlooked: "The librarian and the teacher have a responsibility to educate a student about all aspects of culture and society—the good and the bad."[29]

PART III

It is time for a slightly more subjective analysis of *Little Black Sambo*—and there is admittedly still much room for disagreement. An important question is raised by librarians Keyes and Aiken within the case and by the case author at the end: *"Is Little Black Sambo* harmful?"

It is harmful, in this writer's opinion, for a library to pass on the grossly stereotypic Hutchinson edition (*Chimney Corner Stories*) as the only available edition of *Sambo*. If Ms. Aiken were to allow Ms. Keyes to talk her into removing the Lippincott edition from the school library shelves, such would be the result. Furthermore, if the Sambo story is to be kept on the shelves (and the analyst thinks it should be) then both the Hutchinson and the Lippincott editions should be kept. The Lippincott should be retained because it is superior to the Hutchinson edition; the Hutchinson should be retained primarily because it is part of a very popular children's set and secondarily because it is highly educational for readers to be able to compare different editions of the stories that they read.

Other editions could also be sought, carefully picked by Ms. Keyes to be the least stereotypic in to her opinion. With dozens of editions to choose from and numerous reprintings available, the difficulty could not be too great. Far more difficult would be explaining to a child who wants to read the story, "We cannot show you that book, for your own good."

Furthermore, it bears repeating that it is harmful not to educate in the use of stereotypic books—or books which could be construed as such. Librarians and teachers sensitive to such problems (e.g., Beth Keyes and Priscilla Wirt) should be able to discuss such reading matter with the readers—to describe the historical and social background of such a book and to explain that it was not intended to be what it may seem to be today. (At the very least, readers should be grateful that stereotypes can finally be recognized as such and should appreciate whatever social progress may have taken place since *Little Black Sambo* was first written.) As cited before but worthy of recall, "How is the material intended to be used in the schools? Is the student taught to accept unthinkingly everything he reads, or is he taught to evaluate and discriminate?"[30]

If the analyst were black and only five years old, perhaps more credence could be given to these words. But one white five-year-old (the analyst's daughter) offered some candid comments on *Little Black Sambo*. Since concern has been expressed in the case over the possibility that Sambo has been made to look like a fool, Zoe was asked if she thought Sambo was very smart.

Her eyes lit up and she nodded her head enthusiastically. "Yes! At the end of the story, *he* ate the *tigers!*"

PART IV: CONCLUSION

The words of a wide-eyed five-year-old were hardly meant to be the last word on *Sambo*—but they do say a lot. Beyond her very innocent approach to the story, there is still the need for a very astute educational approach to books such as this one.

The question has been raised, "What approach should Ms. Aiken take with Ms. Keyes at this point?" Since the analyst feels that teachers, librarians, and parents should start working together, it is logical for Ms. Aiken to do basically two things. First, she and Ms. Keyes should discuss *Sambo* much as it has been discussed in this analysis—considering the numerous instances of censorship over the last two decades; the importance for readers to be aware of the existence of stereotyping, however painful to behold; the educational mistake made by benevolent censors in assuming that an idea banned no longer exists. We have reason to believe that these two librarians have had rewarding discussions before and that both are as rational as they are sensitive. The second thing for Ms. Aiken to do, after opening her associate's mind to the many problems involved in the weeding of such a book, is to get her approval for a staff meeting (of teachers and librarians) on the subject of the potential banning of *Little Black Sambo*. Present at this meeting, of course, would be members of the incipient group Teachers against Discrimination— a group of teachers likely to be as uninformed about the background of *Sambo* as is librarian Keyes.

In all honesty, there can be no assurance that talks between the two librarians, joint staff meetings on the subject of book censorship, or eventual school meetings attended by concerned parents would automatically usher in an age of reason and understanding. Such attempts would be just a beginning—but an important beginning—in understanding the historical imperative of preserving books which seem to reflect the mores or stereotypes of the past.

One day teachers, librarians, and parents will start working together, rather than against one another, to protect such a book and to educate young readers to understand it historically. Only such cooperation and diligence can lessen the likelihood that *Little Black Sambo* will continue to be pursued by the most fearful tiger of all—the censor.

NOTES

1. *Newsletter on Intellectual Freedom*, V (April 1956), pp. 3–4.
2. *Ibid.*, XII (July 1963), p. 51.
3. *Ibid.*, XIV (January 1965), p. 12.

4. Dorothy S. Hirshfield, "T.V. Bigotry—It's 'All in the Family' " (1972), p. 15. In this censorship study, someone being polled was asked why he found stereotypic humor so funny. His response was, "What's the difference? The world is in such a state now that laughter of any kind and for any reason is better than no laughter at all."

5. "Sambo Banned by Montgomery County Schools," *Library Journal*, September 15, 1971, pp. 2813–2814.

6. "Sambo Removal Sought by National Black Coalition," *Library Journal*, January 15, 1972, pp. 237–238.

7. Mavis Wormley Davis, "Black Images in Children's Literature: Revised Editions Needed," *Library Journal*, January 15, 1972, pp. 261–263.

8. *Newsletter on Intellectual Freedom*, XXI (May 1972), p. 72.

9. *Ibid.*, XXI (July 1972), p. 117.

10. Davis, *op. cit.*, p. 262. In this article, Bannerman's book was considered "a classic which has been translated into many languages and read all over the world [but] the focus of much controversy because of its caricatured and stereotyped illustrations." The Tenggren edition was put out in 1948 by Simon and Schuster, illustrated by Gustaf Tenggren (#57 in The Little Golden Library series).

11. Jack Nelson and Gene Roberts, Jr., *The Censors and the Schools* (Boston: Little, Brown, 1973), p. 193.

12. Sterling A. Brown, *The Negro in American Fiction* (Washington, D.C.: Associates in Negro Folk Education, 1937), p. 167.

13. Augusta Baker, "The Black Experience in Children's Books—An Introductory Essay," *New York Public Library Bulletin*, LXXV (March 1971), pp. 143–145.

14. Donnarae MacCann, "Sambo and Sylvester," *Wilson Library Bulletin* XXXXV (May 1971), pp. 880–881. Webster's *New International* (second edition) lists "sambo" as a colloquial term for "any Negro"; *The Oxford Dictionary of English Etymology* (London: Oxford University Press, 1966), p. 785, lists that "sambo" was first recorded as a "nickname for a Negro" in the nineteenth century; and the *American Thesaurus of Slang*, second edition (New York: Crowell Co., 1964), pp. 347 and 890, lists "Sambo" as slang for a male Negro and also as "possibly African . . ., the name given second sons."

15. Anne Lyon Haight, *Banned Books: Informal Notes on Some Books Banned for Various Reasons at Various Times and in Various Places* (New York: Bowker, 1970), p. 119. The ADL has, however, actively sought to include in history texts more material on the mass genocide in Nazi Germany.

16. Dorothy M. Broderick, *Image of the Black in Children's Fiction* (New York: Bowker, 1973).

17. Kathleen S. Rau, "Wanted: Black Writers for Black Children's Literature" (1972).

18. Margaret Walker, *Jubilee* (London: Cox and Wyman, 1967).

19. Helen B. Bannerman, *The Story of Little Black Sambo* (Philadelphia: Lippincott, [1951?]), p. 53.

20. Veronica S. Hutchinson, *Chimney Corner Stories: Tales for Little Children* (New York: Minton, Balch and Co., 1925), pp. 69–76.

21. Bannerman, *op. cit.*, preface. See also notes 1, 7, and 10.

22. Dorothy M. Broderick, "Lessons in Leadership," *Library Journal*, February 15, 1971, pp. 699–701.

23. Edna Johnson and Carrie E. Scott, eds., *Anthology of Children's Literature* (Boston: Houghton Mifflin, 1935), pp. 574–575. The aim of *Chimney Corner Stories* was first reported on p. 53 of the *Children's Catalog*, Supplement 3, 1928.

24. David Cohen, "Selection and Racism," *Library Journal*, October 15, 1969, p. 3585. See also note 15.

25. Chandler B. Grannis, "Where Do You Draw the Line?" *Publishers Weekly*, April 14, 1969, p. 73.

26. Lindalee Mesiano, "Even When It Offends," *Library Journal*, May 15, 1969, p. 2031.

27. Bartholomeus Landheer, *Social Function of Libraries* (New York: Scarecrow Press, 1957), p. 110.

28. "An Answer to the Censors," *Wilson Library Bulletin*, XXXVI (March 1962), p. 498.

29. Martha Boaz, "The Student Does Have a Right to Read," *California School Libraries*, XXXXI (January 1970), pp. 63–67. The full quotation by Shaw is cited in this article.

30. Nelson and Roberts, *op. cit.*, p. 193.